Kernel & Warden

A CIP catalogue record for this book is available from the British Library

E-Mail: Binden@kernelwarden.com

ISBN-13: 978-0-9558178-1-6

Dedication

To Sir Winston Churchill for writing such a wonderfully entertaining set of memoirs of the Second World War that inspired this book.

To anyone who is about to read the book. I hope you enjoy it. Please do not take it too seriously or literally. Any opinions or historical overviews are entirely my own summations. Whilst great effort has been taken to ensure the accuracy of historical detail. I reserve the right to be wrong and to misinterpret every day.

Contents

I would like to extend my heartfelt thanks to everyone who helped with the creation of this book.

You know who you are.

Preface

Churchill's Secret Advice

This book will change any perception a reader has of Churchill for the better. The subtitle of the book is "Keeping the Nazi's off the beaches required more than fine speeches". Over the next 250 pages I will share the secrets garnered from my years studying Churchill's approach to running the war in a way that enables the reader to transfer these skills into a modern business environment. I would like to think that I have achieved this feat whilst delivering a thoroughly entertaining and informative read, that has a few surprises thrown in for good measure.

I was born in 1964 a year before Churchill died and, whilst I picked up snippets about the iconic Winston over the years, when his name was mentioned I conjured up the mental picture of a tough leader who saved Britain from defeat in World War 2. I was familiar with the classic quotes from his speeches, "their finest hour", "never surrender", "we will fight them on the beaches". Like most British people of a certain age I knew enough about Churchill to be proud of him and his achievements.

This perception altered irrevocably when I read his WW2 memoirs, which including the appendices run to 5000 pages of tiny text, or 8000 pages of modern print. Reading through them I felt as if Churchill were talking to me, relating the challenges he faced in WW2 and sharing the secret of successfully managing the events that lead to Britain's salvation. Though this took months of reading I was absolutely riveted. Even the appendices containing the thousands of memo's he sent throughout the war were fascinating. Churchill's memoirs are 60 years old. As I read through them time and again the situations he described and the advice he gave drew parallels with business problems and situations that have occurred during my 25 year working career. Whilst I haven't had to make dramatic changes to the way I work, Churchill's secret advice has helped me in many business situations. When I might doubt myself, I reflect upon the lessons I have learned and find the confidence to make the tough decisions and deal with the problems and issues which form my daily business life.

This book is written from the perspective of a person who works within a normal business environment. It is not one of those books written by a retired CEO who wants to tell you how they became successful and how you too can get rich by following their advice. The bookshelves are packed with such tombs, I do wonder if any of these books actually lead to success once the flush of the readers enthusiasm starts to wane. I can assure you that if you follow the secret advice given by Churchill you will make improvements, but I make no promises that you will turn into some overnight success.

I have read several "business improvement books" but I tend to avoid them as in the main they are too much like hard work. I was determined not to add to the list of boring business improvement books that people start but don't finish. To keep your attention I have filled each chapter with fascinating and unusual stories and anecdotes from the war. The memo's I have included have been chosen not only because they add to a particular chapter but also because they offer a fascinating insight into the real issues affecting the daily lives of soldiers and civilians during WW2.

When Churchill became Prime Minister in 1940, he famously stated that he felt as if he had been walking with destiny and that all his past life had been but a preparation for the hour and the trial that was to come. He was 65 and had an amazingly jam-packed lifetime of experience. I can think of no current politician that has one tenth of the life experience that Churchill amassed. Unfortunately, these days he would be considered too old to be taken seriously. Thankfully, this was not the case in 1940.

I came upon Churchill's memoirs by pure chance after listening to Simon Scharma's History of Britain (on my IPOD).

This led me to download Churchill's History of the English speaking peoples, volume 1, as they were mentioned by Scharma. Churchill wrote these books just before the war; however the publishers delayed their release until after he completed his memoirs in the late 50's. The references to his war memoirs fascinated me, and whilst stopping by chance at a second hand book warehouse, I purchased all six original volumes for $40.

It is unlikely that anyone will ever again have to orchestrate the defeat of a Nazi tyrant. The way Winston Churchill managed this task in conjunction with the USA and the rest of the Allies is quite incredible. Reading his memoirs has really changed many of my preconceived ideas about Churchill and the events of WW2.

The memoirs show in detail how good he was as a manager of people, a negotiator and persuader, and how the techniques he used consistently throughout the war helped him keep on top of a myriad of simultaneous events across the globe.

Churchill did not acquire his skills by reading management self-help books or going to seminars given by self-development gurus. To my knowledge, he had never been on a training course on how to develop the ten habits of a highly effective war leader! Churchill had no proper job in the conventional sense. He qualified for a commission in the army not long after he left school. After graduating at Sandhurst Military College he went to India and South Africa as a sub-lieutenant, adding to his income by writing articles for London newspapers detailing his many adventures. He became a member of parliament in 1906 at the young age of 26, gaining his ability to motivate people and manage events through decades of practice. By the time he became prime minister in 1940, he was sixty-five. Most people of this age would be looking forward to a happy life of retirement, not taking on the greatest single challenge to befall a man in recent history.

For many years, Churchill's only income came from writing books, newspaper articles and lecture tours. In spite of his privileged background, he actually had no money. In the pre-war years, he always endeavored to maintain his income within hailing distance of his outgoings.

He was a great believer in trying to make reading an interesting and rewarding experience. His war memoirs span six books which I found to be an incredibly interesting read. Some of the chapters in the second volume "Their Finest Hour" dealing with the fall of France and the Battle of Britain are just electrifying especially to someone British.

One of the most memorable and humorous short stories from "Their Finest Hour", details a meeting at the Russian Embassy in Berlin in November 1940. It was between Hitler, Stalin's foreign minister Molotov, and his German equivalent Ribbentrop. Churchill describes how Hitler tried to enlist Russian support for his campaign against the British, and how Churchill personally intervened to put a spanner in the works. I have detailed an edited extract from the conversations.

The Fuehrer was talking to Molotov and stated *"that if German-Russian collaboration was to show positive results in the future the Soviet Government would have to understand that Germany was engaged in a life-and death struggle, which at all events she wanted to conclude successfully. Hitler stated that after the conquest of England the British Empire would be apportioned as a gigantic worldwide estate in bankruptcy of forty million square kilometers. In this bankrupt estate there would be for Russia access to the ice-free and really open ocean. A minority of forty-five million Englishmen had ruled six hundred million inhabitants of the British Empire. Hitler was about to crush this minority. Germany of course would like to avoid any conflict which would divert her from her struggle against the heart of the Empire, the British Isles. The conflict with England would be fought to the last ditch, and Hitler had no doubt that the defeat of the British Isles would lead to the dissolution of the Empire. It was impossible to believe that the Empire could possibly be ruled and held together from Canada. Hitler went on to say that under those circumstances there arose worldwide perspectives. During the next few weeks they would have to be settled in joint diplomatic negotiations with Russia, and Russia's participation in the solution of these problems would have to be arranged. All the countries which could possibly be interested in the bankrupt estate would have to stop* all controversies among themselves and concern themselves exclusively with the partition of the British Empire. This applied to Germany, France, Italy, Russia, and Japan. Hitler then retired for the night.

After supper at the Soviet Embassy there was a British air raid on Berlin. Churchill had heard of the conference beforehand, and though not invited to join in the discussion he did not wish to be entirely left out of the proceedings. On the "Alert" everyone moved to the shelter, and the conversation was continued till midnight by the two Foreign Secretaries in safer surroundings. The German official account stated:

Because of the air raid the two Ministers went into the Reich Foreign Minister's air raid shelter at 9.00 p.m. in order to conduct the final conversation.

As soon as England conceded her defeat and asked for peace, the decisive question, was whether the Soviet Union was prepared and in a position to cooperate with Germany in the great liquidation of the British Empire. On all other questions Germany and the Soviet Union would easily reach an understanding if they could succeed in extending their relations and in defining the spheres of influence. Where the spheres of influence lay had been stated repeatedly. It was therefore as the Fuehrer had so clearly put it, a matter of the interests of the Soviet Union and Germany requiring that the partners stand not breast to breast but back to back, in order to support each other in the achievement of their aspirations.

In his reply Molotov stated that the Germans were assuming that the war against England had already actually been won. If therefore, as had been said in another connection, Germany was waging a life and death struggle against England, he could only construe this as meaning, that Germany was fighting "for life" and England "for death". As to the question of collaboration, he quite approved of it, but added that they had to come to a thorough understanding. A delimitation of the spheres of influence must also be sought; On this point however he (Molotov) could not take a definitive stand at this time, since he did not know the opinion of Stalin and of his other friends in Moscow on the matter. However, he had to state that all these great issues of tomorrow could not be separated from the issues of today and the fulfillment of existing agreements.

Thereupon Molotov cordially bade farewell to the Reich Foreign Minister, stressing that he did not regret the air raid alarm, because he owed to it such an exhaustive conversation with the Reich Foreign Minister.

Churchill made his first visit to Moscow in August 1942 and received from Stalin's lips a shorter account of this conversation *"which in no essential differed from the German record, but may be thought more pithy"* .

"A little while ago," said Stalin, *"the great complaint against Molotov was that he was too pro-German. Now everyone says he is too pro-British. But neither of us ever trusted the Germans. For us it was always life and death."* I interjected that we had been through this ourselves, and so knew how they felt. *"When Molotov,"* said the Marshal, *"went to see Ribbentrop in Berlin in November of 1940 you got wind of it and sent an air raid."* I nodded. *"When the alarm sounded Ribbentrop led the way down many flights of stairs to a deep shelter sumptuously furnished. When he got inside the raid had begun. He shut the door and said to Molotov: 'Now here we are alone together. Why should we not divide?' Molotov said: 'What will England say 'England,' said Ribbentrop, 'is finished. She is no more use as a Power.' 'If that is so,' said Molotov, 'why are we in this shelter, and whose are these bombs which fall? ' "*

In summary, each chapter of this book stands alone with some of the same events used throughout the book and examined from different angles. In each of the chapters, I have used real stories and situations from 25 years of my own working life as examples to try to illustrate a particular point. Some of the chapters might resonate with the personal experiences of the reader. It would be disappointing if no chapter struck a chord. I hope that a business situation will arise where the reader will stop and think, what would Churchill have done in this situation and take inspiration from the secret advice I have shared.

Chapter 1

The Weapon of Courtesy and Consideration

Churchill was a very demanding boss, driving his staff to the absolute limit of human endurance. Given the life and death nature of the circumstances, it is understandable why they would give their all to the task. He was however demonstrably fair and always courteous in his dealings with those who worked for him. He could have quite understandably acted like a tyrant bullying staff to do his bidding.

Churchill's management style of being demanding whilst at the same time being pleasant and courteous, meant that those he came into contact with not only gave everything, but did so willingly. On numerous occasions, he took time to send messages of thanks or congratulations to those who worked hard and achieved success. He did not give the appearance of taking things for granted. I have included a couple of examples below.

PRIME MINISTER TO MINISTER AIRCRAFT PRODUCTION   1 MAR 44
My congratulations upon the output of aircraft for February, and upon beating the program. Pray convey to all those who have achieved or exceeded their program my best thanks.

PRIME MINISTER TO MINISTER OF WAR TRANSPORT   28 NOV 42
Pray convey to all those in your department who have contributed to the success of "Torch" my warmest congratulations and thanks for the part they played in the preparation and movement of this great armada. It owed much to their skill, industry, and reticence, and they share in the honor of a great achievement.

His sense of decency and fair play, the hallmark of the

western Allies, was to prove invaluable when the war was at its peak in March 1945. The Allies were driving the Germans across the Rhine making rapid progress into Germany. Whilst the victories were difficult, progress was remarkably good.

Russian progress on the Eastern front was much slower. Whilst the Red Army were advancing, the Germans appeared to be fighting much harder for every mile of ground covered.

At this time, a row broke out between Russia, the USA and Great Britain. This was the first major disagreement between the three powers, with the Soviets accusing the Allies of bad faith. During March 1945, a German general had made contact with the Allies to explore potential terms of surrender, hoping to end the war in the North of Italy. The Allies, uncertain if this was a genuine offer, arranged a meeting with the German General and a couple of SS officers in Switzerland. For logistical reasons the Soviets could not attend. At the meeting, the Allies stated that only an unconditional surrender would be acceptable, with all troops required to become prisoners of War. This was important, as it was pointless for the Germans to surrender on one battlefront, only to transfer their troops to another.

Because the Soviets were not at the meeting, they became suspicious of the Allies, assuming that Britain and the USA had struck some sort of deal with Hitler, resulting in the German army fighting harder against the Soviets than the Allies. The tone of the telegrams sent by Roosevelt and Churchill to Stalin protesting the innocence of the Allies was brutal. (see actual memo's below) This was all happening at the same time as the Soviets were effectively trying to annex Poland (later chapter). Eventually, the Allies managed to convince Stalin of their innocence, and the issue blew over.

MOLOTOV TO CHURCHILL (COPIED TO ROOSEVELT)   MARCH 1945
In Berne for two weeks, behind the backs of the Soviet Union, which is bearing the brunt of the war against Germany, negotiations have been going on between the representatives of the German military command on the one hand and representatives of the English and American commands on the other.

MARSHAL STALIN TO PRESIDENT ROOSEVELT   1ˢᵗ APRIL 45

I have received your message on the question of negotiations in Berne. You are absolutely right that, in connection with the affair regarding negotiations of the Anglo-American command with the German command, somewhere in Berne or some other place, "has developed an atmosphere of fear and distrust deserving regrets".

You insist that there have been no negotiations yet.

It may be assumed that you have not yet been fully informed. As regards my military colleagues, they, on the basis of data which they have on hand, do not have any doubts that the negotiations have taken place, and that they have ended in an agreement with the Germans, on the basis of which the German commander on the Western Front, Marshal Kesselring, has agreed to open the front and permit the Anglo-American troops to advance to the east, and the Anglo-Americans have promised in return to ease for the Germans the peace terms.

I think that my colleagues are close to the truth. Otherwise one could not have understood the fact that the Anglo-Americans have refused to admit to Berne representatives of the Soviet command for participation in the negotiations with the Germans.

I also cannot understand the silence of the British, who have allowed you to correspond with me on this unpleasant matter, and they themselves remain silent, although it is known that the initiative in this whole affair with the negotiations in Berne belongs to the British.

I understand that there are certain advantages for the Anglo-American troops as a result of these separate negotiations in Berne or some other place, since the Anglo-American troops get the possibility to advance into the heart of Germany almost without resistance on the part of the Germans, but why was it necessary to conceal this from the Russians, and why were your Allies, the Russians, not notified?

As a result of this at the present moment the Germans on the Western Front in fact have ceased the war against England and the United States. At the same time the Germans continue the war with Russia, the Ally of England and the United States. It is understandable that such a situation can in no way serve the cause of preservation of the strengthening of trust between our countries.

I have already written to you in my previous message, and consider it necessary to repeat it here, that I personally and my colleagues would never have made such a risky step, being aware that a momentary advantage, no matter what it would be, is fading before the principal advantage of the preservation and strengthening of the trust among the Allies.

Churchill then added the comment below regarding the presidents reply, which was written only a matter of weeks before President Roosevelt died.

This accusation angered the President deeply. His strength did not allow him to draft his own reply. General Marshall framed the following answer, with Roosevelt's approval. It certainly did not lack vigor.

PRESIDENT ROOSEVELT TO MARSHAL STALIN   5 APRIL 45
I have received with astonishment your message of April 3 containing an allegation that arrangements which were made between Field Marshal Alexander and Kesselring at Berne "permitted the Anglo-American troops to advance to the east, and . the Anglo-Americans promised in return to ease for the Germans the peace terms".

In my previous messages to you in regard to the attempts made in Berne to arrange a conference to discuss a surrender of the German Army in Italy I have told you that (i) no negotiations were held in Berne; (ii) that the meeting had no political implications whatever; (iii) that in any surrender of the enemy Army in Italy there could be no violation of our agreed principle of unconditional surrender; (iv) that Soviet officers would be welcomed at any meeting that might be arranged to discuss surrender.

For the advantage of our common war effort against Germany, which to-day gives excellent promise of an early success in a disintegration of the German armies, I must continue to assume that you have the same high confidence in my truthfulness and reliability that I have always had in yours.

I have also a full appreciation of the effect your gallant Army has had in making possible a crossing of the Rhine by the forces under General Eisenhower, and the effect that your forces will have hereafter on the eventual collapse of the German resistance to our combined attacks.

I have complete confidence in General Eisenhower, and know that he certainly would inform me before entering into any agreement with the Germans. He is instructed to demand, and will demand, unconditional surrender of enemy troops that may be defeated on his front. Our advances on the Western Front are due to military action. Their speed has been attributable mainly to the terrific impact of our air-power, resulting in destruction of German communications, and to the fact that Eisenhower was able to cripple the bulk of the German forces on the Western Front while they were still west of the Rhine.

I am certain that there were no negotiations in Berne at any time, and I feel that your information to that effect must have come from German sources, which have made persistent efforts to create dissension between us in order to escape in some measure for responsibility for their war crimes. If that was Wolff's purpose in Berne your message proves that he has had some success.

With a confidence in your belief in my personal reliability and in my determination to bring about together with you an unconditional surrender of the Nazis, it is astonishing that a belief seems to have reached the Soviet Government that I have entered into an agreement with the enemy without first obtaining your full agreement.

Finally I would say this: it would be one of the great tragedies of history if at the very moment of the victory now within our grasp such distrust, such lack of faith, should prejudice the entire undertaking after the colossal losses of life, material, and treasure involved.

Frankly, I cannot avoid a feeling of bitter resentment toward your informers, whoever they are, for such vile misrepresentations of my actions or those of my trusted subordinates.

Churchill was deeply struck by the last sentence. He felt that although Roosevelt did not draft the whole message he might well have added the final stroke himself. It looked like a personal addition or summing up, even though he was gravely ill he still wanted to show his anger.

By March 1945 the German army with the exception of Hitler and his immediate circle, knew that they were going to lose the war it was just a matter of time. The Battle of the Bulge was Hitler's last big push and he narrowly lost because of lack of fuel.

Imagine you are a German soldier or officer struggling against the tough, hard fighting, Allied troops and you have to surrender. If you end up as a prisoner of war, you will be treated by the Allies according to the Geneva Convention; there would be a good chance of seeing your family and country again. The Red Army, on the other hand, had a reputation of acting decidedly brutal towards captured prisoners, executing officers and shipping soldiers to far away frozen parts of Russia to be slave workers never to return.

The Soviet army also had a terrible reputation for the way in which they abused any population that they liberated.

In fairness to the Russians, the Germans behaved in the same way. Hitler had instructed his Generals to treat the Russians with greater severity than the British, as they had not signed the Hague Convention on the treatment of prisoners.

Churchill set his stall out early regarding the treatment of prisoners. This was enforced throughout the services as the memo below indicates.

FIRST LORD TO FIRST SEA LORD AND SECOND SEA LORD. 25.Mar.40

I see charges of looting preferred against our men in the German Press. I should not think it necessary to mention this but for the fact that it has come to my notice that the Captain of the Altmark's watch, chronometer and Iron Cross were stolen, and are now in the hands of some of the sailors as souvenirs. Any-thing of this kind must be stopped with the utmost strictness. No souvenir of any value can be preserved without being reported and permission obtained. Personal property of enemies may be confiscated by the State, but never by individuals.

Because the Allies treated the population they liberated or

the soldiers they captured with decency and respect, (the opposite of the Soviets), the German soldiers fought the Soviets so much harder for every mile of ground, knowing that defeat or capture would lead to a bleak future. The evidence was plentiful given the way in which Russia had treated Poland. The Germans knew that land captured by the Soviets would end up as part of a Communist regime. Allied occupied land would eventually end up as part of a democratic society. Given the choice it is hardly surprising that Germans would not have wanted to be under communist rule, and as it turned out in the years following the war with good reason!

By continuing the policy of treating soldiers and civilians harshly, the Soviets made it difficult for themselves. Stalin assumed that the Allies had concluded a deal with the Germans, but he was wrong. He simply failed to understand the difference his brutal policy had on the German army compared to the policy of the allies. The basic principle of self preservation applied, a soldier desperately wanted to be captured by the allies rather than the Soviets.

On a much smaller scale, the Red Army effect regularly applies in business situations. Over the years, I have worked with colleagues who complain that no one in back office departments ever does them any favors or helps them out. Such colleagues will often interact well with their peers and with customers, however staff within the supporting business departments find them difficult to work with.

In a sales role at a previous company, one of my team was a great example of this. For the purposes of this narrative, I will call him Roger. Roger and I had the same role selling for a young successful Telecoms company. This involved a great deal of interaction with different company departments whilst in the office and on the road. Quickly resolving internal issues delivered better service to customers, brought in more business and put additional money in my pocket.

If I visited an internal department shortly after Roger had been there and they realized I was in his team, the staff would automatically be hostile towards me. It would be difficult to receive any assistance and I would have to work hard to demonstrate that not everyone treated people in the same way as Roger.

He took the approach with internal support staff that "I'm really important and you're not, so you had better complete this request and treat it like it is your number one priority". He would never say please or thank you. No pleasantries, no trying to understand the colleagues current workload, or how time consuming his request might be, just "do this because I want you to". He would then complain to everyone that so and so in the billing department was useless and never did anything for him.

Roger was consistent; he behaved like this with all back office departments. His behavior didn't lead to him losing his job, he was actually very good with customers but he didn't attain the success that others had. His approach cost him the difference between doing really well and doing okay. Back office staff would eventually do what he asked, assuming that it was a valid request, but begrudgingly and with the least amount of effort they could get away with.

Thankfully, once the same staff had worked with me, I didn't have to contend with the same issues as Roger. I am no saint, however I discovered early in my career that showing respect for a colleagues role and dealing with them in a reasonable manner, whilst taking a few extra seconds to be pleasant, makes all the difference to how willing they are to help. In effect, I treated back office staff as if they were my customers. Roger just didn't appreciate that good internal business relationships can be the differentiator between being successful and doing okay.

By taking a little extra time to explain why a request needs urgent attention and the difference some help could make, it is amazing how much easier it is to have something prioritized. People like to feel they have contributed; it is just basic human nature. When someone has done an exceptional job, it is important to take the time and say that their help was really appreciated.

Adopting this approach helps us become more effective and efficient, with less effort. Often, even when favors are not required, requests seem to speed through the system and the Rogers of this world find their work requirements taking the longest time possible. When treated decently colleagues spread the word to other parts of the business. One simple act of being pleasant, when making a request, can make things easier when help is required from other parts of the business. The opposite is also true. Take a Red Army approach and resistance can spring up in areas where it is least expected.

Russia could have made it much easier for German soldiers to stop fighting and surrender simply by changing their tactics and treating them decently. This would have prevented the loss of countless Soviet and German lives and enabled the Red army to occupy a larger part of Western Europe than they eventually did, helping them to carve up even more of Europe for their own benefit.

At the end of the war, German soldiers and civilians would travel hundreds of miles to surrender to the Allies rather than risk the consequences of surrender to the Red Army. Were you a German scientist or highly skilled engineer, who would you prefer to work for, the brutal dictatorship of Stalin's Soviet Union or the proven freedom and democracy of the Western Allies? Hundreds of thousands of Germans voted with their feet and the Allies gained enormous benefits and saved thousands of soldier's lives as a result of behaving decently. The Allies strictly enforced adherence to the Geneva convention on the treatment of prisoners and population, knowing that it was the right thing to do. Whilst also recognizing the advantage this policy gave them over the Soviets. What the allies had not foreseen was the unintended consequences this strategy would derive.

One of the key secrets to Churchill's success was that in spite of a reputation for tough talking and firm action, he actually understood and practiced the skill of deliberately treating others with courtesy and respect. He knew from many years of experience that this skill was one of the cornerstones of his success. It is as true today in business as it was during the war, taking the time to treat people decently both at work and in all of life's situations can make the difference between doing well and achieving great results.

Chapter 2

Tell it Like it is, Nicely!

Most people who have an opinion about Churchill would not be surprised to know that he could be both tough and absolutely ruthless. Churchill had developed this capability over the course of his life. He was quite comfortable giving bad news without losing any sleep over it. He was able to do this because he firmly believed that he was acting for the common good. What might surprise the reader is the fact that he would endeavor to be as reasonable and pleasant as possible when having to act in this way. By Ruthless, I mean absolutely life and death ruthless.

It was May 1940 and Churchill had not long been appointed as Prime Minister of Britain. The French were nearing collapse in their struggle against Germany. They were ill prepared to fight such a large, strong and well equipped vicious fighting force which Hitler had amassed on the French border. In the years leading up to the start of the German aggression, in Churchill's view the quality of the French army had deteriorated to the point that Churchill was convinced they would be not be able to hold out for long. The objective was to reduce Germany's war making capacity, in order to weaken the Nazi ability to attack Britain.

A British fighting force of 400,000 men equipped with the best Allied military equipment available at the time was on French soil. Churchill wanted this fine body of troops to do as much harm to "The Hun" as possible. He committed more Spitfires to the fight than was prudent for the defense of Britain for he knew that this awesome new fighting machine was more than a match for anything the Luftwaffe could launch into the air. The Spitfire did good business for every one lost, three

German planes were shot down. Within a few weeks of the start of hostilities, he could sense that the French high command did not have the stomach for a long fight. A growing air of desperation and despondency permeated the frequent meetings with the French military high command. Churchill directed all his efforts into persuading the French to keep on fighting but he knew it was only a matter of days before the end would come and the French would negotiate a surrender.

This was the first major test of his leadership. He had only been in the job a few weeks. A large part of the world was not convinced that Britain could survive the onslaught of the mighty German machine, the greatest army ever assembled on the face of the earth. It all went rapidly from bad to worse and then to disaster. The Germans smashed through Belgium and the French army collapsed. The only question remaining was whether the British army could get out of France intact. The outlook was truly grim. The most optimistic forecast from the British generals was that 50,000 might escape if everything went in Britain's favor. Just about every trained man the British army had was on French soil, so few men would leave the island virtually undefended. In addition all the highest quality military hardware was in France, no matter what happened to the men it would be impossible to get all the military equipment out. Whilst Churchill put a brave face on events he knew that with so few guns and only a small army to defend the mainland from the inevitable German invasion, he needed some kind of miracle. Hitler knew that for his evil scheme of world domination to succeed Britain must be either neutralized or crushed. With Churchill now at the helm, the only option left open was to smash the Englanders, Churchill had made it abundantly clear that if the Nazi's wanted to put their jackboots on British soil they would have to "bring it on". Unlike the French, Churchill knew that cities could be rebuilt, but once the spirit of a nation had been lost, things would never be the same again. It was his opinion that a country who goes down fighting can be reborn, one that capitulates, whilst they still have fight left in them, is doomed forever.

As will be described in a later chapter, whilst Lord Halifax was trying to persuade the war cabinet to seek terms with Hitler, to everyone's surprise, especially Winston's, the end of May

1940 delivered Churchill his miracle. Amid incredible scenes of heroism hundreds of small boats evacuated 350,000 troops from Dunkirk. They ferried backward and forward repeatedly across the channel, despite the peril of air attack and shelling from the shores of France. Small fishing boats and pleasure cruisers joined with the Royal Navy to bring relief to a truly desperate situation. Hundreds of small boats were sunk, killing their heroic captains and crew. Every type of vessel was involved. The people of Britain knew that their very survival depended on the number of men who could be liberated from the bomb drenched beaches of Dunkirk, and everyone capable of helping, gave their all. Even Churchill's own private secretary seconded an old pleasure cruiser from the Thames and ferried many hundreds of soldiers to safety.

Churchill was convinced that Hitler could quite easily have instructed his troops to obliterate the British army had he wished to. One theory Churchill put forward after the war to explain why Hitler did not give this order, was his absolute confidence in victory over Britain and a subsequent negotiated surrender. He wanted the evacuated soldiers to police the Empire once Britain had capitulated. Thankfully, things panned out somewhat differently for Adolf.

Not long after Dunkirk the French army was finally defeated. Despite the tremendous efforts of the brave French troops and the great loss of life inflicted on the people of France, it was all in vain. The Generals and politicians preferred to surrender rather than fight to the bitter end and see Paris destroyed. The Vichy government was created as a puppet for the Germans and over the remainder of the war it was to become the willing supporter of many grisly Nazi schemes. Thankfully, in spite of the terrible risk of capture and the horrendous torture and terror that awaited anyone who was caught, the French resistance immediately sprang to life and proved to the world that whilst the politicians had given up the fight, enough French men and women still cared passionately about their country. Over the next 5 years many thousands would die for the cause of freedom and liberation, amid countless acts of heroism.

With the French army neutralized the overriding issue for the British was the future of the French Navy. France had the fourth biggest fleet in the world, and had state of the art battleships near completion in French dockyards.

The man in charge of the Fleet was Admiral Darlan. Darlan had given repeated assurances to Churchill, that should France be defeated, he would give the command to sail the fleet to Britain rather than see it fall into German hands. Had he stayed true to his word, Darlan would have been acclaimed in France and Britain as a hero. He might have ended up as popular as De-Gaulle, who fled France to set up a French opposition in Britain.

In what Churchill describes as an astonishing act of treachery Darlan reneged on his personal commitment and failed to give the command. According to Churchill, double crossing Darlan had a new ministerial job in the Vichy government and it no longer served his personal interests to move the fleet.

Throughout Churchill's memoirs, he is scathing about certain historical figures but he saves some of his most derisory comments for Darlan, calling him an arrogant self-seeking publicist who threw away the chance to be a great savior of France. Instead over the next few years the Admiral suffered a miserable existence in the Vichy administration weighed down under the yoke of German control, only to be assassinated by his own people. His one redeeming credit in Churchill's eyes was that he never let the Germans have access to the French fleet.

After the miraculous evacuation from Dunkirk, the 350,000 grateful British troops were desperately short of equipment and in particular guns and ammunition. The men escaped, leaving years of British military production behind to be recycled by the Germans. In desperation Churchill asked Roosevelt to sell Britain fifty old American destroyers to help protect the vital convoys crossing the Atlantic. He also asked to purchase a million rifles to re-equip the army. This was in the early days of the war. The Americans wanted to maintain neutrality and whilst Roosevelt was sympathetic to Britain's plight, he was hesitant to supply the weapons, as he and the American high command were not convinced that Britain could survive for very long. It was one thing for Churchill to state in a famous speech that Britain would fight the Germans on the beaches and in the countryside. It was quite another for America to make the mistake of supplying a vast arsenal of guns and ships to Britain, unsure that the

Germans would not be able to point them back at the USA at some time in the near future.

The issue of the French Navy, the perception of Britain, and Churchill's will to fight were all resolved simultaneously. By dealing with the French Navy in a ruthless manner, Churchill sent an unequivocal message to the world that Britain intended to fight on, no matter what the cost and that any suggestion of a negotiated surrender was completely out of the question

Churchill knew that he could not persuade the new French government to hand over the ships very easily despite the obvious fact that with the French additions to the Royal Navy, Britain's chances of survival would improve, giving France the glint of a possibility that one day they might awaken from their German nightmare. To make it easy for the French he gave the Vichy government three options. Hand the ships to the British; scuttle them, or sail them out of harm's way to the Caribbean or Canada. One thing was certain he was not going to allow them to fall into German hands.

The Navy was run by Darlan so all negotiations had to go through him. General Weygand, the French Prime Minister, was informed by Darlan that Britain had given the French Navy only two options, for purely personal reasons Darlan deliberately omitted option three, sailing the ships to the Caribbean. Churchill was acting ruthlessly for the common good however, his third option revealed that he was also reasonable and sensitive to French feelings and public opinion. Had Darlan told Weygand about option three he would have been ordered to accept it.

Retaining control of the French Navy was Darlan's key to power and had the ships been scattered around the world, his power base would have been eroded. Hence the reason why Darlan took the treacherous decision to conceal Churchill's Caribbean option which ultimately led to 1500 French sailors losing their lives. This cold and calculated decision must have weighed heavily on his mind for the short remainder of his life.

To ensure that the French ships did not defect to the Germans, Churchill mobilized the British fleet and squadrons were dispatched to intercept the two main groups of French ships. One of the British Admirals managed to persuade his opposite number in the French Navy to surrender his ships. The other Royal Navy battle group, guarding a large fleet of French ships moored at Oran in North Africa, was not so successful. In essence, there was a standoff. The British Admiral in charge at Oran made repeated attempts to come to a negotiated agreement with the French but to no avail. Churchill was not going to flinch, he knew a lot more was at stake than the fate of the French Navy, the world was watching and any backing down at this crucial point in the war would have far reaching consequences. Unlike Chamberlain the previous Prime Minister Churchill stood his ground and instructed the British Admiral to attack the French ships if they failed to heed a final warning.

The final ultimatum was given to the French. Foolishly they decided to make a run for it and whilst trying to break through the blockade under the cover of darkness they opened fire on the British Navy. All sympathy for the French plight had to be suspended as the British quickly came to battle stations and launched a counter attack. They sank or disabled all French ships, whilst suffering some minor damage themselves. Fifteen hundred French sailors perished despite the best efforts of the British to save as many lives as possible. If Darlan had done the right thing, the Oran incident would never have occurred.

The French public, fed by the propaganda machine of the Vichy government, resented this incident bitterly and could not understand how their Allies would turn on them, so soon after their humiliating defeat at the hands of the Germans. They would not know the truth for many years to come. The sinking of the French ships at Oran sent a message around the world that Britain was deadly serious about fighting to the bitter end and would stop at nothing in the best interests of preserving her freedom. Shortly afterwards the guns arrived from America. A few months later the destroyers sailed across the Atlantic to be put into the service of the British Navy. The deal for the destroyers was long before Lend Lease and involved Britain giving ninety nine year leases for air bases in Bermuda and parts of the Caribbean. After Oran, no one was in any doubt about Britain's resolve to survive. The next big test, the Battle of Britain was to follow.

Whilst the Oran incident illustrated Churchill's well known ruthless streak, it also demonstrated how he went out of his way to act decently towards the French Navy. He insisted on giving plenty of warning to the French, he was desperate to avoid any loss of life. The British Navy did not try to surprise the French or do anything underhand. They were unceasing in their efforts to come to a settlement. In the end, it just was not acceptable to watch the Germans take control of the French Fleet as this would have destabilized the whole balance of British naval superiority over the enemy, the one area in which Britain had the upper hand.

The Churchillian skill of acting both decently and ruthlessly at the same time, was something he was to practice many times during the course of the war. He stated that his decision to sink the ships of a country that Britain had been allies with, only weeks before, was the most difficult he ever had to take. Whilst he did not regret it, he wished that it had been avoidable.

Churchill knew that he had to establish his credentials as a person of stern resolve, if he said he was going to do something or issued an ultimatum then all the governments and people he dealt with needed to know the consequences, should they fail to act. After Oran, his capacity to deliver on a threat or ultimatum was no longer doubted by anybody, friend or foe.

I don't want to give a false impression of Churchill as being some sort of angst ridden leader, who agonized about every tough decision he had to make. There are many examples in the book where it was clear that bad people did bad things, and in those circumstances Churchill had no hesitation whatsoever in taking the necessary steps to bring about their destruction. Without a doubt the greatest crime in history was perpetrated by the Nazi's against the Jewish race during WW2. By 1944 it was becoming clear just how truly dreadful the extent of Hitler's crime was. When I read Churchill's memoirs, I was surprised by how little he had written about the ordeal of the Jews. It was only when I read all the memo's in the appendices that it became clear just how moved Churchill was by their dreadful plight. In what was a very powerful note, he made it abundantly clear what he wanted to happen to the perpetrators.

PRIME MINISTER TO FOREIGN SECRETARY 11 JULY 44
There is no doubt that this [persecution of Jews in Hungary

and their expulsion from enemy territory] is probably the greatest and most horrible crime ever committed in the whole history of the world, and it has been done by scientific machinery by nominally civilized men in the name of a great State and one of the leading races of Europe. It is quite clear that all concerned in this crime who may fall into our hands, including the people who only obeyed orders by carrying out the butcheries, should be put to death after their association with the murders has been proved.

I cannot therefore feel that this is the kind of ordinary case which is put through the Protecting Power, as, for instance, the lack of feeding or sanitary conditions in some particular prisoners' Camp. There should therefore, in my opinion, be no negotiations of any kind on this subject. Declarations should be made in public, so that everyone connected with it will be hunted down and put to death.

An example of Churchill's pleasant ruthlessness came after Pearl Harbor. The declaration of war that Britain made on Japan read :-

FOREIGN OFFICE   DECEMBER 8TH 1941
    Sir,

On the evening of December 7th His Majesty's Government in the United Kingdom learned that Japanese forces without previous warning either in the form of a declaration of war or an ultimatum with a conditional declaration of war had attempted a landing on the coast of Malaya and bombed Singapore and Hong Kong.

In view of these wanton acts of unprovoked aggression committed in flagrant violation of International Law and particularly of Article I of the Third Hague Convention relative to the opening of hostilities, to which both Japan and the United Kingdom are parties, His Majesty's Ambassador at Tokyo has been instructed to inform the Imperial Japanese Government in the name of His Majesty's Government in the United Kingdom that a state of war exists between our two countries.

I have the honor to be, with high consideration, Sir,

Your obedient servant,
WINSTON S. CHURCHILL

Churchill was criticized for the pleasant way he ended the letter. As Churchill put it, "when you have to kill a man it costs nothing to be polite".

Taking this analogy and applying it to business is reasonably straight forward, as it is also highly desirable to create the perception in business of being someone who is prepared to carry out a threat or an ultimatum. When a person will do what they say, when they say it, even if it means there will be unpleasant consequences, they are instinctively treated differently. If they can achieve this whilst demonstrating integrity, being pleasant and avoiding obvious confrontation, they gain and retain respect, even when the outcome is unpalatable. Genuine respect is one of the hardest things to achieve in business and is unquestionably one of the key traits that people aspire to.

It's one thing to manage by dictation, bullying and fear. It is something entirely different to be ruthless, respected and admired at the same time. I would contend that Churchill had the latter in abundance and it was another of the key skills that he practiced, forming one of the cornerstones of his success.

Throughout the chapters of this book I have used examples from my business career to show how Churchill's secret skills can be applied in business. Clearly, these examples pale in comparison to Churchill, as most business examples would do compared to the life and death survival situation that Churchill was in charge of. However I genuinely believe that parallels can be drawn, it is not necessary to be in a life and death situation or to do anything overly dramatic for colleagues or staff to know you are being serious. Being candid, I would probably be described as firm rather than ruthless.

I took on a management role with a new company and started in the summer. In the process, I inherited a team of three people. When December came all of my team vanished for most of the month, they had holiday days left over and wanted to take them before the calendar year end cut-off.

It seemed odd that everyone would leave it so late in the year to take such a large amount of holiday. On investigation, I discovered that company policy was to allocate all fixed public holidays as floating days; staff could either work them or take them off. My team all worked from home as they lived a long distance from the nearest office. They claimed to be working the public holidays from their home office, whilst the rest of the country was on holiday. In reality, they kept their mobile phone on just in case of emergency. By doing this, they accrued additional holiday. They would take five weeks annual leave during the year, then indignantly insist on taking their ill gotten accrued floating days in December.

It would have been easy and personally beneficial to turn a blind eye to this practice, especially considering the rest of the company were largely relaxed about it. Other managers in the company were happy to take advantage. I remember chatting to one manager who had the ludicrous situation of one of his team taking the week before Christmas and the week after as holiday, insisting that she would work from home on the three quiet days between Christmas and New Year. What a likely story!

This extra holiday made my team less effective. I was launching a brand new business service and it was imperative that they put in maximum effort, not easy if they were on leave. I solved the problem by issuing a new holiday directive, this allowed everyone to continue working public holidays, so long as they did so from a company office. No one ever worked them again, as it would have meant at least a one hundred mile round trip.

An option to carry up to five days of annual leave across to the following year was commonplace and was at the discretion of the manager. This just encouraged people not to take their holidays, resulting in greater stress, whilst stopping them spending time with their families. I stopped the carry over and insisted that only one week of holiday could be taken in December. The rules applied to everyone without exception, including myself. From then on, the team took their holidays during the year and in my view were more productive and happier as a result.

Whilst these examples were very low level, they

demonstrated a principled approach and a certain amount of resolve. Nobody liked the new rules, however boundaries had been set which began the process of the team developing respect for me as a manager.

Building on the theme of developing respect, I was in the office sitting near the support team when they overheard me having a conversation with a project manager who had just given me some bad news regarding the delivery of a business service I was trying to launch. This caused a robust argument over the phone. Later on I was told by one of the support team that after the phone call they all looked at each other and said, we had better not mess with that guy; he bites your head off. Whilst I wasn't rude to the project manager I made it clear that the revised proposal was unacceptable and offered advice as to how to make improvements.

It only takes a simple incident like the one described, for people to understand that you can be ruthless and firm when called for. It is unnecessary to be ruthless all the time, as people will understand that certain boundaries exist that would be unwise to cross. Within the boundaries, it is possible to act in an entirely pleasant manner.

Ruthlessness, respect and admiration are probably the hardest things to achieve in business, however to be successful these qualities are not necessarily required. There are plenty of examples of truly dreadful people, who have been successful because they were bullies and treated staff appallingly. Over the years I have met plenty of very wealthy people that fall into both categories. I have spent a great deal of time working with the owners and managers of companies. The conclusion I have drawn is that successful companies run by tyrants, are filled with staff that feel as if they HAVE to perform a job to earn an income and have no connection with the company. The companies I have worked with run by highly regarded and well liked owners and managers are filled with staff that WANT to perform a job and are happy to go the extra mile to help achieve success.

Given the option of achieving success by either being liked and respected or doing so whilst being thoroughly loathed by everyone, I know which I prefer. Based on the people I have met, it would appear possible to choose which option to take.

It would have been easy for Churchill to act in a tyrannical fashion not unlike his counterpart in Germany. One of the surprising secrets that jump out from Churchill's memoirs is that he naturally choose the option of wanting to be liked and respected.

Chapter 3

Invest in Yourself

One of the truly surprising talents that Churchill developed was his capacity to make sure he enjoyed any situation he found himself in, to the best of his ability. Churchill's memoirs clearly described how he took time to re-charge his batteries whenever possible, despite being under almost incalculable pressure. He absolutely subscribed to the work hard play hard approach to life, at a level that most people today would struggle to match.

Churchill spent many months out of the country during the war visiting battle fronts and talking to troops airmen and sailors. It was as a result of his direct contact with the fighting forces that he was able to gauge the moral of the troops. He spent many months abroad on conferences, persuading and cajoling allied and commonwealth leaders to support the war effort, in the way that Churchill specifically wanted them to. He was actually criticized by the press at home for taking too many trips abroad, these criticism's must have been hurtful and appeared very unfair to Churchill, as the trips put a great strain on him. It would have been impossible for Churchill to have had such an extraordinary influence on the direction of the war, if he had stayed in Britain.

It was during these frequent trips to places such as North Africa, America, Canada and Russia that he endeavored to travel in the greatest degree of comfort possible, taking time to enjoy the journey. Whilst negotiating or persuading he would ensure the best use was made of any hospitality on offer. At the end of his trips, he would plan additional time to recuperate and recharge his batteries. If he was going to make complicated decisions with life and death consequences, he needed to be as fresh and alert as possible, for Churchill the downtime was as critical a part of his success as the time he spent in the thick of it.

Churchill's idea of relaxing wasn't like most mortals. He would go to bed very late, sleep for eight hours then lay in until early afternoon reading and responding to a mountain of telegrams, part of the unrelenting decision making process of war. He always travelled with an entourage of secretaries who he dictated to, along with an encryption team responsible for securely transmitting his messages around the world.

One of his favorite locations was Marrakech, he loved to stay in the opulence of the American ambassador's house, which had fantastic views over the Atlas Mountains. In fact, he produced his only painting during the war on one such visit. Churchill was a prolific painter using painting as means of relaxation. He even managed to publish a book on the subject after the war.

Churchill was regularly ill during the war being particularly prone to colds and flu, this meant he was often laid up in bed. Even when he was desperately ill and barely able to walk, he would still attend a conference. His personal doctor worked wonders to keep him fit during the war.

Given the pressures upon him, it would have been completely understandable if Sir Winston had left no time for himself, devoting every single waking minute to the war effort. The impression given is that he was not a particularly religious man, believing that he would stride the earth once, with little expectation of a hereafter. He therefore went to great lengths to enjoy the time available.

There is a great anecdote in his memoirs about an incident, which took place in early 1945. Churchill was on his way back to Britain from a conference with Roosevelt and Stalin in Yalta, Russia. He made a stopover in Egypt to meet an important Arab Prince who had been very loyal to the war effort, providing the allies with oil. The Prince was on board an American battle ship, which had transported him along with his 10 wives, 60 servants and a dozen goats. Dinner was arranged by the Prince's personal assistant who wrote to Churchill informing him that because of the Prince's religion, no alcohol would be permitted during dinner. Churchill was famous for enjoying a drink with a reputation for preferring the finest wines, champagnes and cognacs. There was no possibility whatsoever that Churchill would abstain from a drink during dinner. He diplomatically wrote to the Prince and stated that, whilst respecting His Highness's convictions, abstinence during a meal would offend his own belief that he should be allowed to drink, before, during, and after every meal. Dinner proceeded with drinks and without incident.

For ordinary working people such as I, with a wife and two young boys, cramming lots of fun and excitement into life can be a challenge. My wife and I try to get as much time together as we can, we never tire of each other's company, our idea of heaven is a night away in a hotel on our own. Whilst spending time with the children is great fun, they are now approaching that age when we have to compete with the attractions of a computer and an X-Box. Thankfully, my work is enjoyable, rewarding, pays well and provides plenty of opportunities to do and see different things. Work that enables me to spend time with my family and to stop and smell the roses occasionally is of the utmost importance to me, but this has not always been the case.

Please forgive the negativity of the following few pages, they are intended to illustrate how really poor managers can have a massive impact on the business and private lives of their staff, as a result of the stress they cause.

The job before last was terribly difficult, the kids were young my immediate manager was a decent person but his boss, the director, was dreadful, although even worse examples are detailed below.

The director had without doubt one of the sharpest minds of any person I have ever worked under, along with absolutely no ability whatever to interface with other people. He had no thought for the lives of staff outside of work. Treating them as a commodity to be used without consideration. It was common to work fourteen hours a day, 5 days a week, only to put in half a day at the weekend. He would think nothing of making staff stay late even if they had plans. He subscribed to a blame culture which meant his management team spent their time trying not to do anything wrong, rather than do something creative. Because he was so intellectually sharp, compared to the rest of his management team, his natural disposition was to concentrate on criticizing his team's work. He knew he had the upper hand intellectually and wanted to continually prove it. This constant negativity created great stress and anxiety in advance of his monthly meetings. The guy made the life of everyone who worked in his department intolerable. Everyone, without exception, absolutely loathed him, he created the worst possible working environment for his business and then wondered why results were consistently poor.

Those who know me would not recognize the permanently stressed out person I was then. One day during a moment of clarity amid the chaos, it dawned on me that life was too short to keep burning myself out in a job I resented, working in a climate of fear under a tyrant. Another job was required. I have never looked back since and it is only right to say a big thank you to my old director. After working for him and doing pretty well it gave me the confidence that I could work in just about any environment, for almost anyone.

I am not one of those spiritual types but occasionally I have noticed that life has a habit every now and then of dealing out poetic justice. Shortly after my departure, he moved roles within my old company and started working for a Frenchman, who was so difficult to work for he made my old director look like a saint. To this day I have never heard anyone say a good word about the Frenchman. Although to be fair, women loved his Charles Aznavour French accent, staring dreamily at him during presentations.

The Frenchman had what appeared to be a real hatred for any other human being. When he became MD of Europe, he continued to make my old directors' life hell, bullying him and slowly stripping him of his dignity and self respect. Effectively turning my old tyrant of a director into his little French poodle, he had truly met his match, poetic justice! The Frenchman was fired as MD of Europe, the result of a failed business strategy. My old director went, not long after.

The Frenchman immediately re-surfaced in another high profile business. This coincided with my own move into the same industry. A few years later I was at an event and I overheard someone who had recently finished working for him describing how awful he was. He re-told a great story that really got to the nub of why everyone loathed him. A senior director who worked for the Frenchman booked an annual holiday in the Italian lakes. Months later a board meeting was called, which happened to coincide with the director's family holiday. The Frenchman insisted that he came back from Italy to attend the meeting.

The meeting started to run late so the director stood up and made his excuses, explaining that he had to get back to the airport or he would miss his flight. The Frenchman angrily shouted at him in front of the other directors, "how dare you leave the meeting before it is finished", arrogantly stating "you will just have to get another flight tomorrow", accusing him of disloyalty and not being committed to the company. All the other directors at the meeting knew that it served no purpose for him to remain, it was just one example of the way the Frenchman treated people by bullying them and belittling them in front of their peers. Incidentally, if at this point you sympathize with the Frenchman then this book is probably not for you!

The Frenchman eventually "left" the company, went to another business, then "left" there also, three months later, and not from choice. This same man once threatened a friend of mine that he would immediately sack any of his team, if they gave a bad presentation at a press launch organized to promote a range of new products. My friend, not phased at all, told him that if any of his team failed to perform the Frenchman could sack him instead.

I have been very lucky in my career, having only had one brief stint working directly for a guy who was completely unsuited to his role. He managed to gain the kind of respect you reserve for a neighbors vicious dog. You don't like it, you can't do anything about it, and you want it to go away, but ultimately it could hurt you if you mess with it. Shortly after he took over as the head of my division, I decided it was time to move on.

Whilst he was just trying to put food on the table for his family, in the best way he knew how, I believe he had a hole in his bucket. Whilst difficult to explain without sounding stupid, I like this analogy. Assume that everyone carries inside them a bucket of goodness. Unless a person's bucket is full, they feel out of balance and need to take action to fill it. A decent person will do something good, which will fill their bucket. A bad person, will top up the bucket, by doing something horrible, to someone decent.

In the cases of the three people described, for one reason or another, known only to them, they had big holes in their respective buckets. They needed to treat people badly in order to fill their buckets up and feel good about themselves.

From a productivity perspective, acting like a bully can create a short-term improvement, in the long term it tends to be counterproductive. It is often cited as the catalyst of a blame culture, leading to people doing what they have to, whilst avoiding taking any risks for fear of getting into trouble. Businesses run in this way are just not as effective as those that have contented, motivated staff. It seems a really bland statement to make, however it is surprising how many companies fail to achieve the obvious. For no other reason than they have employed one or two of the wrong people that act as the catalyst for the wrong type of culture within the organization.

Churchill would regularly visit the war zones to get a feel for troop morale. If he sensed that it was low, he would ascertain why. If he concluded that poor leadership was the cause, he would quickly make changes. Above all, he knew only too well that motivated troops can make the difference between winning and losing a battle.

Quick story about a lady who once worked for me. Not long after she started we went on some customer appointments. In the first client's office I noticed that she had brought a laptop computer in with her, I asked why and she said that her previous manager had insisted she take one into every customer meeting. I asked if she was planning to use the laptop and she said no, I thought this a bit odd but ignored it. Then she pulled out a notebook and apologized for only having a ballpoint pen to write with. At this point I thought she had some sort of obsessive compulsive disorder. "Why apologize," I asked. It transpired that her previous manager insisted on the use of fountain pens. I had to do everything in my power not to fall about in fits of laughter.

After the meeting I asked if her old boss had any other rules. It transpired that he insisted women had to wear "power suits"; all the men had to wear hand tailored "Saville Row" type suits, along with expensive shirts, cufflinks, and handmade leather shoes. He issued all new staff with a page of dress instructions. He disciplined anyone who did not adhere to his code. I was astonished that he could not trust well-paid salespeople to dress themselves. The guy was clearly some sort of control freak.

I made it clear to the lady that I trusted my team to dress appropriately without specific instructions. We would regularly joke about the conversation, without thinking of the reason behind it. Later on she realized that enforcing the excessive dress code was just one part of his controlling behavior, which among other things made her feel bullied, and caused her to leave. This lady was one of the best and most successful people I ever employed, a great asset to my business and a great loss to my competitor.

Stopping to smell the roses requires time to be set aside even from the busiest schedule. When work is a constant rush it can take a great deal of effort to stop. It is often more difficult to kick back and relax than to fill days off with a hectic schedule of activities. Sometimes the best plan is one of deliberately doing nothing.

When a job is so consistently demanding that it leaves no time to enjoy life, then that job should be re-evaluated. Notwithstanding financial economical and family commitments it could be better to move on and work somewhere else, or be self-employed, than resent going to work every day. Times are different, we all live in an age when phones and messaging devices keep us in constant contact with the office, creating the opportunity to work all hours of the day and night. It is sad when someone out for a family dinner cannot resist the temptation to respond to a message from work when they hear a beep or feel a buzz. There is no opportunity to "switch off" which eventually leads to a resentment of the job. Amazingly even when on a family holiday they feel compelled to take their laptop "just in case", ending up sitting by a pool watching the kids splash about, whilst being too busy to join in. Scared stiff, that even from thousands of miles away, work will fall apart without them.

Breaking the cycle is not easy, and can take considerable courage. Generally, a good manager will not try to contact a member of staff at weekends or while they are on holiday. They understand that when staff get a clean break from work they perform better when they return. Other managers through incompetence or malice will take as much of someone as they are prepared to give, happily phoning and e-mailing staff at all hours, expecting a quick response without any consideration for their personal circumstances. I am a stickler for not contacting members of my team out of hours, new members of staff are in no doubt that working late into the evening and at weekends is not expected. Far better that employees give everything to the job when they are supposed to, then get some down time, rather than be permanently connected to the umbilical cord of work, leading to reduced effectiveness and poor decision making. Often a job that would take 30 minutes when you are fresh, takes 90 minutes when you are exhausted. This builds on the ineffectiveness associated with being over tired. Causing greater anxiety and leading to the vicious circle that causes job related stress with all the consequent problems for work and family life.

In a previous job, one chap called me the day before going on a two-week holiday to give me his personal mobile phone number because the company mobile wouldn't work abroad. This was just in case any big issues cropped up whilst he was away. I made it abundantly clear that no matter what happened he would not be getting a call from me, I joked that I would sack him if he contacted the office or a colleague. I wanted him to have a real break from work, something unheard of in his previous job. I selfishly denied him the opportunity to feel indispensable whilst on vacation, because I wanted a more efficient and committed team member to return.

It can be very tempting to call or e-mail someone out of hours looking for a quick answer to a problem. It occasionally has to happen but it's the absolute exception. It takes a great deal of self discipline not to, but I am convinced that it's for the best, both for the individual and in the long run for the company.

One of Churchill's secrets, refined over the first 65 years of his life was the discovery that switching off from work meant that when he switched back on he burned brighter for longer. He had worked out what a lot of younger people never quite grasp in these days of hectic communication, that time invested in relaxing is actually a good investment for the business and the individual. He also correctly guessed that taking time out for personal enjoyment and relaxation, even on a small scale, added to the number of years he would reside on this planet. If Churchill could spend time during a war to experience everything around him, making the effort to rest and recuperate, it must be possible for 21st Century workers to attempt to do the same. After all, Churchill lived until he was ninety!

Chapter 4

Make the Past a Positive

I was struck by the phrase "your past can be a bridle or a spur" which Churchill used in his memoirs. In planning for the Normandy invasions, Churchill had on his mind the terrible events of WWI. After he resigned from the government, following the terrible catastrophe of the Dardanelles he joined the army and served for a while in the trenches. He had bitter first-hand experience of the devastation and slaughter that a coup-de-main (the direct frontal attack on a well defended enemy position) could wreak upon an advancing army. Hundreds of thousands of young men, the flower of a generation, had been cut down making such frontal attacks against the Germans across muddy, blood soaked battlefields. These thoughts and memories sat heavily upon him while planning for D-Day June 1944.

The Great War extracted a price in men by the millions on such battlefields as the Somme and Passchendaele. In those days a well developed defense and the use of machine guns could pin down armies for months at a time and kill thousands of young men in a single assault, just to gain a few hundred yards of territory. In WW1 war was different, there were no machines that could easily break through the trenches, each yard of progress was paid for with the blood of youth. It was only towards the end of the first world war that the tank started to change the way wars would be fought in the future. Incidentally the tank was the developed from an idea by no lesser man than Churchill himself. At the beginning of WW1 Churchill saw the difficulties that would face the armies as they squared up to each other on the Western Front he believed that the only way to pierce the thousands of yards of trenches, barbed wire and minefields was to use a mechanical device. Amazingly the Army were not keen on the idea of Tanks, but after many years of development and much cajoling from Churchill they eventually saw the light. The introduction of the tank on a large scale at the end of WW1 had a major influence on the final outcome.

Twenty years later the WW1 method of defending land by building trenches for defense was largely pointless. The strength of tanks and armored vehicles backed up by air power could quickly and efficiently punch a hole through such outdated modes of warfare.

Imagine yourself in Churchill's situation; you have lived through the horrors of World War 1 and here you are about to do the same thing again in 1944. It would be only human if you tried to avoid repeating the same mistake again, only natural not to want to see more young lives sacrificed, this is where Churchill's phrase "your past can be a bridle or a spur" is apt. Just to explain, a bridle is strapped to a horse's head and slows it down when pulled. You can spur a horse on to go faster by the use of a whip. I do not mean to be insulting, but you never know who will be reading this.

Churchill explained in his memoirs that lessons from the past should not hinder doing something in the future, if plans have been made to avoid making the same mistake twice.

In my own career I have certainly not been immune to making mistakes. I have thought twice on many occasions before doing something again that I know has not gone well in the past. The kernel of the idea to write this book was inspired by the phrase "your past can be a bridle or a spur". I can vividly remember the moment whilst I was reading towards the end of the fifth volume of Churchill's memoirs and I came across the phrase. The story related below immediately popped onto my head. I decided a few days later that if Churchill could inspire me to such reflection then maybe others could be inspired in a similar way. The stories and personal examples I share in the book are merely to show how Churchill's skills have related to situations in my own life and career, or how they might help me in the future. To derive the most from the purchase of this book I would recommend that after each chapter you spare a moment to see if situations from your own life and career have any parallels. Or if some of the skills Churchill used to win the war, which I have attempted to identify, could be of help in the future.

During my time at one company I was asked to set up a new service, having had extensive experience of running a very similar operation in a previous job. All was going well and I expected to launch within 3-4 months of kicking off the project.

Whilst driving home one Friday afternoon in October I received a phone call from my office (hands free I might add), the voice on the other end of the line assumed that I knew who he was. I did not have a clue, but carried on as if I did, rather than cause offence. He quizzed me about the service I was launching with a rather negative tone, which was annoying. I remained quiet and attentive because he seemed as if he might be important. Certain characters have the ability to convey their position without actually saying I'm so-and-so and I'm really powerful. He made it clear he was unhappy about what I was doing and wanted to see my manager and myself as soon as possible.

I made a couple of calls trying to find out who on earth he was, they confirmed that he was indeed extremely important and could quite comfortably bury my project if he wanted to.

Not the best news to hear on a Friday afternoon, the next action was a call to his personal assistant to set up a meeting with him just as soon as a space could be found in his diary .

The only slot available for the next two weeks was Monday, three days time! I was exasperated at the prospect of having to spend the weekend creating a presentation to convince this guy who I had never heard of, that I was doing the right thing for the business. It was critical that the project went ahead as I probably didn't have a career in the company without it. Development budget had been allocated, everyone who mattered in the business was completely comfortable with the project. Unfortunately, he could have snatched the rug from underneath me. The job was great, I was well paid and I wanted to keep the rug under my feet.

The conversation I had with my boss at the time has etched in my memory. "Cancel what you are doing on Monday," I said. "We have to go and present the business case for the project to the senior director whom I have just come off the phone to. Incidentally, he's annoyed with you for not telling him about it in the first place". My old boss's response was typical. "Why should I have told him about it, I didn't know he had any interest in the project. These people really wind me up, expecting us to drop everything and jump at their command, anyway, it's nothing to do with him". After further heated discussion mixed with plenty of four letter expletives, we arranged the flights.

On the Monday, we presented our case, the guy was one of those smiling assassins that you meet every now and then. The sort that make all the right noises and tell you they liked the presentation, that they can see the benefits for the business and the potential money the service could make. Then as soon as you walk out of the door they are straight on the phone wanting to kill the project off, which is what happened in this case. We found out the next day, much to our disappointment that he wanted to stop the project dead in its tracks and this is where we get to the punch line. The director had looked after a similar type of business in the far east some years before and had issues with the potential for the service to be used fraudulently, putting the business at risk of bills going unpaid. Even though this was some years before and systems and security measures had much improved, he would just not countenance the idea of launching the same type of service in his company.

He had let his previous experience become a bridle, even after we had presented a compelling case which addressed all the issues, he was adamant about not allowing the service to go ahead. He was not prepared to accept that I had incorporated the lessons of the past into the new plan. I immediately started a campaign of building support within the business to keep my project alive, I had meeting after meeting with everyone who could influence the outcome. A final decision was to be taken at a main board meeting that was scheduled for 2 weeks later, at which, the fate of my project and effectively my future at the company was a small agenda item.

If Churchill had taken this approach we might not have had the Normandy landings in the early hours of June 6, 1944. Whilst the allies would have gone on to win the war, the time it took may have been extended to Hitler's advantage, as will be seen later in the book.

What Churchill actually did was use the lessons from the past, to guide him in considering the issues that presented themselves in 1944. In WW1, air superiority did not count for much, as planes did not have powerful enough guns and could not carry enough bombs to really make a big impact on the ground. In WW2 air superiority was one of the key success factors, in fact it formed the basis of the Allied victory.

Before the landings in France, Churchill took a very active role in the planning and made sure the German defenses were heavily targeted. Focusing the bombing on the locations where the allies would land, in equal measure with the places where they would not. In addition, and of equal importance, all bridges and railway lines leading to the beaches were destroyed, making it difficult for the Germans to send in fresh troops before the allies could safely establish themselves in France. Churchill ensured that the number of troops landed on the first day were considerably larger than the original numbers planned for the campaign. He had a large array of specialized weapons developed to help overcome the considerable German beach defenses, each of which played their part at the right moment. He left nothing to chance, preferring to have the luxury of an overwhelming force of manpower and equipment, minimizing the potential risks and increasing the chances of success.

In the months leading up to the landings elaborate deceptions were planned to try and fool the Germans into believing the attack would not strike at the beaches of Normandy. Churchill had a real issue with the Irish at the time as the German and Japanese had active consulates in Dublin. He wanted to avoid any Germans flying across from Ireland on a commercial flight spotting the allied build up. He instructed that all flights out of southern Ireland should be grounded or else risk being shot down and that all commercial shipping had to stay in Irish harbors until after the attack.

Designation of the landing zones had taken place long before D-Day, the British Commonwealth and American troops had specific beaches allocated. The movie "Saving Private Ryan" gives some idea of the scale and nature of the difficulties facing the Americans at Omaha beach. Whilst the British had difficulties landing, they were not nearly as bad as those experienced by American forces at Omaha. Most of the landing beaches were manned by what Churchill described as low-grade forces. Unfortunately for the Americans, shortly before D-Day the troops at Omaha were replaced by fresh, well-prepared, first-rate German troops. Hence the reason behind the terrible loss of American life on Omaha beach in comparison with the other landing zones.

If you watch all the war movies that have been made over the years you could quite easily draw the conclusion that it was largely American troops taking part in D-Day. In fact, when the landings took place the troops had a split of 65/35 British/American. This ratio had reversed within six months.

During the early planning stages of Operation Overlord it was assumed that a British military commander would be in overall charge of the attempted liberation of Europe. As the planning went on and the size and scale of the operation massively increased, it became clear that within a few months of landing the USA would have the largest forces on the ground. It made sense that the commander in overall charge should be American. The decision caused a great deal on consternation within British military ranks, as up to this point the majority of the fighting had been done by non US forces. Churchill saw the bigger picture and had to deliver the bad news in the knowledge that it was the right decision politically and militarily.

After the Dunkirk evacuation of 1940, Churchill began considering the practicalities of a return to France. The planners assumed that it would be impossible to successfully capture a large port before it was destroyed by the Germans. They had to develop a method of landing the vast quantities of men and the millions of tons of equipment needed to wage war, onto a beach. Given tides and the swell from waves, it was not possible to do this conventionally. Churchill set up a team to look at ways of overcoming this major obstacle, by the time of the D Day landings, a giant floating harbor had been developed called a Mulberry. This was sunk off the beach and bolted together, thus enabling all the supplies to be landed safely. The Mulberry's had difficulty in the first few weeks of the landings due to severe weather but proved themselves to be an invaluable asset.

Of the many inventions that had a direct bearing on the success of the invasion one stands out to my mind, that of Operation Pluto, the laying of a pipeline to pump petrol from the Isle of White across the mine infested English Channel to the Normandy beaches. Churchill attributed this brilliant idea to Montgomery's staff, and it's success was vital to the ongoing effectiveness of the campaign. Lack of fuel was the one critical component that could bring an army to a standstill. As the result of Operation Pluto, this enormous problem was bypassed.

The Germans had not expected the allies to land on the 6th June as the weather had been so poor beforehand. The forecast for the sixth was not considered good enough by the German weathermen. The allies however had little choice. Even though the weather wasn't perfect, they had hundreds of ships loaded with troops who had been kept on board for 3 days. No one was allowed to disembark in order to preserve secrecy. The decision, taken on balance, was to "go now", rather than wait another month and risk even worse weather. The rough landings caused some of the amphibious tanks to sink, but the element of surprise achieved by the allies outweighed these losses.

Churchill was convinced that modern warfare would overcome the problems of the past. He was right. On D-Day, only three thousand men died, and by the end of June, this figure was only eight thousand. Whilst these are large numbers, it only represented a very small percentage of the men landed and was a far smaller number than the operations team had planned for. In one of Churchill's memo's he argues that less troops will be required for re-enforcements, as less men died than anticipated.

The point Churchill was trying to make when he used the phrase "your past can be a bridle or a spur", is that people should endeavor to take positive lessons from the mistakes of the past, and not dismiss doing something just because it went badly the last time. By making the effort to discover why problems occurred and then creating effective plans to avoid them in the future, anything is possible.

Regarding the launch of my new service, the day came for the board meeting, by this time I was confident that I had done everything I could to overcome the objections. I vividly remember sitting with my boss in Alfresco's, an Italian restaurant which overlooks the beach in Brighton, a seaside town on the south coast of England. 65 years before it was covered in barbed wire and out of bounds to the public. I nervously waited for a phone call, we had been advised that going into the board meeting our chances were 50-50 it was early evening and we had just finished a long day at an exhibition, I was just pouring another glass of wine when the phone rang. My boss answered and the relief on his face said everything, our project had been approved. To overcome the security concerns the board had agreed to add more people into the security team to minimize any risk of fraud. Whilst it was a close run thing, we managed to get the right decision. The project went on to deliver a fantastic service that proved to be a huge success for the business.

Chapter 5

Success is Hidden in Details

At the very outbreak of the war, Prime Minister Chamberlain appointed Churchill head of the Admiralty, giving him complete charge of the Royal Navy. He effectively got his old job back, as he had been head of the Admiralty at the outset of WW1, resigning as a result of the Dardanelles disaster. Churchill immediately sent a memo to everyone in his department, stating that he would not take responsibility for any decision attributed to him, which he had not put in writing. He kept to this principle when he became Prime Minister and Minister of Defense in May 1940.

Churchill was a prolific writer of telegrams and ciphers, the wartime equivalent of E-Mail. He would continually dictate memo's to his secretaries, issuing instructions and asking questions of the people and departments that dealt with every aspect of making war. What set him apart from previous Prime Ministers was his habit of attending to detail. The quote from Churchill below sums up his philosophy.

"An efficient and a successful administration manifests itself equally in small as in great matters".

He wanted to know about everything and he looked closely at all areas, he did not leave anything to chance. This created a workload that would have floored a man half his age. To handle such a colossal level of detail, Churchill would typically work 16 hours a day, requiring secretaries to be available around the clock, just to keep up with him. He managed to attain this constant level of productivity by sleeping for an hour every day after lunch. He had picked up this habit when he was a young man on adventure in Cuba with the Spanish army.

Churchill was very explicit, no interruptions during his nap. In fact, he had a golden rule regarding sleep in general, if a German invasion force landed in England, wake him up, otherwise he was not to be disturbed. Remarkably, the D Day landings started on the morning of June the 6th at 4.00am, Churchill found out about the successful landings at 7.00am when he awoke. Can you imagine these days a leader sleeping through such a momentous event!

Having a nap in the early afternoon can really work for some people. I returned from a three week holiday with a five hour time difference and was working from home on my first day back. I woke up very early to catch up on my E-Mail, by lunchtime I was flagging, the jet lag had kicked in and I could barely keep my eyes open. Rather than the usual trick of drinking lots of strong coffee and just pushing through the exhaustion, as I'd not long finished reading the chapter in his memoirs I thought I would try a "Churchill" and go to bed for an hour. Instead of a lunch break, I ate a sandwich at my desk. It took a little while to fall asleep, fifty minutes later the alarm went off. I had probably slept for thirty and felt a bit groggy when I woke up, ten minutes later I could not believe how fresh I felt. I was a new man, full of energy and concentration and able to get through a stack more work with far greater concentration than I had managed in the run up to lunch. I felt fantastic for the rest of the day and into the evening. I thought it might spoil my sleep at night, but it didn't.

It would be great if I could have a "Churchill" every day but given the nature of my job, that is not practical. I would love to have an airline Club Class chair in my study at home, I could then have a lunchtime sleep when I felt the need, again not very realistic. Everyone's circumstances are different and it might not be possible to grab a sleep for most people. If there is any way of squeezing an hour's sleep into a schedule or taking a quick nap in the car, or just sitting in a chair with one's eyes closed for twenty minutes. It is surprising how the body responds to a quick pit stop.

I do wonder if the fact that Churchill took a nap every day

added to his longevity? He died at the age of ninety, he had lived a life filled with the most incredibly stressful events, he smoked huge cigars and was famous for enjoying a drink. By any insurance company's estimate he should have been dead at fifty. It is not impossible to imagine how taking an hours sleep every day could make a big difference to a person's health and overall sense of calm and well-being. I am no doctor but you never know, it might be the secret to a healthier extended life.

Churchill's memoirs contain many examples of his requests for information about a myriad of issues affecting every aspect of the war, both at home and abroad. He was fanatical about checking every detail. From the farming of vegetables to the building of bombers, no area was too small for him. There are quite literally thousands of memo's which Churchill selected to publish at the back of his memoirs. I have selected a few of my favorites below.

The first shows how Churchill was concerned with the everyday safety of the British population. Throughout his memoirs there is a theme of taking officials to task who overstep the mark and become too pernicious in the application of rules.

NOTE BY THE FIRST LORD OF THE ADMIRALTY,   *20 NOV 1939*

I venture to suggest to my colleagues that when the present moon begins to wane the black-out system should be modified to a sensible degree. We know that it is not the present policy of the German Government to indulge in indiscriminate bombing in England or France, and it is certainly not their interest to bomb any but a military objective. The bombing of military objectives can best be achieved, and probably only be achieved, by daylight or in moonlight. Should they change this policy, or should a raid be signaled, we could extinguish our lights again. It should have been possible by this time to have made arrangements to extinguish the street lighting on a Yellow Warning. However, so far as night bombing for the mere purpose of killing civilians is concerned, it is easy to find London by directional bearing and the map, whether the city is lighted or not. There is no need to have the 'rosy glow' as a guide, and it would not be a guide if it were extinguished before the raiders leave the sea: But there is not much in it anyway.

2. *There is, of course, no need to turn on the full peace-time street-lighting.*

There are many modified forms. The system in force in the streets of Paris is practical and effective. You can see six hundred yards. The streets are light enough to drive about with safety, and yet much dimmer than in time of peace.

3. *The penalty we pay for the present methods is very heavy: First, the loss of life: Secondly, as the Secretary of State for Air has protested, the impediment to munitions output; and also work at the ports, even on the west coast:.*

Thirdly, the irritating and depressing effect on the people which is a drag upon their war-making capacity, and, because thought unreasonable, an injury to the prestige of His Majesty's Government: Fourthly, the anxieties of women and young girls in the darkened streets at night or in blacked-out trains:

Fifthly, the effect on shopping and entertainments.

I would therefore propose that as from December 1:

(a) Street-lighting of a dimmed and modified character shall be resumed in the cities, towns and villages.

(b) Motor cars and railway trains shall be allowed substantially more light, even at some risk.

(c) The existing restrictions on blacking-out houses, to which the public have adapted themselves, shall continue; but that vexatious prosecutions for minor infractions shall not be instituted. (I see in the newspapers that a man was prosecuted for smoking a cigarette too brightly at one place, and that a woman who turned on the light to tend her baby in a fit was fined in another.).   .

(d) The grant of these concessions should be accompanied by an effective propaganda continuously delivered by the broadcast, and handed out to motorists at all refueling stations, that on an air-raid warning all motorists should immediately stop their cars and extinguish their lights, and that all other lights should be extinguished. Severe examples should be made of persons who, after a warning has been sounded, show any light.

4. *Under these conditions we might face the chances of the next three winter months in which there is so much mist and fog. We can always revert to the existing practice if the war flares up,*

or if we do anything to provoke reprisals.
  W.S.C.

Churchill was not happy with what he saw as profiteering by Londoners, charging high rents to US military personnel.

PRIME MINISTER TO LORD PRESIDENT, CHANCELLOR OF THE EXCHEQUER, MINISTER OF WORKS AND BUILDINGS, AND MINISTER OF HEALTH   *14TH MAR 44*
  General Bedell Smith mentioned to me yesterday the very high and extortionate prices now being charged to American officers over here for flats and small houses. A medium-sized flat, he said, was £28 a week, and the small house that he occupied was £35 a week. There is no reason why the Americans should not pay a fair and equitable price for accommodation, which they are quite willing to do, but I do not think extortion or profiteering should be allowed.
  I am not certain who deals with this, but would you very kindly give it your attention and let me know, first, about the facts, and, secondly, whether there is any remedy.

PRIME MINISTER TO DEPUTY PRIME MINISTER   *2 APR 44*

  I am sure Bedell Smith would not have mentioned the matter to me if the charges were not excessive. £28 a week for a medium-sized flat and £35 a week for a small house seem outside the bounds of reason. Perhaps these few cases could be examined by Lord Portal himself anyhow, if he gets into touch with General Bedell Smith I should have done my bit.

Churchill wrote an incredible number of memo's regarding farming matters and had a particular focus on chickens and eggs. He sent more memo's on this subject than any other agricultural issue, he appeared to have a real problem with the ministry of food. He felt they were overly officious in administering schemes for keeping chickens. Churchill applauded the local entrepreneurial spirit of hard pressed Britons trying every angle possible to keep eggs on the table.

PRIME MINISTER TO MINISTER OF FOOD   *22 DEC 41*

Your minute about the egg distribution scheme.

The fact that 370,000 small producers have enough gumption to keep chickens is a matter for congratulation; under this heading the only complaint I have heard, is that this practice is not sufficiently encouraged. After all, the backyard fowls use up a lot of scrap, and so save cereals.

I quite recognize your difficulties, with your imports cut to one third, but I hope that you will get in the quantity which you had planned, so that this important animal protein which is so essential in the kitchen should not be deficient.

I couldn't leave out Churchill's note about the American addiction to ice cream

PRIME MINISTER TO MINISTER OF FOOD   *22 SEPT 42*
PROHIBITION OF THE MANUFACTURE AND SALE OF ICE-CREAM
Without definite information as to the saving in transport and man power, I cannot judge whether the destruction of this amenity was worthwhile.
I suppose the large numbers of American troops in this country will have their own arrangements made for them, They are great addicts of ice-cream, which is said to be a rival to alcoholic drinks.
The step should not have been taken without the Cabinet having an opportunity to express an opinion.

PRIME MINISTER TO SECRETARY OF STATE FOR WAR   23 OCT 44
A serious appeal was made to me by General Alexander for more beer for the troops in Italy. The Americans are said to have four bottles a week, and the British rarely get one. You should make an immediate effort, and come to me for support in case other departments are involved. Let me have a plan. with time schedule, for this beer. The question of importing ingredients should also be considered. The priority in issue is to go to the fighting troops at the front, and only worked back to the rear as and when supplies open out.
The question of leave is also pressed seriously. If only a small proportion could have leave it would be much appreciated. Try to work out a thousand a month plan. Could these men come

back across France? I am aware that Marseilles is greatly congested, but are there not other routes which could be used? In this case also priority should be given to the troops who have been engaged in the fighting.

PRIME MINISTER TO SECRETARY OF STATE FOR WAR   20 NOV 44
   Good. Press on. Make sure that the beer, four pints a week, goes to the troops under the fire of the enemy before any of the parties in the rear get a drop.

When Churchill took over at the admiralty he checked if the sailors at the large naval base in Portsmouth had enough warm coats, and if there was enough entertainment in Portsmouth to keep the sailors occupied during shore leave. Not the sort of thing someone in Churchill's position would normally take an interest in. There was a clear intention in his deliberate approach to managing the detail, by delving down to this level, he put everyone below him on notice that he had the desire and the capacity to get involved to the tiniest degree. The consequence of this approach was to motivate the people who worked in the admiralty to be equally as diligent. If they did not, then the chief could hold them to account for any of their shortcomings, sloppiness, or the cutting of corners at any time.

The example of making sure the sailors were well looked after and the matters raised in the memo's I have included also highlight Churchill's appreciation that it is people at the top who make the policies, whilst the people at the shop front turn policy into reality, or victory, in the case of war.

During a committee meeting discussing the effect of German bombing in 1944 it was highlighted by one of the officers that German bombs developed a 30% greater bomb blast per pound than British bombs. Churchill immediately demanded to know why this was the case. It transpired that the Germans added aluminum powder to their explosive mixture, which increased the effective blast. In 1940 aluminum was a scarce commodity in Britain, all available aluminum went into making fighters and bombers, British bomb producers had taken the decision not to use aluminum. This decision had remained unchallenged for four years, despite the fact that aluminum was in plentiful supply in

1944. The Battle of the Atlantic had been won and shipping was getting through in ever increasing numbers. This limitation meant that the RAF needed to send more bombers to Germany to have the same overall blast impact as the Luftwaffe, when they attacked Britain. This oversight by the bomb manufacturers was limiting the effectiveness of the British war effort. Churchill immediately gave the instruction to build all new bombs with the revised explosive mixture, to the detriment of the German population.

Another example of attention to detail involved the diet of the troops. In 1940 essential food imports from around the world were decreasing as merchant ships were continually being sunk by U-Boats. In fact two thirds of the British pig population had to be slaughtered in 1940 because the ministry of supply was unable to import the necessary feed to sustain such a large population. Churchill created a scientific committee to investigate the nutrition of the troops and the British people. The committee recommended the rationing of tea and promoted the idea that all troop meals should consist of a high-energy diet of vegetables, nuts and pulses. Churchill immediately intervened and asked professor Lindeman (the scientist he trusted most of all) to evaluate the proposals. He concluded that limiting tea would be counterproductive for the war effort as it was one sure way of upsetting the working population. In those days the British drank a great deal of tea! Churchill was not happy with the troop rationing proposals either and stated that, "All the food faddists and nut eaters I have ever known died young after a long period of senile decay". He insisted that the troops received rations of meat and vegetables, and concluded that one easy way to lose the war was to upset the soldiers by putting them on a vegetarian diet. He also insisted that tea remained in plentiful supply for as long as possible.

It is astonishing, that with the fall of France and the Battle of Britain to contend with, Churchill could find time to attend to such matters.

Another example of Sir Winston managing detail had a significant effect on the War and in particular, greatly contributed to the turnaround in the fortunes of the British army.

In the early part of the war the Italians had been ejected from

North Africa as part of the British army's western desert campaign. These victories were the first real success the army had achieved and for some time it looked like the war wasn't going to be as difficult as everyone thought. Unfortunately the Italian army was of a very low caliber and everything changed when Hitler decided that he could not afford the loss of prestige caused by the abject failure of his Italian axis partner. He dispatched a number of German divisions, they had superior equipment, were better organized and had in Rommel a formidable General. He was determined to take the fight to the British and reverse the Italian territorial losses, and that is exactly what happened. The Germans quickly started to win back the Italian territory lost to the British, ending with what Churchill considered a humiliating defeat. The heavily fortified port of Tobruk which had been won at great cost against the Italians and was a crucial port for delivering vital materials to the allies, surrendered, to a German force one third its size.

Churchill heard about the surrender whilst he was at a strategy and planning conference in Washington. President Roosevelt delivered the news to him personally. He was devastated and took it very badly. He resolved to make changes to the command structure in the western dessert. Winston reshaped the organization so that Generals had more focus on fighting and less time was wasted on matters that could be handled by back office staff.

The US had just introduced the Sherman tank, which was widely regarded as the finest tank in the world at the time, far superior to anything the British had. Churchill discovered that when the British tanks engaged the German Panzers they were soundly beaten. Not surprisingly, in a tank battle, how good your tanks are is a crucial factor. The British tank was better than the Italian, but no match for the German machines. Over the course of the war there was a race by the protagonists to build tanks with ever bigger guns and thicker armor. The tanks that started the war were like pea shooters compared to the tanks that ended it.

Whilst talking to my mother about this book she related a story about my grandfather who was in the army engineering corp and was stationed in North Africa during the original western dessert campaign against the Italians. He had noticed a flaw in one of the tank designs which put the tank crews at great risk. He took it upon himself to devise an additional steel plate to re-enforce a strategic weak spot on the British tank. This modification was so successful that it was implemented across all of the existing and new tanks, helping to save countless lives by giving increased protection to the occupants when the tank was attacked.

When an army knows that the opposition's tank has them outgunned and has armor thick enough to withstand the shells they are firing and every time they are directly hit, the power of the enemy's shell pierces through thei armor destroying the tank, it is clear they are fighting with a massive handicap. The burden and psychological effect that an army carries knowing they are effectively fighting with one hand tied behind their back must be difficult for a commanding officer to overcome.

At the time of the Tobruk humiliation the USA had started mass-producing Sherman's and the first 300 tanks were on their way to a division of US rangers. When Roosevelt broke the bad news he asked Churchill if there was anything he could do to help, in desperation Churchill asked if Roosevelt could divert the tank shipment from the eager American troops and have them shipped across the ocean to North Africa. Roosevelt did not hesitate.

Churchill then went to Cairo where the command structure for the British army was based. Churchill altered it by stationing a senior British minister in Cairo so that the time consuming politics of war, and the massive administration headaches associated with such a large campaign, could be handled by an experienced politician. Enabling senior commanders to position themselves closer to the action and to take responsibility for a smaller theatre of war.

It was at this time that one of Britain's most famous field marshals took over the crucial task of commanding the British Eighth army, nicknamed the Desert Rats. After much consideration Churchill originally appointed General Gott as commander of the Eighth Army. In one of those twists of fate which Churchill's memoirs throw up time after time, the next day General Gott was due to have a well earned weekend break and had decided to spend some time in the hustle and bustle of Cairo recharging his batteries. Tragically, on the plane journey into Cairo he was shot down on what was supposed to be a safe route, in fact Churchill had used it the day before. Churchill needed to act quickly and immediately appointed Field Marshall Montgomery to what must have seemed a daunting task. Montgomery was actually working with Eisenhower in England on plans for the D Day invasion when the news came of Gott's premature death. He immediately flew to North Africa and seizing his big chance for fame and glory started to shake things up.

Monty revised the tactics the Army used when engaging the German Panzers, in particular he had the brilliant strategy of using large caliber field guns at close range to disable them. Until Monty came on the scene the Germans had been crushing the British and had them on the retreat, it was touch and go if the allies could hold Egypt. If this crucial country had fallen it would have been a disaster for the allies, leaving the Germans with a free reign in North Africa. Giving them easy access to the Middle East and the wealth of the oil fields, whilst making the task of defending the Mediterranean almost impossible.

By the time Montgommery launched the counter offensive against the Germans at the famous battle of El Alamein in November 1942, he had the benefit of leading the attack with the best tank in the world, the American Sherman. The Germans must have received an almighty shock when their tanks were suddenly ineffective against a faster, more powerful, better armored tank than their own. They would finally "get some" and understand the terror that the British tank crews had felt, going into battle for the previous twelve months. By May 1943, the British army had reversed their earlier territorial losses and effectively kicked the Germans out of North Africa. This gave an enormous boost to the moral of the Allied troops and showed the British and American people that the German army were not invincible, they had sent their best men and equipment and had been soundly beaten.

Monty was undoubtedly a superb General who employed creative tactics to great effect and was to show his exceptional qualities time and again throughout the remainder of the war.

However, great tactics would have only been part of the difference at El Alamein. The deciding factor on the battlefield must surely have been the better tanks, a direct result of Churchill's detailed understanding of tank warfare and his audacious request of Roosevelt. Apart from a few hiccups, the Allies turned the victory at El Alamein into something of a winning habit, in Churchill's view they didn't lose any more significant encounters for the remainder of the war.

In trying to use an example from my own business experience, to put the chapters into a modern context, it is difficult to find anything that does not pale into insignificance in comparison with Churchill. If I am being brutally honest, I am not the best example of someone who keeps to the habit of managing the detail nearly enough. At the same time, it is impossible to manage all the details of a business all the time without everything coming to a grinding halt.

In reality, it is best to manage as much of the detail as possible, taking a balanced view, making compromises on occasions, whilst sticking to the important things.

I mentioned in an earlier chapter how I had been asked in a previous company to set up a new business based on my industry experience. I had a very clear idea of what I wanted and what requirements customers had. One of the crucial elements was to ensure that the service was securely available via the internet enabling the customers to do as much for themselves as possible. In the previous company everything had been done by e-mail with countless staff sat at computers collecting e-mails and processing orders. The service I wanted to launch needed to evolve beyond e-mail and become fully automated. I did not want humans involved in the processes whatsoever, being a great believer that the less people in a process, the greater the reliability of the service.

It would have been very easy in the early stages of the project to rush it out to market and capture some business as a result of compromises on delivery and the details behind the service. However, if I had stuck 100% to every single detail, the service would have taken eighteen months to launch and not the six months required to meet the business plan. I had meeting after meeting and battle after battle making sure my vision of the service and its core operation remained consistent. In reality I had to compromise on occasions, apart from anything else, no one would have wanted to work with me if I didn't. I can remember a number of occasions having really heated discussions with different people in the business, because I was convinced I was right.

I lost count of the number of situations when I was told something wasn't possible, only to find a solution myself then take it back to the person who said no, for implementation.

Churchill used to infuriate the different wartime departments because he would not necessarily believe what they told him. He relied on his own knowledge and a number of people he really trusted to double check things, when he wasn't confident that he was receiving a full picture.

After the new service was launched to customers a number of issues were discovered. I was the developers' worst nightmare as I refused to allow problems to drag on in the way they usually did. I insisted that the issue took priority and was fixed in a timely manner.

By holding on to what I wanted and not compromising on the important details, I managed to launch a service which was market leading and which went on to be incredibly successful, delivering in excess of $300M worth of business in the years that followed.

When considering this chapter on the habit of detail and what an amazing practitioner of this skill Churchill was, a chap I worked for in my last company immediately springs to mind. As I stated earlier I am a reasonable practitioner of keeping on top of detail but this senior director was unquestionably the closest I have come to working with someone who upon reflection I would now consider as having a "Churchillian" attention to detail. He was in charge of a large sales operation with an annual turnover of $800M and had responsibility for 1100 people. The sales director before him was a typical old-fashioned sales animal, delegating in such a poor way that he did not have a great deal of knowledge about what happened within his organization. He relied on information from the small group who reported to him directly. Once a month he would meet with his team for a business update, were his team would tell him why they missed their numbers the month before and how it would be much better next month. There was the odd flourish of success, but overall he ran a sales business that was inefficient and ineffective.

Unfortunately for the old sales director, his boss, the MD of the company, had lost confidence in his monthly sales estimates after they had been consistently missed. The business needed accurate information from the sales force to enable the rest of the company to correctly scale to meet predicted demand. Too high an estimate and the business would waste money, too low and it would be unable to deliver orders on time, leading to customer dissatisfaction and lost business.

The new sales director was appointed, and he completely shook things up. Out went guesswork and excuses for missed sales estimates and in came new processes and systems, these quickly transformed the accuracy of the forecasts by capturing the sales information directly from the sales force. This new level of detail was used to create sophisticated sales modeling tools that gave accurate predictions of what was going to be ordered and when. In addition to the new processes, his approach to business was very similar to Churchill, he was an absolute stickler for detail. Nothing was too small or insignificant for him to enquire about. He also followed the Churchill principle of appointing people he trusted within the business to audit processes and procedures. They made sure that the information he was being fed by one part of the sales organization was cross referenced and confirmed by an independent department. He even had his own equivalent of Professor Lindeman, (the scientist Churchill relied upon most during the war and who eventually became Lord Cherwell) a lady who would check out the facts of a situation and give him an unbiased view.

He rigidly enforced adherence to the new processes. This was perceived by the managers who worked for him as a lack of trust, and in reality, despite pleasant words to the contrary, it probably was. These after all were the same managers that contributed to the previous regime. In effect, they needed to re-earn the trust of the new man, he wanted to know about everything, and appeared to have the capacity to digest and comment on every detail.

Instead of a monthly catch up meeting, every week the first reports would have a two/three hour conference call covering every aspect of the business. This consisted of a report that categorized issues into Red for very serious and business affecting, Amber for serious issues that needed dealing with and Green for good news, big new orders etc. The report also had an action list, which covered tasks that needed completing by a certain time. At the beginning of each month his team would have to give a detailed estimate of all the business they expected to be ordered in the following month. Each week on the conference call they would have to detail their progress against meeting the estimate. On the same call a comprehensive list of all the larger business opportunities over a certain size was monitored, with detailed updates required every week. By running the conference call to such a detailed level he was able to keep a firm control of exactly what was going on within his business.

This process was then cascaded down the sales organization, each manager who was required to attend the sales directors call had to do a similar call with the managers who reported to them. This in turn enabled them to gather the information required for the sales director. A monthly meeting still took place, going into even more detail, covering planning and development.

A classic example of how he managed business compared to the previous chap, was when issues were escalated to him. If he was asked to help with a problem that needed raising in the red section on his weekly call, extensive detail and evidence would be required to prove that everything possible had been done to try to fix it beforehand. No escalation was supported unless a thorough investigation had taken place. This approach halted managers pushing issues onto him that should have been resolved had they tried hard enough.

The output of all this change and the approach of managing by detail was a complete turn-around in the fortunes of the company. Confidence was restored in the sales organization, enabling the planners to accurately build capacity and recruit staff.

After a great deal of initial hostility it had the same effect on the company as Churchill had when he took over as Prime Minister. Everyone knew they couldn't get away with being sloppy anymore and this completely changed the culture of the business for the better. The years following his arrival saw the business flourish until it was so successful that it was bought by a competitor.

The sales director was one of the rare people I have met in business that combined excellent business skills with an affable nature and a ruthless streak. He had the desire and capacity to work fourteen hours a day, enabling him to deliver relentless management of the detail.

He was the first Sales Director I had worked under that took this approach to business. Shortly after he started implementing his program of change I had a similar reaction to the other managers in the business, who were used to a larger-than-life sales director that oozed charisma. Whilst the new systems and procedures were difficult to get used to, at no point did I feel that he was introducing anything that prevented the sales teams from performing to the maximum. The methods were just so completely different to anything I had seen before. It was only some years later, whilst reflecting on my past for the purposes of this chapter that I realized how good he was, and the similarity of his approach to business with that of Churchill's methods for managing the detail of war.

Managing the detail for most people is something of a habit and with good and bad habits, there is a tendency to drift in and out of them. Even Churchill, who at the outset of the war was probably the greatest practitioner of managing detail in the world, had his moments later on, when he wasn't quite as effective as in those early days. No one is perfect and it is unlikely that many can manage all of the detail all of the time like my old sales director.

I always assumed from the impression I had of Churchill, that he would have concentrated on the big picture and the general strategies of war making. One of the great secrets that was revealed to me within the first book "The Gathering Storm" was just how wrong my perceptions of Churchill were. I firmly believe that Churchill's desire to understand and constantly challenge along with his grasp of detail was one of the main pillars of his success. What comes across loud and clear from his memoirs is that the more you practice managing detail the more good flows from it.

Chapter 6

Stand Firm

By the time I had finished reading Churchill's memoirs, my original admiration for the role of America in WW2 had increased immeasurably. I had heard of Roosevelt but it was only through Churchill that I discovered what a truly great man he was. Especially the way he stood by Churchill and Britain throughout the dark, early days of the war. Europe and Britain owe him the most immense debt of gratitude. It is blatantly obvious to any Brit with the slightest grasp of history that without the help and sacrifice of the US, German would be the first language of Great Britain. It was the help that the US gave Britain before Pearl Harbor which came as the greatest surprise to me and which Churchill so eloquently details.

The time between June 1940 after the fall of France and December 1941 before Pearl Harbor saw Britain in the greatest danger, as the brave men and women of the tiny, densely populated island stood alone as the last surviving democracy in Europe. Determined to repel the mighty German mechanized war machine, backed by Mussolini and the Italian fascists and fully supported until June 1941 by the Russians and their wealth of natural resources. All desperate to see the downfall of Britain and its Empire resolved to carve it up into pieces for themselves. Churchill knew that Britain needed to survive until he could persuade the Americans to somehow join the war. He knew Britain had no real prospect of conquering Germany without direct US intervention. His plan was simple, survival at any cost, until the new world came to the rescue of the old.

War is an expensive business and by November 1940, Britain was broke, the bulk of her foreign reserves had been used up buying supplies to keep the population nourished and to purchase the essential weapons needed to stop the light of freedom and democracy being extinguished. The majority of these supplies came principally from the USA and had to be shipped in hazardous convoys across the North Atlantic. In her desperation Britain had to sell off any companies operating in America for the best price they could get. Courtaulds was a well-known example. Britain was burning money at an unsustainable rate, a war cannot be won without a plentiful supply of weapons, which consumes vast quantities of a nations treasure.

Roosevelt struggled to persuade the American people of the case for spending $billions helping Britain. In June 1940, the USA was so certain that Britain would lose to Germany that they asked for all the British Navy ships and munitions be sent across the Atlantic to stop them being used against America after the Nazi's inevitably crushed Britain. Churchill told Roosevelt to take a hike.

Churchill wrote to Roosevelt alerting him of the impending crisis. He pointed out that if Britain could not be sustained due to lack of arms and equally as important, a lack of the imported essentials needed to feed the people, then America would be next. Considering that Roosevelt had promised during his 1940 election campaign that no Americans would be going abroad to war Churchill's negotiation position at this point might on the face of it, have seemed very weak, however, by proving to Roosevelt that without Britain's survival America would suffer a terrible fate; the problem became a shared one, which they both needed to resolve.

The letter which he sent to Roosevelt was regarded by Churchill as one of the most important letters ever to pass between two governments, it is nearly 4,000 words long and is a masterpiece of persuasion. In it Churchill produces a compelling argument before making his request. I have included it in this chapter for those that might be interested. He laid out his case brilliantly and it certainly had the desired effect.

10 DOWNING STREET, WHITEHALL   DECEMBER 8, 1940

My dear Mr. President,

1. As we reach the end of this year I feel you will expect me to lay before you the prospects for 1941. I do so with candor and confidence, because it seems to me that the vast majority of American citizens have recorded their conviction that the safety of the United States as well as the future of our two Democracies and the kind of civilization for which they stand are bound up with the survival and independence of the British Commonwealth of Nations. Only thus, can those bastions of sea-power upon which the control of the Atlantic and Indian Oceans depend be preserved in faithful and friendly hands. The control of the Pacific by the United States Navy and of the Atlantic by the British Navy is indispensable to the security and trade routes of both our countries, and the surest means of preventing war from reaching the shores of the United States.

2. There is another aspect. It takes between three and four years to convert the industries of a modem state to war purposes. Saturation point is reached when the maximum industrial effort that can be spared from civil needs has been applied to war production. Germany certainly reached this point by the end of 1939. We in the British Empire are now only about half-way through the second year. The United States, I should suppose, is by no means so far advanced as we. Moreover, I understand that immense programs of naval, military, and air defense are now on foot in the United States, to complete which certainly two years are needed. It is our British duty in the common interest, as also for our own survival, to hold the front and grapple with the Nazi power until the preparations of the United States are complete. Victory may come before two years are out; but we have no right to count upon it to the extent of relaxing any effort that is humanly possible. Therefore I submit with very great respect for your good and friendly consideration that there is a solid identity of interest between the British Empire and the United States while these conditions last. It is upon this footing that I venture to address you.

3. The form which this war has taken, and seems likely to hold, does not enable us to match the immense armies of

Germany in any theatre where their main power can be brought to bear. We can however, by the use of sea-power and air-power, meet the German armies in regions where only comparatively small forces can be brought into action. We must do our best to prevent the German domination of Europe spreading into Africa and into Southern Asia. We have also to maintain in constant readiness in this Island armies strong enough to make the problem of all overseas invasion insoluble. For these purposes we are forming as fast as possible, as you are already aware, between fifty and sixty divisions. Even if the United States were our ally, instead of our friend and indispensable partner, we should not ask for a large American expeditionary army. Shipping, not men, is the limiting factor, and the power to transport munitions and supplies claims priority over the movement by sea of large numbers of soldiers.

4. The first half of 1940 was a period of disaster for the Allies and for Europe. The last five months have witnessed a strong and perhaps unexpected recovery by Great Britain fighting alone, but with the invaluable aid in munitions and in destroyers placed at our disposal by the great Republic of which you are for the third time the chosen Chief.

5. The danger of Great Britain being destroyed by a swift, overwhelming blow has for the time being very greatly receded. In its place there is a long, gradually maturing danger, less sudden and less spectacular, but equally deadly. This mortal danger is the steady and increasing diminution of sea tonnage. We can endure the shattering of our dwellings and the slaughter of our civil population by indiscriminate air attacks, and we hope to parry these increasingly as our science develops, and to repay them upon military objectives in Germany as our Air Force more nearly approaches the strength of the enemy. The decision for 1941 lies upon the seas. Unless we can establish our ability to feed this Island, to import the munitions of all kinds which we need, unless we can move our armies to the various theatres where Hitler and his confederate Mussolini must be met, and maintain them there, and do all this with the assurance of being able to carry it on till the spirit of the Continental Dictators is broken, we may fall by the way, and the time needed by the United States to complete her defensive preparations may

not be forthcoming. It is therefore in shipping and in the power to transport across the oceans, particularly the Atlantic Ocean, that in 1941 the crunch of the whole war will be found. If on the other hand we are able to move the necessary tonnage to and fro across salt water indefinitely, it may well be that the application of superior air-power to the German homeland and the rising anger of the German and other Nazi-gripped populations will bring the agony of civilization to a merciful and glorious end.

But do not let us underrate the task.

6. Our shipping losses, the figures for which in recent months are appended, have been on a scale almost comparable to those of the worst year of the last war. In the five weeks ending November 3 losses reached a total of 420,300 tons. Our estimate of annual tonnage which ought to be imported in order to maintain our effort at full strength is 43 million tons; the tonnage entering in September was only at the rate of 37 million tons, and in October of 38 million tons. Were this diminution to continue at this rate it would be fatal, unless indeed immensely greater replenishment than anything at present in sight could be achieved in time. Although we are doing all we can to meet this situation by new methods, the difficulty of limiting losses is obviously much greater than in the last war. We lack the assistance of the French Navy, the Italian Navy, and the Japanese Navy, and above all of the United States Navy, which was of such vital help to us during the culminating years. The enemy commands the ports all around the northern and western coasts of France. He is increasingly basing his submarines, flying boats, and combat planes on these ports and on the islands off the French coast. We are denied the use of the ports or territory of Eire in which to organize our coastal patrols by air and sea. In fact, we have now only one effective route of entry to the British Isles, namely, the Northern Approaches, against which the enemy is increasingly concentrating, reaching ever farther out by U-boat action and long-distance aircraft bombing. In addition, there have for some months been merchant-ship raiders both in the Atlantic and Indian Oceans. And now we have the powerful warship raider to contend with as well. We need ships both to hunt down and to escort. Large as are our resources and preparations, we do not possess enough.

7· *The next six or seven months will bring relative battleship strength in home waters to a smaller margin than is satisfactory. Bismarck and Tirpitz will certainly be in service in January. We have already King George V, and hope to have Prince of Wales in the line at the same time. These modern ships are of course far better armored, especially against air attack, than vessels like Rodney and Nelson, designed twenty years ago. We have recently had to use Rodney on transatlantic escort, and at any time when numbers are so small a mine or a torpedo may alter decisively the strength of the line of battle. We get relief in June, when Duke of York will be ready, and shall be still better off at the end of 1941, when Anson also will have joined. But those two first-class modern 45,000 ton, 15-inch-gun German battle-ships force us to maintain a concentration never previously necessary in this war.*

8. *We hope that the two Italian Littorios will be out of action for a while, and anyway they are not so dangerous as if they were manned by Germans. Perhaps they might be! We are indebted to you for your help about the Richelieu and Jean Bart, and I daresay that will be all right. But, Mr. President, as no one will see more clearly than you, we have during these months to consider for the first time in this war a fleet action in which the enemy will have two ships at least as good as our two best and only two modem ones. It will be impossible to reduce our strength in the Mediterranean, because the attitude of Turkey, and indeed the whole position in the Eastern Basin, depends upon our having a strong fleet there. The older, un-modernized battleships will have to go for convoy. Thus even in the battleship class we are at full extension.*

9· *There is a second field of danger. The Vichy Government may, either by joining Hitler's New Order in Europe or through some maneuver, such as forcing us to attack an expedition dispatched by sea against the Free French colonies, find an excuse for ranging with the Axis Powers the very considerable undamaged naval forces still under its control. If the French Navy were to join the Axis the control of West Africa would pass immediately into their hands, with the gravest consequences to our communications between the Northern and Southern Atlantic, and also affecting Dakar and of course thereafter,*

South America.

10. A third sphere of danger is in the Far East. Here it seems clear that Japan is thrusting southward through Indo-China to Saigon and other naval and air bases, thus bringing them within a comparatively short distance of Singapore and the Dutch East Indies. It is reported that the Japanese are preparing five good divisions for possible use as an overseas expeditionary force. We have today no forces in the Far East capable of dealing with this situation should it develop.

11. In the face of these dangers we must try to use the year 1941 to build up such a supply of weapons, particularly of aircraft, both by increased output at home in spite of bombardment and through ocean-borne supplies, as will lay the foundations of victory. In view of the difficulty and magnitude of this task, as outlined by all the facts I have set forth, to which many others could be added, I feel entitled, nay bound, to lay before you the various ways in which the United States could give supreme and decisive help to what is, in certain aspects, the common cause.

12. The prime need is to check or limit the loss of tonnage on the Atlantic approaches to our island. This may be achieved both by increasing the naval forces which cope with the attacks, and by adding to the number of merchant ships on which we depend. For the first purpose there would seem to be the following alternatives:

(1) The reassertion by the United States of the doctrine of the freedom of the seas from illegal and barbarous methods of warfare, in accordance with the decisions reached after the late Great War, and as freely accepted and defined by Germany in 1935. From this, United States ships should be free to trade with countries against which there is not an effective legal blockade.

(2) It would, I suggest, follow that protection should be given to this lawful trading by United States forces, i.e., escorting battleships, cruisers, destroyers, and air flotillas. The protection. would be immensely more effective if you were able to obtain bases in Eire for the duration of the war. I think it is improbable that such protection would provoke a declaration of war by Germany upon the United States, though probably sea incidents

of a dangerous character would from time to time occur. Herr Hitler has shown himself inclined to avoid the Kaiser's mistake. He does not wish to be drawn into war with the United States until he has gravely undermined the power of Great Britain. His maxim is "One at a time".

The policy I have ventured to outline, or something like it, would constitute a decisive act of constructive non-belligerency by the United States, and, more than any other measure, would make it certain that British resistance could be effectively prolonged for the desired period and victory gained.

(3) Failing the above, the gift, loan, or supply of a large number of American vessels of war, above all destroyers, already in the Atlantic is indispensable to the maintenance of the Atlantic route. Further, could not the United States Naval Forces extend their sea control of the American side of the Atlantic so as to prevent the molestation by enemy vessels of the approaches to the new line of naval and air bases which the United States is establishing in British islands in the Western Hemisphere? The strength of the United States Naval Forces is such that the assistance in the Atlantic that they could afford us, as described above, would not jeopardize the control of the Pacific.

(4) We should also then need the good offices of the United States and the whole influence of its Government, continually exerted, to procure for Great Britain the necessary facilities upon the southern and western shores of Eire for our flotillas, and, still more important, for our aircraft, working to the westward into the Atlantic. If it were proclaimed an American interest that the resistance of Great Britain should be prolonged and the Atlantic route kept open for the important armaments now being prepared for Great Britain in North America, the Irish in the United States might be willing to point out to the Government of Eire the dangers which its present policy is creating for the United States itself

His Majesty's Government would of course take the most effective measures beforehand to protect Ireland if Irish action exposed it to German attack. It is not possible for us to compel the people of Northern Ireland against their will to leave the United Kingdom and join Southern Ireland. But I do not doubt that if the Government of Eire would show its solidarity with the democracies of the English-speaking world at this crisis a Council for Defense of all Ireland could be set up out of which the unity of the island would probably in some form or other emerge after the war.

13. The object of the foregoing measures is to reduce to manageable proportions the present destructive losses at sea. In addition, it is indispensable that the merchant tonnage available for supplying Great Britain, and for the waging of the war by Great Britain with all vigor, should be substantially increased beyond the one and a quarter million tons per annum which is the utmost we can now build. The convoy system, the detours, the zigzags, the great distances from which we now have to bring our imports, and the congestion of our western harbors, have reduced by about one-third the fruitfulness of our existing tonnage. To ensure final victory not less than three million tons of additional merchant shipbuilding capacity will be required. Only the United States can supply this need. Looking to the future, it would seem that production on a scale comparable to that of the Hog Island scheme of the last war ought to be faced for 1942. In the meanwhile we ask that in 1941 the United States should make available to us every ton of merchant shipping, surplus to its own requirements, which it possesses or controls, and to find some means of putting into our service a large proportion of merchant shipping now under construction for the National Maritime Board.

14. Moreover, we look to the industrial energy of the Republic for a reinforcement of our domestic capacity to manufacture combat aircraft. Without that reinforcement reaching us in substantial measure we shall not achieve the massive preponderance in the air on which we must rely to loosen and disintegrate the German grip on Europe. We are at present engaged on a program designed to increase our strength to seven thousand first line aircraft by the spring of 1942. But it is abundantly clear that this program will not suffice to give us the weight of superiority which will force open the doors of victory. In order to achieve such superiority it is plain that we shall need the greatest production of aircraft which the United States of America is capable of sending us. It is our anxious hope

that in the teeth of continuous bombardment we shall realize the greater part of the production which we have planned in this country. But not even with the addition to our squadrons of all the aircraft which, under present arrangements, we may derive from planned output in the United States can we hope to achieve the necessary ascendancy. May I invite you then, Mr. President, to give earnest consideration to an immediate order on joint account for a further two thousand combat aircraft a month? Of these aircraft, I would submit, the highest possible proportion should be heavy bombers, the weapon on which, above all others, we depend to shatter the foundations of German military power. I am aware of the formidable task that this would impose upon the industrial organization of the United States. Yet, in our heavy need, we call with confidence to the most resourceful and ingenious technicians in the world. We ask for an unexampled effort, believing that it can be made.

15. You have also received information about the needs of our armies. In the munitions sphere, in spite of enemy bombing, we are making steady progress here. Without your continued assistance in the supply of machine tools and in further releases from stock of certain articles, we could not hope to equip as many as fifty divisions in 1941. I am grateful for the arrangements, already practically completed, for your aid in the equipment of the Army which we have already planned, and for the provision of the American type of weapons for an additional ten divisions in time for the campaign of 1942. But when the tide of Dictatorship begins to recede many countries trying to regain their freedom maybe asking for arms, and there is no source to which they can look except the factories of the United States. I must therefore also urge the importance of expanding to the utmost American productive capacity for small arms, artillery, and tanks.

16. I am arranging to present you with a complete program of the munitions of all kinds which we seek to obtain from you, the greater part of which is of course already agreed. An important economy of time and effort will be produced if the types selected for the United States Services should, whenever possible, conform to those which have proved their merit under the actual conditions of war. In this way reserves of guns and ammunition and of airplanes become interchangeable, and are by that very fact augmented. This is however a sphere so highly technical that I do not enlarge upon it.

17· Last of all, I come to the question of Finance. The more rapid and abundant the flow of munitions and ships which you are able to send us, the sooner will our dollar credits be exhausted. They are already, as you know, very heavily drawn upon by the payments we have made to date. Indeed, as you know, the orders already placed or under negotiation, including the expenditure settled or pending for creating munitions factories in the United States, many times exceed the total exchange resources remaining at the disposal of Great Britain. The moment approaches when we shall no longer be able to pay cash for shipping and other supplies. While we will do our utmost, and shrink from no proper sacrifice to make payments across the Exchange, I believe you will agree that it would be wrong in principle and mutually disadvantageous in effect if at the height of this struggle Great Britain were to be divested of all saleable assets, so that after the victory was won with our blood, civilization saved, and the time gained for the United States to be fully armed against all eventualities, we should stand stripped to the bone. Such a course would not be in the moral or economic interests of either of our countries. We here should be unable, after the war, to purchase the large balance of imports from the United States over and above the volume of our exports which is agreeable to your tariffs and industrial economy. Not only should we in Great Britain suffer cruel privations, but widespread unemployment in the United States would follow the curtailment of American exporting power.

18. Moreover, I do not believe that the Government and people of the United States would find it in accordance with the principles which guide them to confine the help which they have so generously promised only to such munitions of war and commodities as could be immediately paid for. You may be certain that we shall prove ourselves ready to suffer and sacrifice to the utmost for the Cause, and that we glory in being its champions. The rest we leave with confidence to you and to your people, being sure that ways and means will be found which future generations on both sides of the Atlantic will approve and

admire.

19. If, as I believe, you are convinced, Mr. President, that the defeat of the Nazi and Fascist tyranny is a matter of high consequence to the people of the United States and to the Western Hemisphere, you will regard this letter not as an appeal for aid, but as a statement of the minimum action necessary to achieve our common purpose.

After receiving the letter Roosevelt was observed reading it over and over, he was trying to consider the right response. The letter builds brick by brick a solid and compelling argument, it had a profound impact upon Roosevelt, who was already supportive towards Britain's desperate plight. The letter spelled out in no uncertain terms how critical it was for the President to act and the desperate need for him to do so quickly. In 1939 total US military production was tiny. It takes years for a country to get onto a war footing and build up to a peak of munitions output. To put America's position into perspective, little Holland produced more weapons than the mighty USA in 1939. Roosevelt knew that America needed Britain to struggle on until the USA was in a position to defend itself from any direct threat from the Nazi's. It was 1943 before US military production reached its stride. By that time Pearl Harbor had happened and everything was different.

It was not realistic for the Americans to lend money to Britain, the amount would have been so large that repayment would have been impossible. The American constitution prevented Roosevelt from just giving Britain the desperately needed arms. Roosevelt and his aides delved into history and discovered the lend-lease bill, passed in 1894. Lend-lease was at once brilliant and easy for Roosevelt to explain to the American public. The new bill was passed by Congress in March 1941, nine months before Pearl Harbor and gave Roosevelt the power to sell, transfer, exchange and lend equipment to any country to help defend itself against the Axis powers. The amount of money involved in the first act was a colossal $50 billion with additional top-ups during the remainder of the war. $31 billion from the first tranche went to Britain. In Roosevelt's, own words, "imagine your neighbor's house catches fire and your neighbor needs to borrow your hose to put it out. You don't wait until your neighbor gives you the fifteen dollars, the hose cost, before giving it to him, you lend it on the basis that he will give you the hose back when he has put out the fire." This in simplicity is what Roosevelt did for Britain, he loaned Britain all the planes, tanks, ships and guns that America could make, using its vast production capacity. Britain did not have to pay for any of this vital equipment; it was on loan until the end of the war. Any useful equipment that remained at the end of the war was shipped back to America by a truly grateful nation.

With the passing of the act Britain's prospects improved dramatically. By Churchill's calculation the benefit of the Lend-lease act to Britain was an increase in production capacity that an equivalent growth in the population by 10 Million working people would have brought, a 25% increase. At that time Britain was under constant bombardment from the Luftwaffe and was straining every sinew to survive, the difference Lend-Lease made to Britain was the difference between survival and extinction. This American act of generosity borne out of principled self-interest should be remembered forever, both in Britain and throughout Europe. To bring America to this point took a tremendous effort of negotiation and persuasion from Churchill as can be seen in his memo, it must stand as one of his greatest achievements. Sadly the British minister who conducted the talks in Washington on his behalf was unable to see the fruits of all his hard work, he died shortly after the policy became public.

Without Lend Lease, Britain would almost certainly have perished. Churchill persuaded Roosevelt that if Britain lost the war against Germany, then it would only be a matter of time until the USA suffered at the hands of the Germans, both in terms of trade and militarily. If Britain had become another German precinct the Germans would then have possessed the largest Navy in the world and would have added the massive British war making capacity to that of Europe and Russia. Even without Japan, they could have potentially held the USA to ransom unleashing the deadly U-Boat menace against American shipping and strangling the USA's ability to conduct international trade, leading to economic collapse.

Clearly it is a matter of what if's, but it is possible that after the Germans had defeated Russia (which would have been very likely with no US Lend-Lease supplies to help them through the first German onslaught), the Nazi's would have consolidated their position in Europe. Over time they could have developed something along the lines of operation Sea Lion (Britain) or Barbarossa (Russia) where they would meticulously plan every detail of what would have been their biggest operation. It is unlikely that they would have directly landed on American soil they would have stood a better chance invading Canada and Mexico where they could build vast armies against little opposition, until they had the strength to attack the USA from multiple positions along the Canadian border. Then simultaneously attacking the southern states of America via Mexico, aiming for the Texas oil fields. Whilst potentially using Bermuda as a stronghold from which to attack the Eastern Seaboard. This offensive could have been coordinated with a Japanese attack on Hawaii. Giving the Japanese the opportunity to capture the Island and use it as a base for further attacks against the west coast of America. Pure conjecture, but however it happened, WW2 would have eventually landed up on America's door step.

Roosevelt understood that Lend Lease wasn't just about helping Britain; it was to protect America's short and long-term security interests. Britain fought to save herself and by doing so simultaneously protected America from ruin. As Roosevelt put it, far better to help your neighbor by lending him a hosepipe than to have to put out a fire at your own house once the fire has spread.

At the beginning of the War, British scientists had been working on the development of a totally new type of bomb, the Atom bomb. The team all worked in the newly created Department for Tube Alloys, the code name of the department that would ultimately lead to the total transformation of modern warfare. British scientists convinced Churchill that given enough resources, they could build a bomb in time to have an effect on the war. A weapon with the ability to eliminate whole armies at a stroke could have delivered Britain from evil, in the department for tube alloys potentially lay the answer to Britain's collective prayers. The major issue for Churchill was the cost, so he decided that the best way to achieve his objective was to get the Americans involved. In January 1942 shortly after Pearl Harbor Churchill had the first combined war conference with Roosevelt in Washington. He needed to convince Roosevelt, to part with the cash to build a bomb, so he took the key members of the department for tube alloys along for the ride.

It transpired that American scientists had also been working on the theory of building an Atom bomb, however, in Churchill's view they lagged behind the British. Churchill was adamant that a bomb should be built. If America was unconvinced about the chances of success, then Britain would go on ahead single-handedly. He did not want this new weapon built in Britain as German bombing or agents could have destroyed it at any time. He designated Canada as the best place for developing the bomb, it was a far safer environment, with the vast open spaces offering great potential for secrecy.

The estimated cost of building the bomb in 1941 was $750M, the equivalent of $15BN in today's money. No small sum, for a country desperately short of cash. Thankfully, it didn't get to the point where Britain had to go it alone, in typical Churchill style he managed to get everything he wanted. He scheduled a meeting with Roosevelt and the British scientists, they convinced the president that it was possible to build a bomb in time to have an influence on the war. Once Roosevelt was convinced by the scientists, Churchill knew that there was no way he would countenance Britain having exclusive rights and access to such a powerful weapon. He immediately came on board and negotiated an agreement with Churchill, enabling British and US scientists to pool their research and to fully collaborate on the development of the bomb, on America soil. All fully funded by Uncle Sam. The agreement was subject to the sharing of future developments and knowledge between the 2 great powers. This was no small achievement, he not only persuaded the US to fund the development of the bomb, but also made sure that by the end of the war Britain technically had an equal partnership in what was to become the defining weapons technology of the age. The Manhattan Project was born.

In writing his memoirs Churchill was adamant that without his intervention there would ultimately not have been a

Hiroshima or Nagasaki. Churchill contends that had America not dropped at least one of the two bombs on Japan the Japanese would not have surrendered. This he believes would have led to the deaths of hundreds of thousands more Allied and Japanese soldiers. According to Churchill, the Emperor was determined to see every soldier dead rather than surrender. The allies could well have believed this at the time, as the Japanese had been the early practitioners of suicide bombing, by way of Hari Kiri, the practice of flying planes into Allied warships. In addition, the army regularly committed ritual suicide rather than surrender. The Emperor had given an imperial order that the thousands of allied POW's captive in Japan, should be executed if Japan was invaded.

When I embarked on the long road of reading his memoirs I had no idea that Churchill had played such an influential part in the development of the bomb, and that his determination and hard negotiation tactics had played such a decisive part in the history of nuclear weapons technology.

After the Allied victory over Germany, Churchill was gravely concerned that the Russians were going to occupy most of Europe. The Russians had gone from allies of the Germans at the beginning of the war to impoverished underdogs at the point in June 1941 when the Germans turned against them and opened up an eastern front. Everyone assumed the might of the German army would quickly crush the Russians. However, they became conquering heroes who considerably reduced the length of the war by destroying large parts of the German army on the eastern front. Albeit at a cost in human life that is difficult to comprehend.

Churchill was convinced that the Soviets wanted to set up pseudo Russian governments in all the countries they occupied, effectively making them Russian satellites. They had already managed this in Poland with the Lublin government, contradicting the agreement and solemn promises they made at both the Tehran and Yalta conferences. The Russians promised free and fair elections in all the territories they would control at the end of the war, a map was drawn up with a geographical split of land the Russians and the allies would occupy. The countries occupied by the allies were able to choose their government in democratic elections. The countries under the sword of Stalin were free to vote for the government that Stalin chose and were likely to be executed if they didn't like it. The reality for the countries liberated by Russia, is that the war didn't end in May 1945, those poor unfortunate peoples effectively swapped one ruthless evil regime for another. It would be many decades later before they would enjoy the fruits of freedom and democracy. History proved Churchill correct.

At the Potsdam conference after victory in Europe, the Russians attempted to occupy more of Europe than was originally agreed between the allies. They expected to strong arm the USA into concessions as they were convinced that America needed Russian help to defeat Japan. Shortly into the conference, news came through to Churchill and Truman (who had taken over from Roosevelt) that the "babies had been born".(the two bombs that dropped on Japan were subsequently code named Little Boy and Big Boy). This was the code for announcing the successful testing of an atom bomb in the Arizona dessert. This simple message heralded the birth of the nuclear age.

Shortly afterwards Churchill had a private meeting with Stalin and explained the development. The Russians would have quickly understood the ramifications of the western allies owning the first weapon of mass destruction. The Americans would not need Russian help with Japan after all. They knew that Stalin was no longer the biggest kid in the schoolyard and his bully boy tactics would not work whilst the Soviets had inferior technology. It would be some years before Russian secret agents working within the allied nuclear programs would provide them with the knowledge to build a bomb. By that time Europe had stabilized and Russian territorial ambitions had to be put on hold.

Whatever people's opinions about the rights and wrongs of the bomb, its existence materially changed the outcome of the war in Japan. This saved countless lives and stopped further Russian territorial gains in Europe to the benefit of those countries lucky enough to have been under allied occupation.

Given the amount of research taking place in both Britain and America, the development of a bomb at some point in the 20th Century was a certainty. By Churchill negotiating hard with Roosevelt in January 1942 the technology ended up in the right hands.

It will probably not be any surprise to the reader that Churchill was a tough negotiator. This particular skill of Churchill's unlike a significant number of the others alluded to in this book is not exactly a secret. The surprise in his memoirs, were the situations and events where he applied his tough negotiation tactics. Such as the story he relates about how he directly intervened in Greek affairs to stop them going the way of Poland and becoming a communist state. Unlike the Atom Bomb negotiations, which were carried out in secret, this decision and the subsequent operation cost over a thousand British lives and initially proved extremely unpopular in both Britain and America. Churchill received a lot of bad press at the time for what people assumed to be one monarchy supporting another. Everyone accused him of supporting the Greek King at the expense of democracy, treating Greece like a dominion of the British empire. Churchill in fact, despite the headlines, wanted to save Greece from becoming another communist satellite under Stalin's control. Given the way things panned out, the Greek people have a great deal to be thankful for. Greece held a special significance for Churchill, in the early days of the war when Britain and her commonwealth allies were the only ones pointing guns at the axis powers, he made great sacrifices in the western dessert army to save her. He sent 50,000 troops to help the stoic Greek people defend their soil from the Nazi's & Mussolini's Italian fascists. He took this decision, because at the beginning of the war Britain had signed a solemn treaty with the Greeks guaranteeing that Britain would come to their aid if they were invaded. Even though he didn't believe the operation could be ultimately successful, he knew that as a matter of honor Britain should keep its word and be seen by the rest of the world to have done so. The operation failed, resulting in the deaths of thousands of Allied troops, although as will be seen in a later chapter they did not die in vain, the delay to the Germans caused by the British troops arrival played a key part in Russia's salvation.

By the time the war was drawing to a climax in the winter of 1944 Churchill had become exasperated with the Greek resistance which was made up of two factions; one loyal to the

King and democracy, the other communist supported by the Soviets. From 1941 onwards Britain had given help to both groups, the common enemy was German and anyone who would fight the Germans deserved support regardless of their politics. Unfortunately, the two factions seemed more intent on fighting each other than fighting the enemy. British agents stationed in Greece continually reported skirmishes between the two elements. The communists appeared to be concentrating their efforts on trying to eliminate the democratic resistance, in order to facilitate the easier installation of a communist leadership loyal to Stalin after the war.

At the Tehran conference Churchill had negotiated a deal with Stalin that in return for Britain keeping out of Polish affairs the Soviets would keep out of Greece. His settlement with Stalin assumed Poland would be a democratic state with free and fair elections and not the Soviet puppet regime it became.

By October 1944, Stalin had clearly shown his hand with regard to Poland and the particular style of democracy he promoted once the Red Army occupied a country. Stalin continually protested his innocence whilst refusing steadfastly to allow allied inspectors to monitor the Polish situation. Stalin had a very simple method of dealing with democracy and the democratic process, he murdered everyone associated with it. So that by the time inspectors arrived it was too late to monitor anything, as there was no one left on the democratic side to cause any problems. Stalin used this process time and again putting in his stooges and assassinating democracy. The Polish government in exile had its spies in Poland and kept Churchill informed of the deteriorating situation.

Churchill was deeply concerned that Greece would end up as another Soviet backed government. To avoid this happening he ordered the British army to keep a force of 5000 soldiers near to Greece ready to move in once the Germans had evacuated. He knew that it was critical he act immediately before the communists filled the political vacuum.

In November 1944 the Germans abandoned Greece leaving the communists and the rebels loyal to the king to fight it out in bitter house to house combat. Churchill who had been monitoring the situation closely immediately gave the order for the British troops to take control of Athens. This proved to be considerably more dangerous and difficult than he envisaged. The communists put up a determined resistance and the British army had to fight street by street to wrestle control of the Greek capital from them. The British troops involved had been battle hardened fighting the Germans in Italy so it was only a matter of time before they had Athens under control. According to Churchill he did not believe that Stalin had double-crossed him by actively backing the communists, it was the faction themselves that were bent on taking over the country. However, had they succeeded, the Soviets would have soon had their hands on the levers of Greek power.

After taking control of Athens and the surrounding area, the British commanders on the ground told Churchill it would be impossible to clear Greece of communists without committing vast amounts of additional troops, which simply was not practical. They explained that using guerrilla warfare tactics, the communist resistance could keep a large British force under constant strain by hiding in the vast mountainous regions and attacking at will. With the war still to be won on the mainland Churchill couldn't afford to tie up his resources dealing with an internal Greek issue. He was convinced that the only solution was a negotiated settlement. For obvious reasons the Greek factions detested each other and in Churchill's view if you left a Greek man alone in a room, he would pick an argument with himself.

It was Christmas Eve December 1944, the last Christmas of the War. Clementine, Churchill's wife had everything arranged and all the family and an array of guests were at Chequers, the country retreat for British Prime Ministers. All had settled into their rooms and were eagerly awaiting Winston's arrival. Celebrating Christmas during the war was a difficult business, although by 1944 things had improved considerably over the earlier war years. As ever Clementine had gone to enormous lengths, she was determined to make this one extra special as she was confident it would be Winston's last as Britain's war leader, and who could know what the future held. The beautifully decorated tree, cut down from Roosevelt's own special forest at his private house, was shipped over as it had been since 1941.

Chequers was decked out beautifully everyone was just waiting for the main attraction and then came the phone call. It is difficult to imagine how angry Clementine must have been when Churchill phoned to give her the shattering news, "Darling Clemmie it is with great regret that I have to inform you that I will not be home for Christmas, I have to fly off immediately to deal with the deteriorating situation in Greece lest I fear it will end up as another Communist vassal state. Do send my apologies to the guests and tell them that I hope to be home for new year."

Clementine would no doubt have recognized the worthy nature of the mission but I doubt many wives would be very understanding in such circumstances. So on Christmas Eve 1944 Churchill flew to Greece with a small entourage.

Churchill's memoirs contain a significant amount of text detailing the Greek situation. By personally going to Greece, he demonstrated to the protagonists, that he was deadly serious about resolving the issue. Churchill had identified the impressive figure of Archbishop Damaskinos as a good man to act as leader, although he had initially been a bit skeptical. After meeting him on Christmas Eve he came to the conclusion that the Archbishop had the widest Greek interests at heart and as a man of the cloth was someone both sides would probably trust.

Churchill managed to pull the leaders of all the factions together in one room on Christmas day, despite the open hostility between them. He opened up the meeting and explained that they would have to come to an agreement before the meeting was over, he literally would not let them leave the room until a working arrangement had been thrashed out. Armed British guards blocked the exit with orders to shoot anyone who tried to leave.

After long hours of heated discussion, agreement was reached between the bitter enemies. Churchill then had to convince the King of Greece to give up his title as monarch and to implement a democracy based on free and fair elections. Initially the King was hostile to the idea, however after some very frank discussions with Churchill, a few days later the King appointed Damaskinos head of the government. Greece (courtesy of direct intervention from Churchill), avoided the grizzly fate that befell Poland, Romania, Czechoslovakia and Hungary. The democratic solution also proved to his critics that Britain was not trying to support the Greek monarchy. Churchill firmly believed that there was no point winning the war if you could not offer a lasting democratic peace. He knew by December 1944 that Britain could not save Poland from communism. Greece however was different, as Britain had greater forces available to help determine a successful outcome.

Before reading Churchill's memoirs, I was unaware that he had saved Greece from communism, or that over 1000 British service men had given their lives in the street fighting necessary to allow the democratic process to have a chance. Churchill's commitment to what he believed in, and his tough stance with the Greeks, in the face of harsh criticism from both Foreign and British press, ultimately saved Greece and demonstrated once again that Churchill had no hesitation in standing firmly behind his convictions.

In the world of business things are not so dramatic, to find a comparison is impossible and this is especially the case with regard to my own career. However, as the idea behind the book is to interpret Churchill's skills and apply them in a modern business setting I have detailed an example of a business situation from my career, where my own dogged determination made a difference. At a company I recently worked for I launched an incentive program to take a group of customers on a business incentive to Las Vegas. It was entirely my idea and if the incentive failed, totally my responsibility. I was confident that our customers would seize the opportunity to win an all expenses paid trip to Vegas. Most of the businesses we dealt with were small and run by the person who owned them, the day had long passed when such incentives were commonplace. The rationale behind the incentive was to use the prospect of the luxurious trip to persuade customers to direct new business to my company instead of the competition. This worked assuming our service and pricing was in line with other industry offerings.

It launched in October with great fanfare, the incentive ran until the following March, when the winners were to be announced. This gave them six months to place what was seen as a fairly modest amount of new business in order to qualify for such an awesome trip. My fellow managers thought it was a great idea, my team thought it would help them hit their targets, and our customers made all the right noises.

Unfortunately the incentive was a resounding failure, instead of twenty winners bringing in lots of new business, five winners delivered about one third of anticipated sales. Thankfully, only a small amount of money was required to be spent before the number of winners became apparent. It was a huge disappointment for the marketing team that had supported my plan. I was embarrassed by the scale of the failure but I was not repentant. I had pulled together what I thought was an excellent incentive, it had delivered additional business and had not cost a great deal. It was still good value for money, however, it had widely missed the mark in terms of additional business. I had to make a decision, I could accept it as an abject failure and try to quickly move on, send the few winners to Vegas or give them some money in lieu of cancellation. Alternatively I could learn from my mistakes and try again. I really believed in the incentive idea so I decided to push for it to be re-launched. The feedback I had received the first time around was almost entirely positive. Whilst the customers were keen in principle, they were also lethargic. I assumed the trip was so good it would sell itself, which it clearly had not. I was certain that with a greater degree of promotion from the sales teams, it would work better the next time.

After countless meetings, conference calls and E-mails I managed to convince the company to carry the original budget for the incentive over to the following year and give me another chance. This was no mean feat as I was met continually with the accusation that the trip had failed so miserably last time, why should we put our effort and money in to it again. Without getting into the boring details, in short the trip was re-designed. The qualification criteria was changed, which delivered improved engagement for customers and more profit for my company. I ensured the sales team put greater focus on the incentive and constantly hounded everyone to promote the trip effectively.

My determination paid off, second time around the incentive was a resounding success, delivering millions in extra business for the company. I had the pleasure of hosting the trip along with my boss, we all stayed at the Four Seasons, which is a fantastic hotel and is distinguished from the rest of the Las Vegas hotels by its quiet refined ambience. On arriving I had lunch with a few customers out on the terrace and Yoko Ono was sitting across from us, it was that sort of place. If customer's can't enjoy themselves on an all expenses trip to Vegas then there is something wrong with them. The majority of the party was male and it would be fair to say that some of them relied on the maxim that what happens in Vegas stays in Vegas. If you will indulge me I will share a couple of stories, but no names. I promise they are absolutely true and not exaggerated in any way. As the saying goes, the truth is stranger than fiction

One of the customers decided he was going to be very naughty and a have a private Vegas style party in his room. Now I am no great judge of character but I would never have guessed in a million years that this guy would be in to that sort of thing. He went to the bar in a nearby hotel and got chatting to a lady who specialized in fulfilling the personal needs of a certain type of Las Vegas tourist. He asked her to meet him back at his room and bring a girl friend, he also asked her to bring some herbal coca plant extract. Half an hour later they knocked on the door, after some discussion a fee was agreed for their services. In what can only be described as an astonishing act of stupidity, he then snorted what he thought was a line of the plant extract, but what actually turned out to be horse tranquilizer! He woke up a few hours later, completely disorientated not knowing what had happened to him. He had been robbed of all the valuables in his room, along with his credit cards and all his cash. He was so confused that he phoned his wife in England to tell her everything that had happened. Everything! Clearly his wife was less than impressed with his antics and told him to phone the Police, which he duly did. They took him to the hospital where he was checked over to make sure nothing even more serious had happened to him. After a few stern words they sent him back to his hotel room with his tail between his legs.

I wouldn't have found out about the story only he missed the fantastic helicopter ride down the Grand Canyon giving the excuse that he had overslept, which I thought was odd. On the last night I asked a guy who knew him why he hadn't made it and to my amazement he recounted the whole story. I was completely stunned and virtually speechless, I've never so much as puffed on a cigarette and I think twice before taking a painkiller, what an eye opener!

I was amazed that the guy telling me the story was so calm. Until he went on to tell me that whilst very drunk in the early hours, at great expense, he had invited 4 ladies back to his room to put on a private "Las Vegas" style performance for him. Ironically he was so drunk that despite spending so much money he couldn't perform the part of the leading man in his own show. The ladies had raided his mini-bar and ordered champagne on his room account. The whole evening cost him $3,000. I then understood why Vegas has the nickname of Sin City.

The problems for the horse whisperer were not over as once the drugs had worn off he had to try and bridge the canyon between himself and his wife as the magnitude of his stupidity slowly dawned on him. As a postscript to the story a couple of months later I was having Christmas lunch with another of the Vegas winners who told me that things had just started to quiet down between horse boy and his wife, when a credit card statement for $5000 dollars of medical expenses from the Las Vegas hospital landed on his doormat. Just a few weeks before Christmas. His insurance company refused to cover his medical bills stating that the injury had been self inflicted, and who can argue with that conclusion.

Whilst not all of the customers behaved in a saintly fashion they all had a fantastic time. The success of the second attempt, made all the hard work of persuading the company to give me a second chance worthwhile.

One of the surprising aspects of the trip was how well relationships developed with customers. The incentive trip was to be purely for fun and relaxation, with an unwritten rule that no "work" discussion was to take place, in such a relaxed atmosphere it was easy to form mutual business friendships.

After the trip, I lost count of the times that these close relationships proved beneficial for both the customers and myself. Something I would never have predicted, a very definite, but tangible benefit of the incentive.

It is embarrassing, trying to describe a scenario from my ordinary life, to highlight an example of a Churchill skill. In one sense, the examples are insignificant compared to negotiations for an atomic bomb or saving a country from communism. In another, the same principle applies, whether it is for a bomb or a business incentive. If you really believe in something, you should negotiate and persuade as hard as possible to achieve it.

Chapter 7

Stay Objective

Churchill used the phrase "your own words can make a tasty dish" in his book to explain to the reader that as he grew in years, he concluded, that it was not a disaster to radically change a course of action. Especially if it resulted from a wrong decision or fresh information which lead to a re-evaluation of the facts. Whilst this principle should apply in business I have been in situations too often where I have thought a business decision taken some months before was being doggedly followed. Despite clear evidence that business circumstances had changed which required a re-think.

At sixty-five when he took control of the war, Churchill was completely comfortable radically changing his decisions. Clearly, no one makes decisions or plans believing they are wrong. Unfortunately too many people, once they have decided on a plan, see it as a weakness or the cause of lost pride or integrity to change their mind.

Churchill would not advocate somebody constantly chopping and changing, trying to do business with such people would be incredibly difficult. However, there will be times and they will hopefully be rare, that for any number of reasons, plans have to be abandoned or a strategy radically altered.

Churchill took the view that abandoning a broken plan at the earliest opportunity was better for everyone concerned. Carrying on when there is an obvious problem and hoping for the best is a recipe for disaster. Far better to acknowledge a mistake, make any necessary explanation, apologize and take the medicine. Trying to brave it out in the face of probable failure or the hope of a change in circumstances is neither a plan nor a strategy.

Shortly before France surrendered to the Germans, Britain desperately tried to keep them fighting, as mentioned earlier. The British still had 400,000 troops and associated equipment in France. Without their return, defending Britain against the inevitable German assault would have been a challenge of the greatest magnitude.

A plan to incorporate France into the union of Great Britain emerged, effectively creating a country under one government, based in London, which included France and all the French dominions.

A 300-word Declaration of Indissoluble Union was drawn up offering French people the opportunity to become citizens of Great Britain. I have copied it below as I thought it might be of interest.

DECLARATION OF UNION

At this most fateful moment in the history of the modern world the Governments of the United Kingdom and the French Republic make this declaration of indissoluble union and unyielding resolution in their common defense of justice and freedom against subjection to a system which reduces mankind to a life of robots and slaves. .

The two Governments declare that France and Great Britain shall no longer be two nations, but one Franco-British Union.

The constitution of the Union will provide for joint organs of defense, foreign, financial, and economic policies.

Every citizen of France will enjoy immediatef citizenship of Great Britain every British subject will become a citizen of France.

Both countries will share responsibility for the repair of the devastation of war, wherever it occurs in their territories, and the resources of both shall be equally, and as one, applied to that purpose.

During the war there shall be a single War Cabinet, and all the forces of Britain and France, whether on land, sea, or in the air, will be placed under its direction.· It will govern from wherever it best can. The two Parliaments will be formally associated. The nations of the British Empire are already forming new armies. France will keep her available forces in the field, on the sea, and in the air. The Union appeals to the United States to fortify the economic resources of the Allies, and to bring her powerful material aid to the common cause.

The Union will concentrate its whole energy against the power of the enemy, no matter where the battle may be.

And thus we shall conquer.

It was hoped that if the French accepted the proposal and became British whilst Britain was still unconquered, they might be more determined to fight on. The French army would join the British and, more importantly, the French Navy would come under British control. The charter, proposed to the French Prime Minister at a meeting outside Paris, received brief consideration but was quickly re-buffed. The plan was rejected for plenty of reasons, including the likelihood that Hitler would be harder on the French for agreeing to such a proposal. Plus French suspicion that Britain might be looking to expand the Empire by taking control of French colonies as a result of the deal.

It now seems completely implausible that the French would accept such an offer, but in those dark days of early 1940, desperate men took desperate measures.

After the French prime minister refused the offer, rather than press ahead with the plan, Churchill dropped it, even though a great deal of effort had gone into preparing the charter for the French people. It was far better to recognize the plan as a dud and move on than to try to persuade the French people directly once their Prime Minister had effectively given up control to the Germans.

Another example that demonstrates Churchill's willingness to put his weight behind new ideas and to change his mind occurred towards the end of the war. At the time there were competing interests for how best to take the fight to the Germans. One plan was to invade Norway in revenge for the British getting a thorough thrashing by the Germans there in the early days of 1940. Britain had tried to invade Norway to prevent the Germans getting access to Swedish iron ore transported through Norway.

In order to give any operation a reasonable chance of success the RAF would need to be able to position sufficient air power off the coast of Norway to provide air cover for the landings. Given how thinly spread the Navy was at the time, the allies could not have amassed enough aircraft carriers to give a landing the support that military planners would require. Without airpower it would have been a non-starter.

At around this time a British inventor had devised a process that mixed ice with wood chippings, which when frozen created an incredibly tough material that took a long time to defrost. Churchill was so impressed with the idea, that he decided to demonstrate it to the next Joint Chiefs of Staff meeting.

With everyone sitting comfortably the secret session began, Churchill explained the invention to the committee and asked the inventor to bring in a block of ice that had been subjected to the new process. To demonstrate its strength Churchill pulled out a pistol and fired a shot at the block of ice. The material was so strong that it ricocheted off the ice and just missed one of the US Generals. At which point the security guards came rushing in thinking there had been an assassination attempt. Thankfully, all was well.

Everyone was impressed with the invention. The plan, which looking back could be considered ambitious to say the least (but I suppose you could use the phrase "he who dares, wins" about it), was to break off a large sheet of ice from the Arctic cutting it into the shape of a long runway using ice breaking boats. The sheet of Ice would then be sprayed with sea water and subjected to the wood pulp process. This exercise would be constantly repeated, until the newly cut sheet of ice had sufficient mass to allow it to hold the weight of required aircraft. Along with the buildings and fuel stores required to make it into a floating airfield. Whilst this process would have taken some considerable time, it would have been a great deal quicker and less expensive than building an aircraft carrier, hence the attraction of what on the face of it seems an implausible project. Once the preparation was finished, tugboats would then attach cables and tow it to the Norwegian coast. A sheet of ice that had been transformed into a giant floating airfield, capable of handling enough planes to allow an attack to take place.

You have to consider when judging the plan that this was the same country which conceived, and built, the bouncing bomb. Successfully destroying a significant part of the Ruhr valley industrial production, though no one thought that the huge structure of a dam could be bombed successfully.

Churchill pressed ahead with the development of the floating airfield project and a large team was engaged to examine the practicalities of putting the plan into action. At the point when it became clear the allies would not be invading Norway, Churchill quickly took the decision to bury it. There was no point wasting further valuable time and resources on the scheme. Even though it had the attraction of being so unique that to pull it off would have been a tremendous achievement.

It would have been a remarkable sight, an enormous great floating sheet of ice transformed into an airfield, the wood pulp process would have given it amazing properties helping it to withstand attack by enemy aircraft. Imagine the photographs and archive footage. You could just see the faces of the Germans defending the Norwegian coast as this great big flat white object floated into place, bristling with hundreds of spitfires and bombers.

Churchill was tremendously keen on seeing the idea come to fruition but once the circumstances changed, he had the courage to drop it.

Another example of Churchill having an idea for a new type of war making machine and then having the courage to drop it, once circumstances changed, was the story of Cultivator No 6. He had the idea when he was First Lord of the Admiralty during the "phony war" period. A time when the Royal Navy engaged the enemy but there wasn't much action on land or in the air.

OVERVIEW OF CULTIVATOR NO6 IN CHURCHILLS OWN WORDS

During these months of suspense and analysis I gave much thought and compelled much effort to the development of an idea which I thought might be helpful to the great battle when it began. For secrecy's sake this was called "White Rabbit No. 6", later changed to "Cultivator No. 6". It was a method of imparting to our armies a means of advance up to and through the hostile lines without undue or prohibitive casualties. I believed that a machine could be made which would cut a groove in the earth sufficiently deep and broad through which assaulting infantry and presently assaulting tanks could advance in comparative safety across no-man's-land and wire entanglements, and come to grips with the enemy in his defenses on equal terms and in superior strength. It was necessary that the machine's cutting this trench should advance at sufficient speed to cross the' distance between the two front lines during the hours of darkness. I hoped for a speed of three or four m.p.h.; but even half-a-mile would be enough. If this method could be applied upon a front of perhaps 20 or 25 miles, for which two or three hundred trench-cutters might suffice, dawn would find an overwhelming force of determined infantry' established on and in the German defenses, with hundreds of lines-of-communication trenches stretching back behind them, along which reinforcements and supplies could flow. Thus we should establish ourselves in the enemy's front line by surprise and with little loss. This process could be repeated indefinitely .

When I had had the first tank made 25 years before, I turned to Tennyson d'Eyncourt, Director of Naval Construction, to solve the problem. 'Accord-ingly I broached the subject in November to Sir Stanley Goodall, who now held this most important office, and one of his ablest assistants, Mr. Hopkins, was put in charge with a grant of £100,000 for experiments. The design and manufacture of a working model was completed in six weeks by Messrs. Ruston-Bucyrus of Lincoln. This suggestive little machine, about three feet long, performed excellently in the Admiralty basement on a floor of sand. Having obtained the active support of the Chief of the Imperial General Staff, General Ironside, and other British military experts, I invited the Prime Minister and several of his colleagues to a demonstration. Later I took it over to France and exhibited it both to General Gamelin and later on to General Georges, who expressed approving interest. On December 6 I was assured that immediate orders and absolute priority would produce two hundred of these machines by March, 1941. At the same time it was suggested that a bigger machine might dig a trench wide enough for tanks.

On February 7,1940, Cabinet and Treasury approval were given for the construction of two hundred narrow "infantry" and forty wide "officer" machines. The design was so *novel that trial units of the main components had first to be built. In April a hitch occurred. We had hitherto relied on a single Merlin-Marine type of engine, but now the Air Ministry wanted all these, and another heavier and larger engine had to he accepted instead. The machine in its final form weighed over a hundred tons, was seventy-seven feet long, and eight feet high. This mammoth mole could cut in loam a trench five feet deep and seven-and-a-half feet wide at half-a-mile an hour, involving the movement of eight-thousand tons of Soil. In March, 1940, the whole process of manufacture was transferred to a special department of the Ministry of Supply. The utmost secrecy was maintained by the three hundred and fifty firms involved in making the separate parts, or in assembling them at selected centers. Geological analysis was made of the soil of, Northern France and Belgium, and several suitable areas were found where the machine could be used as part of a great offensive battle plan.*

    But all this labor, requiring at every stage so many people to be convinced or persuaded, led to nothing. A very different form of warfare was soon to " descend upon us like an avalanche, sweeping all before it. I lost no time in casting aside these elaborate plans and releasing the resources they involved. A few specimens alone were finished and preserved for some special tactical problem or for cutting emergency anti-tank obstacles. By May, 1943, we had only the pilot model, four narrow and five wide machines, made or making. After seeing the full-sized pilot model perform with astonishing efficiency, I minuted "cancel and wind up the four of the five 'officer' type, but keep the four 'infantry'-type in good order. Their turn may come". These survivors were kept in store until the summer of 1945, when the Siegfried line being pierced by other methods, all except one was dismantled. Such was the tale of "Cultivator No. 6". I am responsible but impenitent.

The story of Cultivator No 6 shows how Churchill was capable of developing new ideas and devices for taking the attack to the enemy. It also shows how he was perfectly comfortable dropping his own pet projects once he was persuaded that their fighting value had sufficiently diminished.

Whilst writing this chapter the following example from my own business career immediately sprang to mind, it is a story that highlights how Churchill's approach would have worked, and how mine didn't.

Some years ago, I had a role as a marketing manager for a global company that produced and sold photocopiers and laser printers, among other things. I was responsible for the creation of marketing plans to promote the printers in the UK and across Europe.

For a long time we had been desperate for a low cost, high speed, black and white laser printer. The company specialized in big printers, however, by offering a low-end printer at the right price we could open the door to more customers. Once they were happy we could then introduce the higher end machines.

Finally, product development created a printer that fitted the requirement. We put together a huge plan to market the printer across Europe with a very big six-figure budget. We set the PR team to work, ten different countries had new adverts created and space was booked in magazines all across Europe.

This was all taking place in November. Everyone was excited, finally we could take the business to the next level. The campaign was high profile with the CEO of Europe taking an active interest. Thousands upon thousands of the printers were stacked high in the newly automated warehouse. We received the go-ahead; adverts were booked for the January editions of relevant magazines. The competition did not have a clue what was going to hit them. They would be ashen faced and left floundering once the campaign hit the streets. It was over for them they just did not know it yet. At least that is what we thought!

It was mid November when I started to get some disturbing reports about the performance of the printers. Naturally concerned, I put a team together to look into the matter. After exhaustive testing, they discovered the most bizarre problem I had ever encountered in my business career. If customers switched off both the printer and the heating at night causing the office temperature to drop significantly, the first 10 pages the printer churned out in the morning were completely solid black. If the printer stayed switched on, or if the office heating stayed on overnight, the printer was fine. A very unusual and disturbing problem!

The printer's target market was small business, the sort that would probably switch the printer and the heating off to save on energy bills. By early December we knew that we had a big issue, there was no way we could fix the printers in time for the campaign launch in January. A crunch decision was required, either press on knowing we would be selling faulty printers, or take the brave decision to pull the campaign. We could then fix the printers and try again in three of four months.

If I had stayed true to Churchill's principle of the chapter, I would have bravely insisted that we pull the campaign and take the consequences on the chin, whilst blaming the manufacturer of the printer for the issues. All would have been well and I could have re-launched the campaign in the early spring confident in the re-engineered printer. With hindsight, which is one of the very few exact sciences, this is what should have happened, but it did not.

I put the issue to my boss who then raised it with the head of marketing for Europe, I also made sure I had an e-mail chain to cover myself if everything went wrong, which it did, in a big way. (Incidentally, when Churchill was a soldier and was commanded to pass military orders to other officers he always insisted on having them in writing). The decision was made at a very high level to press on with the campaign, sell thousands of printers and hope that not too many ended up in cold offices. As mentioned in an earlier chapter, hope is neither a plan nor a strategy and in this particular case, luck was not on our side.

By February we were inundated with printers that we knew had a problem before we even sold them. A plan was put in place to get them swapped by the manufacturer for new ones. The strategy was to brave it out until April, when we relied on the weather warming up to stop the flow of returns, which amazingly it actually did.

Over the summer, more inventory of cold resistant printers arrived. I am not in a position to give you either a happy ending or any ending for that matter; I decided to leave the company in the August of that year. The debacle of the cold weather printers was the last straw for me.

The problem caused major issues for every company that bought our printers and supplied them to other companies on our behalf. Every end user that bought one began to associate my company with the manufacture of rubbish. This did terrible damage to the reputation of the company as a whole, impacting on other product areas. Confirming the old adage that a company is only as good as it's worst product. Back office support for the good products suffered badly, because staff could not cope with the issue of dealing with the cold weather printers.

Sales teams were de-motivated; they spent all their time receiving abuse from their customers for selling them such a bad product. Distributors who had bought the printers to sell on to smaller companies were swamped with complaints and stopped buying any products until the problem was resolved. Finance spent all their time raising credits and could not get cash in from customers, because they refused to pay invoices until credits were raised.

This was overall, an unmitigated disaster and entirely the companies fault. They had the information in time to stop the problem from happening; they could have kept their reputation intact and saved themselves and their employees from a torrid year. Instead, they employed that age-old business strategy of hoping that by some miracle, the problem would just go away and all would be well in the end.

Years later when writing this chapter it is blindingly obvious that it would all end in disaster unless they had had the equivalent of winning the business lottery. I was much younger then, and I would like to have been able to write that I heroically stopped the problem before disaster struck, like some hero from WW2 saving the day. In reality I take my share of the blame for letting it happen, I was young, ambitious and keen to progress, rocking the boat too much could have jeopardized my career. Given the same circumstances 10 years on, I would not let such a campaign go ahead and would now go as high as required to get it stopped.

In my view Churchill would have pulled the campaign without hesitation.

Chapter 8

Focus on the Payoff

This book aims to identify a number of Churchill's lesser known traits that could be applied in business. One of the great talents that Churchill possessed was a knack for spotting inventions that could make a difference in the advancement of the war effort. He was passionate about encouraging the development of new technology that could hurt the enemy. His many years of experience had also taught him that whilst new technology could be a powerful aid it was not a solution in itself.

There are some great examples of the influence a new technology had on the outcome of the war. However, the deciding factor for Churchill was the practical deployment against the enemy, and the realistic measurement of its success. He placed more importance on these aspects than on the invention itself.

Since Churchill published the second volume of his memoirs "Their Finest Hour" in which he claims that Britain soundly beat the Germans new research by historians would class the Battle of Britain technically, as a score draw. The French had surrendered; the Germans were using Northern France for what was to be the second to last stop, on the way to complete domination of Europe. Hitler's plan A was to achieve air superiority and then offer Britain generous peace terms, installing a puppet government probably including the fervent British Nazi Oswald Mosley. Britain would have been reduced to a grim Nazi supporting regime, not unlike the Vichy government. Plan B was to invade Britain, which would have succeeded eventually given Nazi air superiority and the lack of weapons on British soil to put up a strong defense.

A slight digression. On the subject of defending Britain in the event of attack I found a really interesting pair of Memo's in "Their Finest Hour". There was a proposal for the Police to unwittingly assist the Germans by preventing civilians from trying to fight them. Once Churchill found out he resoundingly rejected it, his ethos was that in the event of invasion "everyone should have the opportunity to kill a Hun"

PM TO LORD PRIVY SEAL & HOME SECRETARY   3.AUG.40

The attached memorandum by Lord Mottistone on duties of police in the event of invasion raises a very difficult question, and one that must be speedily settled. We cannot surely make ourselves responsible for a system where the police will prevent the people from resisting the enemy and will lay down their arms and become the enemy's servant in any invaded area. I confess I do not see my way quite clearly to the amendments required in the regulations. In principle however it would seem that the police should withdraw from any invaded area with the last of His Majesty's troops. This would also apply to the A.R.P. and the fire brigades, etc. Their services will be used in other districts. Perhaps on invasion being declared the police, A.R.P., fire brigades, etc., should automatically become a part of the military forces.

PRIME MINISTER TO HOME SECRETARY   12 AUG.40

The drafts [about instructions to police in case of invasion] sub-mitted do not correspond with my view of the recent Cabinet decision. We do not contemplate or encourage fighting by persons not in the armed forces, but we do not forbid it. The police, and as soon as possible the A.R.P. services, are to be divided into combatant and non-combatant, armed and unarmed. The armed will co-operate actively in fighting with the Home Guard and Regulars in their neighborhood, and will withdraw with them if necessary; the un-armed will actively assist in the "stay put" policy for civilians. should they fall into an area effectively occupied by the enemy, they may surrender and submit with the rest of the inhabitants, but must not in those circumstances give any aid to the enemy in maintaining order, or in any other way. They may assist the civil population as far as possible.

Hitler had very successfully employed a program of eating up one nation at a time. He would firstly promise his target country that he would not invade them, then he would do exactly that, whilst promising the neighboring country that he would not invade them, and so on. This carried on until Western Europe had been digested leaving just Russia and Great Britain to be sorted out. Thankfully Britain turned out to be a bit too rich for his palette.

One of the major differences between the First and Second World War was the importance of air power in battle. The British had learned a harsh lesson when in February 1940 they had tried to force a landing in Norway. The plan had been to prevent the Germans from getting access to Sweden's vast supplies of iron ore which they were planning to ship via Norway. This was a strategic target, anything that would hinder Germany's ability to produce steel for their highly mechanized army would be a great help to the war effort. It was the first major operation of the war and Britain would need to gain a great deal more experience before they would be any match for the Germans. The British tried to make a landing against well-fortified German positions, without protection from the air. Norway was beyond the reach of fighter cover at the time. Many Royal Navy ships were sunk during the course of the attack. Eventually enough troops were landed, but the inexperience of the army and it's command led to a botched operation. The lack of air support for the offensive and the limiting nature of the operation brought home to the British just how much the game had changed, leading to a dramatic re-think in future tactics.

The spectacular failure of the Narvik operation caused such an uproar at home that a vote of no confidence was demanded in the house of commons, questioning the capability of the Conservative government. Whilst the vote was won, sufficient people voted against the government and the Prime Minister Neville Chamberlain, that his authority was fatally weakened, he had no choice but to resign. In May 1940 he handed the most difficult job in the world to Winston Churchill, such was the bleak outlook that about the only person who thought they had any hope of success was Winston himself. He immediately set about forming a coalition government incorporating people from all of the major parties. To get Britain on a proper war footing he needed the full support of parliament. Over the course of the war as fortunes ebbed and flowed Churchill also faced a number of votes of no confidence but always won them convincingly.

The British soon learned that a land battle or a sea engagement near to shore would be difficult to win, without at least a minimum of parity in the air. Successfully forcing a landing against well-fortified positions would require air superiority.

June 1940 and the commanders of the German army began massing troops along the coast of Northern France, orders were given for thousands of ships to congregate in the ports and inlets with the intention of carrying the Teutonic invaders across the English channel. They weren't the first to try, it had been 1000 years since any country had managed to successfully complete the task, despite many attempts. However, before the troops would climb on board any of the vessels the German army command insisted that Goebbels and his Luftwaffe make the sky safe. After many years of building and training the best army in the world, Hitler's generals were not prepared to let the RAF send half of it plunging to the depths of the ocean, for want of air protection. Whilst all the buildup was taking place it fell to Goebbels to deliver on his promise to Hitler. Without victory in the air, there would be no invasion. In the summer of 1940 Germany had yet to taste the bitter fruit of defeat. Had the armies demand for air superiority been met it was a distinct possibility that the landings would have succeeded. Leaving Britain to go the same way as France, despite the rhetoric of Churchill's speech stating that "We will fight them on the beaches and in the hills, we shall never surrender".

Hitler probably joked with his generals on hearing threatened countries say they would fight to the death, just before they surrendered. The reality in my own uneducated opinion is that Britain, when faced with overwhelming odds, and the successful landing on British soil of such a huge and deadly force, would have eventually capitulated.

This nightmare did not turn into reality, because of the effective use of available technology and a crucial home advantage. Britain, inspired by Lord Beaverbrook, the minister in charge of aircraft production, had managed by a massive effort to build up a large quantity of Spitfires in anticipation of the air battle. Beaverbrook was able to keep production going during the conflict at sufficient levels to replace a large proportion of the damaged fighters.

When it came to dueling in the air, on paper the German Messerschmitt was technically faster than the Spitfire, had excellent, accurate guns and therefore should have been able to comfortably beat the world's most famous plane. The Meshersmitt however, had two incredibly important weaknesses, it was only faster than the Spitfire at high altitude and could not stay in close combat for more than about ten minutes without needing to return to France to re-fuel. The British engineers had specifically designed the Spitfire for dog fighting and optimized them for low altitude. The British strategy was to make the Germans stay low where they had the advantage.

The home team had other benefits, pilots could stay longer in the air and if shot down, they were more likely to survive and fly again. German pilots bailing out would spend the rest of their time in a British POW camp. Remarking on this advantage one of the door attendants at a club Churchill frequented, announced using a football analogy, "I see we've made it to another European Championship final and it's to be played on home ground". A fine example of British gallows humor!

It is difficult to accurately label any invention or device as the one that made the decisive difference in the war, in my view if any invention can lay claim to that accolade it has to be Radar. Chronologically the Battle of Britain was the most important engagement in the war, on the basis that if Britain had lost, everything else that followed would not have happened. In the Battle of Britain the Spitfire was the king of the skies but the Spitfire would not have been able to successfully engage in battle without first being scrambled in time and then being directed to where the action was, all of this was made possible by the use of Radar. Hence my claim.

Churchill had been following the progress of Radar development before war broke out and upon becoming Prime Minister he made the deployment of the Radar defenses a priority of critical importance. Britain had few advantages over the Nazi's and he wanted to make the most of what was available. A mammoth effort of logistics and engineering ensured that a whole series of radar stations were put in place along the south and east coast of England before the battle began. The winning combination of the most effective fighting machine in the air coupled with the new radar technology, along with the skill and courage of the fighter pilots, made the German task a difficult one. The battle raged in the skies between August and October and was a desperately close fought business. At one key point in the middle of September, at the very peak of the fighting, Churchill made a visit to air command. He was talking to the head of the RAF and was being shown a map detailing the deployment of fighters in the air. Churchill asked what reserves were on the ground and where they were stationed. The Air Marshall told him that every serviceable fighter was currently in the air and there were no more reserves. Given that all the fighters were engaged in dogfights with the Germans, it would be fair to call it a pivotal day in world history.

Historians would say that despite claims at the time that the British shot down three German planes for the loss of each one of theirs, in reality, the ratio was closer to one for one. Britain was able to produce more planes per month than the Germans and eventually the Germans had to stop, otherwise they would have had insufficient fighters to defend the homeland from bomber attack by the British.

At the battles of Trafalgar, Waterloo and Blenheim, following long preparation the issue settled itself in a few days; the Battle of Britain however, lasted about two months from start to finish. It started slowly in August, reached a peak in September and petered out in October.

Churchill detailed in his book how Hitler made a massive strategic error during the Battle of Britain, letting Britain and the world off the hook when they were most vulnerable. Towards the end of September the Germans had become increasingly effective at bombing the runways of the southern fighter airbases. So much so, that it was becoming almost impossible to station sufficient fighters to deal with the ever-increasing threat from the air.

It reached a critical point, the RAF had one day left when they had enough serviceable airfields to effectively station fighters for the defense of Britain against the Luftwaffe, then all of a sudden and without any apparent reason the bombing of the airbases stopped and the Germans started heavily bombing London instead.

Churchill is convinced that had the Germans continued bombing the airbases, instead of diverting to London, they would have probably won the Battle of Britain. In his memoirs he describes a number of situations where chance played it's part in the outcome of the war.

Whilst on the subject of the fortunes of war another example of incredible mischance occurred before it ever started. When I read the few paragraphs that described the missed opportunity I was struck by how luck, both good and bad appeared to play a significant role in the build up and in the eventual outcome of the war. Long before the story of Valkyrie, immortalized in the Tom Cruise movie, and before the Germans invaded Czechoslovakia, a number of Generals under Hitler's command were convinced that he was leading Germany to disaster. One incredibly brave man General Halder conspired with the chief of police and other prominent Generals to remove Hitler from power. One of the Generals was to keep a division of Panzers just near the capital. When the signal was given they would occupy all the important ministries and the police chief would arrest Hitler, Himmler, Goering and Goebbels. Everything was planned meticulously all they needed was to wait for Hitler to stay overnight in Berlin. Halder received word that he was leaving Berchtesgaden and was due to arrive in Berlin before midday. The Generals decided to invoke the plan and set the time as 8.00pm that evening. Then Neville Chamberlain unwittingly botched it, he decided to fly to Berchtesgaden and scheduled a meeting with Hitler regarding the Czechoslovakian crisis that same day, in doing so he caused Hitler to leave Berlin not long after he arrived. The plan was put on hold. The Generals were gravely concerned about the Czech crisis because they knew that the Army was still getting up to fighting strength and would not be able to successfully attack the very heavily fortified Czech frontier. Hitler managed to persuade Chamberlain and the French to force the Czech government to hand over the disputed territory without a fight. Impressed by Hitler's ability to win large amounts of territory by bluff, General Halder dropped the plan which was not uncovered until after the war. A few days later Chamberlain gave one of his famous speeches.

How horrible, fantastic, incredible, it is that we should be digging trenches and trying on gas-masks here because of a quarrel in a far-away country between people of whom we know nothing! I would not hesitate to pay even a third visit to Germany, if I thought it would do any good. I am myself a man of peace to the depths of my soul. Armed conflict between nations is a nightmare to me; but if I were convinced that any nation had made up its mind to dominate the world by fear of its force, I should feel that it must be resisted. Under such a domination, life for people who believe in liberty would not be worth living: but war is a fearful thing, and we must be very clear, before we embark on it, that it is really the great issues that are at stake.

Churchill wrote hundreds of pages on why he believed the war could have been avoided, had Britain and France possessed the nerve to stand up to Hitler in the 2 years before the war. Hitler kept on calling their bluff whilst he built up the strength of his army until he didn't need to bluff any more.

After the Battle of Britain in the autumn of 1940 Churchill gave one of his legendary speeches to the house of commons where in his own inimitable manner he described the immense struggle that had strained the air defense mechanism of the RAF to its limit and beyond. He praised all the people who had played their part in it but stated that at the very pinnacle stood the brave and fearless fighter pilots who had to face the enemy in mortal combat, and who prevailed. He coined the very apt phrase that "never in the field of human conflict was so much owed by so many to so few". Always a master wordsmith he got it absolutely spot on, when you consider that as few as a thousand British and Allied pilots were responsible for forcing a draw in a battle where a draw was a good result. Those one thousand pilots, using their courage and skill, along with the best that British technology had to offer at the time, saved the western world from an unimaginably grim future. The people Churchill could not mention in his speech due to the secret nature of Radar were the boffin's, the men and women who developed such radical and effective technology for its time. Without which the Battle of Britain might have had an entirely different outcome. Not nearly so romantic or glamorous, and definitely not as dangerous, but to re-word Churchill's famous phrase for them "never in the field of technological advancement has so much been owed by so many to a single invention" the people of Britain and those liberated in 1945 owe an immense debt of gratitude to those unsung heroes, the boffin's.

Both of the principal protagonists who squared up to each other in 1940 believed that technology held the key to victory. Having sat through hundreds of meetings and presentations regarding the latest class of weapon, Churchill had developed the skill of quickly getting to the nub of a proposition. He was not fazed by clever inventions he just assessed them against a criteria of effectiveness against the enemy, cost, timescale to produce, scalability of production and practical deployment in the field of battle.

As Hitler never got the opportunity to write his memoirs one must assume he went through a similar process, however he didn't have Winston's experience. In WW1 he was an ordinary private in the German army whilst Winston was First Lord of the Admiralty, as a result of his superior knowledge and experience Churchill was able to make better informed decisions about where to invest time, money and resources.

Hitler consistently boasted that some secret invention or other being developed by his scientists would be the crucial new factor in delivering the victory he so desperately craved. This over reliance on technology was to prove part of his undoing in the end.

One of the best known examples of this was the development of the V1 flying bomb and the V2 rocket. Hitler invested huge resources into these two programs, determining that the British would not have an effective response to a fast flying bomb, which they eventually did, and to the V2 rocket, which Hitler correctly predicted could not be stopped. The V2 shot straight out of the sky plummeting vertically at over a thousand miles an hour causing great devastation.

The V1 and V2 were the most advanced military technology of their time, the problem for Adolf was the cost. Each V1 was eight times more expensive than a fighter plane to produce and took twice as long. Similarly the V2 rockets cost 20 times more and took 6 times longer to construct. If Hitler had not been so obsessed with developing the rockets, (which were undoubtedly a marvel of engineering) and had concentrated on the most effective use of resources to support the war effort. He would have concluded that making fighters and bombers was his most effective route to success. Instead, the dazzle of using the latest technology to develop new and sophisticated weapons turned his head. Had he concentrated on the planes it would have enabled the Germans to bomb the Russians and the British with greater venom and intensity and would have improved the defense of France from attack by the allies. Making the allied task of achieving air superiority over northern France, which was a prerequisite before D-Day, much harder.

When the V1 bombs started dropping in London they initially caused great panic. They were indiscriminate and very inaccurate, the random nature of the bombing caused immense concern to Londoners. At least with the V1 the pulsing noise from the jet engine meant that you could hear it coming, which is where the name of doodlebug came from, when the pulsing stopped it would be a few seconds before an explosion was heard. The V2 rocket on the other hand was so quick it made no sound.

Initially London's air defenses struggled to cope with the V1. It was difficult for a fighter to shoot a V1 down in mid-air and anti aircraft guns could not hit them as they were small and fast. Hitler in the early stages must have felt vindicated by his decision to take such a big gamble. Luckily at about the same time, the British were supplied by the USA with a new anti-aircraft proximity shell, which used a magnetic fuse that would explode when it passed near to a V1, reducing the requirement for pinpoint accuracy.

The V1's attacked London from a consistent direction either from Holland or Northern France and subsequently crossed onto the British mainland within a narrow corridor. Churchill decided to mount a major offensive against the V1, and as the result of an incredible piece of planning and logistics, the British moved all the anti aircraft guns from the outskirts of London to the coast over a weekend. This involved laying 10,000 miles of phone cable and electrical wire and was a staggering feat of engineering.

The British were then able to shoot down about 90% of the V1's as they came along the narrow corridor. The Germans could not understand how Britain became so accurate almost overnight. It was easier to shoot down V1's than a fighter or bomber, as they flew in a straight line. With the help of new technology from the USA, Britain was able to master the V1 bombs. This effectively neutralized them as a threat and made all of Hitler's research, time, effort and cost associated with the V1 development, the best that Nazi science could deliver, almost pointless. Hitler must have been devastated. Britain with the help of the USA had once again foiled his fiendish plot. Without his efforts however, the introduction of modern Jet planes would have taken considerably longer.

It was all well and good Hitler using this amazing technology. It was far more expensive to produce and when it did succeed in hitting a target, it was not particularly effective in terms of the damage it could cause, when balanced against the extra cost of each V1. It transpired that ordinary high explosive bombs dropped conventionally from the air at a much lower cost, killed more people and caused more damage. Hitler must have hoped the new weapons would have terrorized the British public to such an extent that they would force Churchill to sue for peace.

Hitler could rightly point to his second and even more amazing technological advance, the V2, as an outstanding success which delivered everything his Nazi scientists promised him. It was impossible for the allies to defend against, it was reasonably accurate and killed indiscriminately. The ideal weapon to strike terror into the hearts of the Englanders. The war office was so concerned about the public reaction to the V2 which caused such big explosions without any air raid warning or noise that they tried to keep the cause of the explosions secret.

Blaming them on burst gas mains. Hitler was furious, he finally had a new weapon of terror, that really worked, and should have been causing great upset to the British public. Instead they were completely ignorant of his incredible weapon of Nazi destruction. Livid that their new toy was staying hidden, they leaked news of the attacks to the New York Times. This was then picked up by the British press. These silent killers carried about the same payload as a V1 but were the most effective weapon developed during the war, except for the Atom Bomb.

Unfortunately for Germany it was too little, too late. The cost and the resources required to make V2's, effectively stole capability from ordinary aircraft research and production. This took valuable capacity away from the defense of the army on the ground. The technology and its wondrous potential had seduced Hitler, he bet everything on it and it cost him dearly. By not being able to defend the army with greater numbers of combat aircraft, the allies overran Germany before Hitler could build enough rockets to make a real difference to the outcome of the war.

Whilst the technology was far in advance of the allies, as Churchill had learned, technology alone would not win a war.

Everyone who knows about the war will have probably heard about the V1 and V2 rocket, the surprise for me came when Churchill pointed out the folly of Hitler's gamble.

The next battle formed part of what Churchill called the wizard war. A time when scientists battled to outsmart each other away from the gaze of the public. It was October 1940, the Battle of Britain had ended and the Germans had set their sights on bombing Britain into submission, in particular hitting the weapon production factories across the length and breadth of Britain. To do this effectively, the Germans developed a method of targeting their conventional bombers using radio beams directed from different parts of Europe, towards the UK. Pointing the radio beams in such a manner, that they crossed over at the exact location of the targets. By using radio detection technology, the German pilots just had to follow a set flight path and listen to the radio signal, once they heard the correct sound the pilot could press a button and know that he had accurately released a reign of destruction upon his designated target.

Through their network of spies, the British found out about the radio direction bombing technology, and set about trying to foil it. They did not want to jam the signals as the Germans would then know the British were onto them and revert to conventional methods. They considered that it would be far better to try and fool them. They discovered that by amplifying one of the radio signals they were able to send the German bombers off course and fool them into unknowingly dropping their bombs in the safety of open countryside. Eventually the Germans realized that their systems had been compromised and had to go back to using normal navigation techniques.

The Germans then devised another type of radio directional technology called Knickerbein, which was a far more sophisticated method of directing the planes. This new technology based on radio pulses, was even more accurate and meant that the German bombers could fly and drop bombs in bad weather, thus preventing British fighters from engaging them or anti aircraft guns from shooting them down. This could have left Britain defenseless to highly accurate bombing whenever the weather over the mainland was bad, a pretty regular occurrence in Britain.

A young British scientist called R V Jones had been working in the department responsible for devising solutions to the German beam threat, and through a number of coincidences he had become suspicious about the development of the new Knickerbein device. He managed to piece together information from many different sources, and found that his suspicions were confirmed when a German bomber pilot was shot down and interrogated about the new radio equipment in his plane. After months of frantic research, the Knickerbein technology was eventually mastered by the British. This time they went to even greater lengths to fool the Germans into thinking they had been successful. For a while, the Luftwaffe would fly their bombers at night in bad weather and drop their bombs, believing that they were successfully destroying their designated target. Once the planes had unloaded the British would light huge fires, set up in open fields to simulate the effect of bombing. Tricking the German Pilots into thinking that they had successfully hit their targets.

One friend of Churchill's commented that on a weekend vacation in the country he had seen a hundred German bombers unload a thousand bombs onto an open field in the middle of nowhere. Churchill just smiled knowingly, but could not explain the phenomenon. Very few people knew what the brilliant British scientists had achieved.

At that same time during the war, Churchill was becoming increasingly annoyed and frustrated with the Irish. They had declared neutrality at the beginning of the war and had subsequently denied the British Navy any access to their ports. This caused tremendous problems for Britain and made it far more difficult to defend the Merchant Navy from the threat of U-Boats in the Atlantic. Whilst Churchill was seething with the Irish politicians and especially the Irish Prime Minister DeValera, he recognized that despite the enmity that existed (based on hundreds of years of bitter history), a large proportion of the Irish population wished Britain well in the fight against tyranny. They knew that life under the Nazi's would be much worse than the form of democracy and freedom that they had finally grasped from the clutch of the British, who were still providing subsidies to help Irish farmers, which they could ill afford. Churchill talked about stopping the subsidies but he did not state in his books whether Britain actually followed through on the threat. Churchill summed up his feelings for the Irish in his final speech of the War, I have included the relevant extract below.

The sense of envelopment, which might at any moment turn to strangulation, lay heavy upon us. We had only the North-Western Approach between Ulster and Scotland through which to bring in the means of life and to send out the forces of war. Owing to the action of the Dublin Government, so much at variance with the temper and instinct of thousands of Southern Irishmen who hastened to the battle-front to prove their ancient valor, the approaches which the Southern Irish ports and airfields could so easily have guarded were closed by the hostile aircraft and U-boats. This was indeed a deadly moment in our life, and if it had not been for the loyalty and friendship of Northern Ireland we should have been forced to come to close quarters or perish for ever from the earth. However, with a restraint and poise to which, I say, history will find few parallels, His Majesty's Government never laid a violent hand upon them, though at times it would have been quite easy and quite natural, and we left the Dublin Government to frolic with the Germans and later with the Japanese representatives to their hearts' content.

When I think of these days I think also of other episodes and personalities. I think of Lieutenant-Commander Esmonde, V.C., of Lance-Corporal Keneally, V.C., and Captain Fegen, V.C., and other Irish heroes whose names I could easily recite, and then I must confess that bitterness by Britain against the Irish race dies in my heart. I can only pray that in years which I shall not see the shame will be forgotten and the glories will endure, and that the peoples of the British Isles, as of the British Commonwealth of Nations, will walk together in mutual comprehension and forgiveness.

In the extract above Churchill states that *"His Majesty's Government never laid a violent hand upon them"* I would not question Churchill's word, but I believe he had the satisfaction of knowing he had some payback. There was an odd incident in 1941 when Dublin was bombed, this caused great outrage in Ireland and especially when it transpired that a squadron of German bombers had "accidentally" dropped their payload of bombs over Dublin. The Irish population were informed that the mistake was the result of the German pilots flying over a blacked out Britain, crossing the Irish Sea and bombing a brightly lit Dublin. At the time this was considered to be a plausible explanation.

Churchill gave his readers a big clue to the actual reason behind the attack. He deliberately mentioned this incident in the same chapter he discussed how the British had mastered the Knickerbein technology. I am convinced that he instructed the British scientists to direct the German bombers to Dublin, ensuring that the Irish lost confidence in the Germans and to punish them for denying the Navy access to their ports. It seems remarkably unlikely that even in bad weather the German Pilots would have avoided Britain altogether, accidentally dropping their bombs with great accuracy upon Dublin. Hundreds of miles past their original target. Churchill was quite correct when he said the British didn't lay a finger on Ireland, the unwitting Germans did it for them. To prove that it was the Irish politicians and not the people that Churchill had disdain for, I have detailed the heroic story of Paddy Finucane

Churchill mentioned in his final speech the number of Irish heroes that gave their life to help the allied cause in spite of their country's neutrality. He included the story of the fighter ace Wing Commander Finucane, an Irish volunteer in the RAF. This example of courage and heroism must have tugged so much at Churchill's heart that he included a small passage about how Paddy met his end. This was unusual in his memoirs as the war was so replete with acts of heroism, that he must have taken the decision not to mention too many individual cases, for want of offending those he left out.

Wing-Commander "Paddy" Finucane, D.S.O., D.F.C. and two bars, was killed at the age of twenty-one in July 1942, when, after continuous exploits, he was leading a fighter wing in a mass attack on enemy targets in France. It was always said that the Luftwaffe would never get him, and it was actually a ground shot from an unusual single machine gun post which hit his Spitfire. He flew slowly out to sea, talking calmly to his comrades. Finally, when ten miles from the French coast, he sent his last message, spoken probably as his engine stopped: "This is it, chaps." He crashed from about ten feet above the sea, and his machine sank at once.

Finucane had always vowed not to be taken prisoner, and it was probably this that made him fly out to sea rather than inland, where he would have had a good chance of survival.

The "Battle of the Beams" ended in the summer of 1941, with the start of "Operation Barbarossa" the German invasion of Russia. The German focus shifted away from Britain and the mass bombing reduced significantly. Hitler left it to the U-Boats to try and starve Britain into surrender, whilst he dealt with Stalin.

By the time the bombing campaign against Britain was

renewed in 1944, new guidance methods and the use of RADAR in planes rendered the beam technology obsolete.

I had to go back many years to the early part of my career for an analogy that chimed with this chapter, one of the fun aspects about writing this book was how it encouraged me to take a trip down memory lane and how much I enjoyed analyzing events that occurred many years ago with a fresh perspective.

At the age of 25 I made a radical change to my life, I gave up a career as a software programmer and embarked on a career in sales. My first job was with a well-known company selling photocopiers. By the time I joined, their best years were behind them. However, their training was second to none which presented a real opportunity for someone like me with no prior sales experience.

The copiers we sold were expensive compared to the competition. To overcome this obstacle, we had weeks of training to help persuade potential customers that the additional benefits of the advanced technology were just what they needed. Our copiers had far greater sophistication than anything our new competitors had developed, it was easy for a new recruit to be convinced of their superiority after six weeks of residential training.

It is amazing what a new young recruit will believe, it reminds me of a story I read in the memoirs of a secret agent who spent many months in France. She had been held captive at a school in the South of France and was talking to her young German guard, he said to her that after the war Hitler was going to reclaim Shakespeare and Voltaire for Germany. As the British and French and stolen them from their rightful home. Amazed, the agent asked the German guard why he believed they had been stolen. Responding with an air of absolute certainty he stated that at school they had been shown that Shakespeare was originally German. The Englanders had cleverly managed years ago to translate his plays from German to English, and to pass him off as an English playwright. Being in a rather vulnerable position and not wanting to upset the fellow she decided not to avail him of the truth.

Whilst my training did not fall into the category of

brainwashing like the German guard, I was certainly trained to believe that my products were far superior to other companies, it was just a matter of explaining the differences and the customers would be only too pleased to sign the requisite paperwork. As I quickly discovered the reality was somewhat different, most of my potential customers wanted a photocopier to simply be able to do what it said on the tin, photocopy. They just wanted to put a piece of paper on the glass or in the feeder, press a button and get out something that looked like the paper they put in. My company's copiers did this; they just did it for a lot more money.

The competitors copiers were not as good, but in reality, they were more than adequate for the job. They cost less, because the manufacturers concentrated on building a copier to the specification the market wanted, at a price the end users would be happy to pay.

We were told to concentrate on how robust our copiers were when selling, and to bring to the customer's attention the rather flimsy nature of the competitors machines. Robustness is a fine quality especially if you are using the copiers in a military zone; it is not really a huge differentiator under normal office conditions.

Our copiers could do the most amazing things with paper, once it had exited the copier. Stapling, folding, making booklets, you name it, our copiers could do it. Unfortunately for the sales force, the number of customers requiring such extensive functionality were few and far between, most customers just wanted to copy, whilst the more sophisticated possibly wanting to staple. Something my copiers did and so did our competitors.

I have been in the sales business for over twenty years. There will be some salespeople reading this thinking that due to my inexperience I was unable to sell the features and benefits of my machines over the competition. That I was using the age-old salespersons excuse of blaming price or anything else they can think of to mask their failure. In fact, considering it was my first sales position, I was rather successful; I won an incentive trip to Bermuda after nine months.

Quick story about Bermuda, Churchill stopped there after his first conference with Roosevelt in early 1941. British Spitfires nearly shot him down on his way back home.

He had flown from Washington to Bermuda in a brand new Boeing flying boat to rendezvous with a battleship for the return journey. He was so impressed with the plane and the pilot that he asked if it would fly him all the way back to Britain. The pilot did a few calculations and confirmed it was possible. After a few arguments, the chiefs of staff agreed that it would be safer to fly home, rather than risk the German subs trying to hunt him down. The Germans knew he had been to America due to the press coverage surrounding the trip and would be trying to get him.

The Boeing took off and had flown for about eighteen hours, by which time the Scilly Isles should have been visible off the south west coast of England, however due to low cloud they were not spotted, after a few anxious moments, the pilot was advised to fly north immediately. Had they continued, in another five minutes they would have been flying over the German anti aircraft batteries of northern France. That wasn't the end of their problems, as unfortunately, they were now heading to Britain on the same flight path used by the German bombers. They had to maintain radio silence and could not relay their location, for fear of alerting the Germans. A British Radar station detected them and scrambled four Spitfires to shoot them down. Thankfully, the fighters did not find the Boeing and its precious passenger; had they done so it could have been the worst example of shooting down by friendly fire in history.

Twenty years on it is easy with hindsight to see where the problem lay for my old employer, hindsight being a particularly wonderful gift. A radical shake up of production processes and a total re-vamp of the business was required to compete with the new low priced products coming in from the Far East. Something that is easier said than done. When I won my incentive trip, the company chartered a private jumbo jet to fly all the winners from England to Bermuda. This represented a small percentage of the UK direct sales force. Six years later the business did not employ any direct sales people and sold via third parties. Thankfully, even though they are a considerably smaller company, they are still in business today.

Coming from a technical background, I understand how the seduction of the latest technology can be very compelling, almost regardless of cost. Unless evaluation of the actual payoff takes place with an accountant-like ruthlessness, devoid of seduction, then large sums of money can be wasted, buying technology to chase a non-existent competitive edge. When in reality less money spent refining existing systems could have delivered a better result.

Churchill had the benefit of hindsight after the war; it was easy to see that if Hitler not been so obsessed with rocket technology and built fighters and bombers in their place, the Germans would have had a far greater chance of defending themselves against the allies. Thankfully, for humanity's sake, this was not the case.

Those scientists who developed Germany's rocket technology did not get the opportunity to go back to their pre-war jobs. Both the Allies and the Russians were desperate to get their hands on such highly skilled individuals, most of them were captured by one side or the other. They started a new career supporting the Cold War with the development of intercontinental ballistic nuclear missiles. They also significantly contributed to the technology that put men on the moon. Hitler's investment wasn't able to help him save the Nazi ideal, but it certainly didn't go to waste.

Chapter 9

Support the Arguments You Lose

Churchill did not always get what he wanted, especially towards the end of the war. I was taken aback by the way he maintained a positive outlook and the vigor with which he fully supported initiatives he violently disagreed with. It struck me that his particular talent of being able to rationalize decisions in this manner would be especially useful if more people in business could copy it.

A couple of events stand out in his memoirs to highlight the point. The campaign to conquer Italy and operation Anvil, the plan for landing troops in the South of France to coincide with the D-Day invasion.

After the decisive victory over the Germans in North Africa in the summer of 1943, Churchill persuaded the Americans to continue taking the fight to the Nazi's and to turn their attention to the island of Sicily. This next move was not as obvious as it might seem, around this time there was considerable debate between the allies. Should they consolidate their forces and begin the build up to D-Day or continue attacking the Nazi's and their Italian fascist partners. The argument prevailed that the best way to support the Russian's, who were committed in battle on a massive scale, was to keep fighting the Germans and thus tie up men and resources that might otherwise be transferred to the eastern front.

Churchill's ultimate agenda was to defeat Mussolini and kick the Germans out of Italy before the D-Day landings. Once the American's had tasted victory in Sicily he was convinced that he could persuade them to carry on a full scale operation in Italy.

The Americans were against the Italian plan, after Sicily they wanted to save men and equipment for simultaneous attack on Normandy(Overlord) and the South of France(Anvil). They didn't want a war on Italian soil to jeopardize the main objective. Churchill on the other hand didn't want hundreds of thousands of soldiers sitting idly waiting for D-Day whilst he could have them fighting "The Hun". He wanted to get through Italy and be ready to move onto Vienna in Austria to coincide with D-Day. He considered it vital to have the allies in Vienna before the Russians. Churchill never fully trusted the Russians to keep their word about promoting democracy in Europe after the war. Why would a communist regime that was suffering terrible hardship and sacrificing millions of lives, give up the land it conquered. Even when Stalin gave his word, signing solemn agreements with Roosevelt and Churchill promising democracy and freedom to all liberated lands, the clue to the likely outcome was in the word "communist". To be on the safe side Churchill wanted the allies to occupy as much land as possible when the Nazi's finally capitulated.

The Americans could not be persuaded by his arguments. The issue at stake was the preparation for D-Day. The military planners wanted all the troops and landing craft earmarked for D-Day safely out of harm's way, months before the big show. Landing craft were a precious resource in war and they did not want to risk anything before the big event. Churchill had the opposite view he wanted to keep the troops fighting Germans for as long as possible, returning them just in time.

After countless meetings and memo's which included many direct appeals to President Roosevelt, Churchill finally lost the argument. After victory in Sicily significant numbers of troops and equipment were taken from the theatre of war. He accepted the losses and with the remaining resources he planned a limited campaign to attack the Italian mainland. He managed to retain enough specialist craft to support a landing and at the end of summer 1943 the allies were back on European soil, taking the fight to the Nazi's. The allied planners intended to continue removing troops in anticipation of D-Day, immediately after the Italian landings, thousands of troops went back to England. Weakening the ability of the army to break out of the foothold they had created on the Italian coast.

To meet his commitment to D-Day whilst still giving the Italian campaign a chance, Churchill drafted in troops from across the British Empire along with divisions and brigades created from soldiers who had escaped German occupation, such as the Polish and Free French. Eventually they succeeded in breaking out of their bridgehead and fought all the way to Monte Cassino, half way up the leg of Italy. This is where the struggle intensified, as the Germans had built up their defenses and were determined to make a stand. Just when the Allies needed additional troops, more had to return to England, delaying victory by months. Whilst Churchill was naturally disappointed, he had given his commitment to the D-Day preparations and bore the setback stoically. He believed that both D-Day and the Italian campaign could have been fully accommodated but he could not bring the American's around to his way of thinking. Whilst US forces played an active and significant role in the Italian campaign, had the forces not been weakened the campaign would have concluded long before the 5th June 1944, the afternoon before D-Day.

Churchill stated on many occasions that he would fully support a majority decision once it was finalized, even if he had argued passionately against it. "If we are going to be fools, then we will make sure we play the part of fools to the utmost of our ability"

Quick anecdote about how desperate the Germans were to kill Churchill. Shortly after the Casablanca conference where Churchill had lost the argument for a more comprehensive Italian campaign, a famous British actor from the forties was tragically killed. Lesley Howard was the star of many movies, but is particularly remembered for the famous 1940's movie "Brief Encounter". He had been holidaying in Lisbon, Portugal, in 1943 and had caught a commercial flight back from Lisbon to London. This coincided with Churchill returning from the Casablanca conference. For reasons that Churchill found difficult to understand, a German spy based in Lisbon spotted a man in a heavy coat wearing a hat similar to his and smoking a cigar. He thought it was Churchill taking a commercial flight back from the conference on his own. As if! He radioed this information to

German fighter command who then dispatched a fighter and shot the plane down, killing everyone and depriving Britain and the world of an immensely talented actor.

Churchill could not believe the Germans had been so callous and naïve as to shoot down innocent passengers without being certain of the facts. The Germans would have been far better off forcing the plane to land and capturing the person they had mistaken for Churchill. Leaving the remaining passengers to complete their journey.

Churchill was tremendously frustrated at the limited American support for his Italian ambitions. He had an exceptional dislike for operation Anvil. The American project to land an army in the South of France which would eventually link up with the troops from Normandy. He considered Anvil to be of considerably less military and strategic value than taking Italy and moving on to Vienna. No matter how hard Churchill tried to persuade the Americans that it was a waste of time, they were adamant that it should go ahead. Again, once the decision was final, he fully supported it, ensuring that it received total British cooperation. Even though operation Anvil was ultimately successful, on reflection after the war Churchill still thought he was right. Believing that it made a negligible contribution to the ultimate victory, especially when he compared Anvil against the sacrifices in Italy that enabled it to happen. Reflecting in the early fifties when he published "Triumph and Tragedy". The last of his six volumes of memoirs, he was convinced that history had proved correct his assertions about Anvil, as great sacrifices had to be made by the Allies to extricate the Russians from Vienna during the post war period.

Winston's ability to fully support the operations he didn't want, with as much vigor as those he cherished came as a complete surprise to me, it was a capacity that I greatly admire.

Ask any company owner or senior executive and they would commend Churchill's approach as a highly desirable employee characteristic. In business, everyone has an opinion and whilst there are always competing interests and agenda's, decision making will often involve some sort of compromise. Most employees like myself do not have the luxury of making decisions entirely on their own. There are times when a consensus view from a meeting, or an instruction from a senior manager seems completely wrong. A colleague might be totally convinced that they are right about an issue and no matter how hard they try to convince other colleagues of the case, no one will listen. When this sort of situation happens, they can have a tendency to do as little as possible to support the decision, dealing with any aspects they might be responsible for, in a half-hearted manner.

In my role as a manager, individuality and discussion is actively encouraged. I am always open to a suggestion that might improve a business process or enhance a project. Even when I have my heart set on a particular program, if someone else can put forward a coherent reason to drop or significantly amended it, then I will change my position. There is no point clinging on to a plan for the sake of pride, when faced with clear evidence it will not work.

My biggest challenge is when I have to implement a new company policy that I fundamentally disagree with, knowing that as a manager I have no choice. My responsibility is to explain the policy in the best way possible and bring the team with me. Doing this, whilst retaining credibility, can be challenging. Ultimately as a manager that is what I am paid to do, achieve results within a business framework, decided by the people I work for. I always have the option of leaving if I don't want to do the job.

On many occasions I have implemented policies and decisions that I believe to be completely wrong, and argued vehemently in their favor when challenged by colleagues, staff and customers. This is when another one of Churchill's tricks for venting his anger is really useful.

To get things off his chest Churchill would write a memo detailing what he really felt about a situation and would not hold back from being offensive. He would then simply not send it. I imagine the writing down of his feelings was somehow cathartic. The next day he would dictate a more appropriate response. The research for this book has taken a number of years (honestly!) and during the course of writing the book I was holding down a full time job. As with any role there are times when I have not agreed with a policy or decision, I get particularly annoyed when I consider injustices have been done to my team. Especially where it concerns their pay. One issue (detailed below) had me so incensed that I decided to put Churchill's technique to the test. I wrote an E-mail that I subsequently didn't send, I printed it out and deleted it from my company PC. I have detailed the E-mail I didn't send below and followed it on with the one that was ultimately sent, once I had calmed down.

From: Shovel, Binden
Sent: October
To: Commission Appeals Group
Subject: Payments - October Payroll

To the commission appeals group

Mike Gray has 200 customers, he was given another customer from a different department, the systems make it difficult to identify exactly where it came from.

When the account transferred it billed Zero, Mike contacted them and they stated that they wanted nothing to do with our company.

5 Months later finance had finally shut down the account and without telling anyone in my division they applied an outstanding debt of -$43k onto Mike's figures costing him $6,483 in lost commission.
I have sent detailed letters of explanation to the appeals team and they have point blank pig headed refused to accept that the -$43k should come off Mike's figures.

He had nothing to do with the customer before they were transferred, they had no interest in our company. The negative figures relate to business they did 18 months ago. Mike therefore correctly concentrated on trying to do business with the other 199 companies on his account list.

I know there is a rule in the pay scheme which states that any debt queries should be flagged to the commission administrators within 3 months of taking over an account, but frankly this is nonsense in this case due to the zero billing and the number of accounts Mike has to look after. This rule is intended for lazy account managers that look after 5 to 10 accounts not the guys who look after hundreds.

I appealed to the commission appeals group stating the case for the anomaly and they flatly rejected it, simply quoting the relevant clause in the commission scheme. What is the f*$£^ng point of having an appeals group if they simply quote the rules and won't venture outside of them. Even when the injustice of the f*$£^ng case is as plain as can be. They might as well not exist for all the b$*&%y use they are.

Are they saying that because of the total intransigence of the appeals process when an account that does no business is transferred between account managers they should waste valuable selling time checking out debt history issues instead of doing the job the company pays them for. Namely, managing customers that want to do business with this company.

These idiots have no idea what an impact they have on the moral of the sales teams when they treat people in this way. You can guarantee that Mike has told everyone what a bunch of wa$%&rs the commission appeals people are and what a waste of time it is to even try and raise an appeal. He will tell all and sundry that the company are ba£$%^&s who will shaft you as soon as look at you, and that everyone had better start spending loads of time checking customer histories at the beginning of each new year. To make sure they don't get tripped up by the rules. That is going to have a really positive impact on performance!!!
The rule that Mike is being shafted by is now being completely misinterpreted and applied in a punitive way to the absolute discredit of the commission appeals panel.

I cannot express my total and utter disdain for this whole process highly enough.

My one wish is that someone in the business wakes up and smells the f*$£^ng coffee and changes this whole procedure which is now a laughing stock.

The officious application of the rules to the detriment of the salespeople whilst ignoring all reasonable explanation is a stain upon this business. I would go as far as saying it is the stinking baby puke on the carpet of this company.

Binden

It was surprising how writing the memo somehow made me feel better. I rarely get so boiled up that writing a Churchill memo is required, but I have to say that I would use the technique again if I felt the urge. It is difficult to explain why it seems to work, you will just have to give it a try and see if it helps you. Churchill did this a lot so I guess there must have been something in it.

The memo I eventually sent is detailed below. It is always good to calm down before sending memo's which are likely to prove contentious. I have made the mistake once or twice in my career of sending an emotionally charged E-mail only to regret doing so an hour after hitting the send button. I then quickly sent a memo apologizing for being unprofessional. I now know to pause for reflection before composing a potentially prickly response. Churchill usually slept on the matter before sending the final response to an issue where he had originally written an offensive note, and that's not bad advice.

From: Shovel, Binden
Sent: October
To: Commission Appeals Panel; My Boss
Cc: Grey, Mike
Subject: RE: Commission Payments - October Payroll Further Formal Appeal to Commission Panel

Folks

I wish to formally re-appeal this credit coming off Mike Greys figures for next month's appeals panel. If I cannot appeal back to the panel then could you advise me on how I might take this matter further.

Mike Grey has 200 accounts, in May of this year a number of what could only be described as very small accounts we placed with Mike. As a salesperson Mike's first duty is to make sure he maximizes the business potential from his customers and drives the revenue required to hit his target. The account that has the $43k negative applied to it due to bad debt, had 0 billing when it was passed to Mike. When he contacted them he was told in no uncertain terms that they had no interest in doing business with our company.

At this point any account manager would simply park them on the back burner until a service came along that might be of potential interest to them.

If they were a large customer with big billing I could understand that an account manager would go into great detail with finance to make sure that billing etc was in order, for such small accounts with so little billing, how large could a bad debt situation be, $5k at most.

Mike has been docked $43,000 which represents 5% of his annual target, because he didn't investigate the potential for a bad debt write off on an account with 0 billing.

I was under the impression that the reason for the appeal process was to look at individual cases and decide if the rules have been applied fairly.

I fail to understand how anyone looking at this case cannot see that whilst the 3 month rule has not been adhered too, there are extenuating circumstances that should allow for the credit to be taken off Mike Greys figures.

Mike appears to be getting punished for finance not being able to collect money over what must have been a very long period of time and deciding to write an account off without any recourse to Mike. Just to be absolutely clear no billing has been added to Mike's figures from this account, it was all accrued on Mike's figures long before the account was handed over.

If the rules are to be applied in such a rigid fashion then at the beginning of the year when accounts are transferred, the business will come to a standstill whilst account managers spend all their time delving in to every little detail of an accounts billing and lodging potential claims. Just in case something pops up outside of 3 months.

I cannot believe that when the rules for credits were first devised that they intended it to have such harsh consequences on an individual with 200 small accounts.

I would kindly ask you to review this credit and take it off Mike's figures.

Regards

Binden

Just for the record the appeal was not successful!

Back to the point of the chapter after that little digression, if I cannot explain why something needs doing when one of the team disagrees with me, then I will do my best to clarify the situation. On rare occasions, I might have to demand that a team member complete an action, even when I cannot persuade them of a good reason why. This is the point when you need someone to do something they do not agree with, giving it their full commitment without constantly complaining.

During the war, an event in one part of the world would have a knock on effect, thousands of miles away. Only those with an overarching view of all events could possibly foresee the consequences. Sometimes a person who has to do something they disagree with, cannot hope to know or understand the reasons behind the decision, because they just do not have all the facts. Sometimes in business, you have to trust that for better or worse those above you know what they are doing and just get on with it. I have certainly been in the position where I have thought some of the strategies and decisions of companies I have worked for were strange and potentially damaging. Only to find out weeks or months later that they were absolutely correct once the background to the decision had been revealed.

In my view, it takes a lot of discipline, self-confidence and inner strength to demonstrate motivation for something you disagree with. It is easy to grumble and be half-hearted about a decision. The colleagues and managers I enjoy working with most are those who can get on with the job whilst staying positive. These coincidentally, tend to be the most successful.

Chapter 10

It's About the People

Ask anyone with an opinion about Winston Churchill and they will probably tell you that he was a great leader and an amazing speaker. That he displayed incredible strength of character before and during the war. He was also known for always having a witty response or put down for any situation or event. Half the people asked will probably try and quote you their favorite Churchill one liner. I doubt anyone will mention that he possessed amazing people skills, or that he had a soft romantic side which he held onto throughout the torrid unending pressure of war. He never appeared to lose his ability to make those whom he encountered from all walks of life, feel special.

One example stands out for me, the story of Major General Orde Wingate from Edinburgh. If people live on in print then I dedicate this book to the memory of Orde Wingate. He gained a reputation in the army as the leader of the irregulars in Abyssinia. Some years before the war Italy had occupied Abyssinia, whilst Britain and other countries had colonized other parts of Africa during previous centuries, by the 1930's the world community judged such aggression as wholly unacceptable behavior.

At the outset of WW2, the British gave arms and military support to the Abyssinian people to help them break free from the Italian fascists, which they did successfully. Wingate was a military liaison between the British and the Abyssinian soldiers, advising them on the best way to oust the Italians.

After a distinguished military career, Wingate went to the Far East to fight the Japanese. At the time, standard military practice was to progress in battle as far as the means of supply would allow. An army requires feeding, watering, and to be provided with bullets. It can only progress on any scale if supplies can be kept flowing to the troops. The capacity to deliver the essentials along the supply line determines how many soldiers can go into battle.

Orde Wingate developed a technique for guerrilla warfare against the Japanese. This involved parachuting a large group of men behind enemy lines, whilst creating a line of supply via airdrops. At the time, this was a radical approach to jungle warfare and caused havoc for the Japanese. Orde's style of warfare made a significant contribution towards defeating the Japanese in the Burmese jungle in the latter stages of the war. The technique seems obvious now; however, at the time the airplane in warfare was being completely re-evaluated. Larger planes could fly further, with heavier loads, enabling sufficient regular drops of supplies to be a realistic prospect.

Wingate had been in the jungle for months and was on his way back home for a well-deserved break. Churchill heard that he was landing at an airstrip in the early evening west of London. He decided to invite him to dinner, that very night!

Wingate was taken by car to Downing Street, still in the same smelly clothes he'd travelled in on his three day journey. He must have been very pungent when he sat down to dinner with the Prime Minister. Churchill was greatly impressed by Wingate and thought him an exceptional soldier with a great career ahead of him. Wingate was a Zionist and had been talent spotted as a potential candidate to lead an Israeli army after the war. During desert Churchill asked Wingate to travel with him to a secretly organized conference arranged in Quebec, with Roosevelt. It was 9:00pm; the train was to leave in an hour. He told Wingate that one of his staff would organize fresh clothes for the trip.

Wingate readily agreed to Churchill's request to join him (how could he refuse?), but mentioned that it was a great shame he would not get to see his wife whilst he was on leave. His wife did not even know that he was on British soil, it was two years since they had last seen each other and he missed her dreadfully. He had tried to block her out of his mind during his time in the jungle. This stopped him from losing concentration. He had thought of little else except throwing his arms around her on his long and arduous three-day journey back home.

All Churchill's conferences were top secret, with no one outside a small group of planners knowing where or when they would take place, for obvious security reasons. After Wingate left the room, Churchill made a few enquiries and discovered that Mrs. Wingate lived in Edinburgh. He knew the journey to Quebec involved a train journey to Scapa Flow in Scotland and then a voyage by war ship to Canada.

As I mentioned earlier, Winston was somewhat of a romantic, and at this point he demonstrated one of the traits that made him the great person he was. Without telling Major General Wingate, Churchill instructed his private office to contact the Edinburgh police. They knocked on Mrs. Wingate's door at four in the morning and told her to pack a bag for cold weather. Mrs. Wingate did not have a clue why but followed instructions. She was taken to Edinburgh train station where Churchill's special train made a detour to stop and pick her up. As she stepped onto the train from the freezing platform in the dead of night it is hard to imagine the joy and surprise she must have felt. After two long lonely years of struggling on her own, their he was, her Orde standing with arms open wide ready to give her the hug she had longed to feel. She had been startled by a knock on the door in the middle of the night, only to be told by a policeman that she had 30 minutes to pack a bag. Mrs. Wingate was then whisked off to the station alarmed and confused. It had all been worth it as there she was on Churchill's train heading for a week in Quebec.

They stayed at the luxury Hotel Chateau Frontenac where the conference took place. Given that everyone lived on rations in Britain, the luxury of the cruise and sumptuous hotel must have been a fantastic treat. Not to mention the opportunity to spend some "quality time" with her husband in luxurious surroundings.

Incidentally I can recommend the hotel, it is perched at the top of Quebec City in a spectacular location, and is truly impressive. I stayed their years ago on a company incentive trip.

Churchill wanted to share Wingate's special type of insurgency with the British and American chiefs of staff. Wingate had built up quite a military reputation and Churchill knew that Roosevelt liked to meet great soldiers. So to cap it all Orde Wingate and his wife met Roosevelt whilst at the conference.

Churchill instinctively arranged for Mrs. Wingate to board the train as a surprise for both of them, without giving it too much consideration. Undoubtedly, this would have left a lasting impression with Wingate, his wife, and everyone who knew them. Wingate no doubt would have told his fellow soldiers who in turn would have spread the story. Until very soon half the army would have heard it. This must have improved morale by proving that whilst Churchill had the weight of the war on his shoulders, he still had time to do something exceptional for a soldier.

Another famous war hero of the time, who went along to meet Roosevelt at the same conference was Guy Gibson. The squadron leader of the Dam busters. He was fresh from leading the bouncing bomb attack that famously destroyed the Mohne and Eder Dams.

The story of King Peter of Yugoslavia (now Serbia and Croatia) is a another touching example of Churchill's romantic sense of fair play and decency. The dashing young King had fled from his kingdom after the Nazi's invaded, like many Royals from occupied Europe he ended up in London. He joined the RAF and wanted to get married to Princess Alexandra of Greece & Denmark, the woman he loved. This caused a great row between the other Yugoslav exiles as the tradition going back centuries was for Kings not to marry before going in to battle. Peter was having none of it and insisted that he be allowed to marry. Eventually an appeal was made to Eden the foreign secretary who consulted Churchill.

PRIME MINISTER TO FOREIGN SECRETARY   11 JULY 43

About King Peter's marriage, we should recur to first principles.

The whole tradition of military Europe has been in favor of "les noces de guerre", and nothing could be more natural and nothing could be more becoming than that a young king should marry a highly suitable princess on the eve of his departure for the war. Thus he has a chance of perpetuating his dynasty, and anyhow of giving effect to those primary instincts to which the humblest of human beings have a right.

2. Against this we have some tale, which I disbelieve of a martial race, that the Serb principle is that no one must get married in war-time. Prima facie this would seem to condone extra-marital relations. Then a bundle of Ministers that have been flung out of Yugoslavia are rolling over each other to obtain the shadow offices of an émigré Government. Some are in favor of the marriage, some are not. The King and the Princess are strongly in favor of it, and in my view in this tangle they are the only ones whose opinions should weigh with us.

3. The Foreign Office should discard eighteenth-century politics and take a simple and straightforward view. Let us tell the King and his Ministers we think the marriage should take place, and if the King is worthy of his hazardous throne we may leave the rest to him.

4. I. may add that I am prepared to go into action in the House of Commons or on any democratic platform in Great Britain or the United States on the principles set forth above; and I think the Cabinet ought to have a chance of expressing its own views. We might be back in the refinements of Louis XIV instead of the lusty squalor of the twentieth century. Are we not fighting this war for liberty and democracy? My advice to the King, if you wish me to see him, will be to go to the nearest Registry Office and take a chance. So what?

King Peter married his princess in March 1944, the year following this memo. Rather tragically he was never able to go back to his homeland as the communists under Marshal Tito took control of Yugoslavia. He settled in America and died at the age of 47 in Los Angeles, following a failed liver transplant. He is the only foreign King buried in American soil.

A further example of Churchill's consideration for others came just after the D-Day landings, when he travelled to France, quite close to the fighting front. He was on a tour of the different battalions and had stopped for lunch. After the break, he climbed into his Jeep to see another area of fighting when his personal body guard realized that he hadn't brought a gun for Churchill. A normal precaution in case they came under attack. The bodyguard took the drivers gun and gave it to him. Churchill then angrily turned to his bodyguard and said, "If I have the driver's gun, what is he going to use if we come under fire." The bodyguard looked at him sheepishly. Churchill gave the driver back his gun and told him to carry on driving, stating that he would take his chances if they were ambushed.

You can guarantee that the whole army on the front would have known of this incident within a couple of days. Again demonstrating that Churchill treated everyone equally and would not countenance putting an ordinary soldier in danger for the sake of himself.

You can't be a romantic without some recourse to flowers. Churchill was frustrated that the coal hearted people in the transport department, could not find it in within themselves to squeeze some flowers onto the trains, for delivery to the wider population. In 1943 the war was far from over and it was a time of great deprivation. He knew that by getting flowers to the cities the men and women of great Britain would have the possibility of a little extra romance in their lives, with the consequent lifting of their spirits. The memo below gives an overview of the problem.

PRIME MINISTER TO MINISTER OF WAR TRANSPORT   3 MAR 43
This note from your office about the ban on the transport of flowers by rail certainly does not give me what I want. I asked that some effort should be made to ease up this war on the flowers, in which your department is showing an undue relish. What is the difference now and what was done last year?

PRIME MINISTER TO LORD PRESIDENT   6 MAR 43
TRANSPORT OF FLOWERS
I am distressed that your Committee should not have seen their way to agree to any relaxation of the ban on the transport of flowers by train. I recognize that in present circumstances the provision of special trains for flowers cannot be justified; but surely some half-way house can be found between the provision of special facilities and the complete abolition of the traffic.

I should be glad if your Committee would give immediate consideration to an arrangement whereby such limited transport capacity as can properly be made available for flowers, without

damage to essential war purposes, and having regard to the
hardships and restrictions imposed on the travelling public, can
be fairly distributed between the growers. In this way a
legitimate outlet would be provided for as high a proportion of
flowers as can be carried to our big cities, and the temptations to
a black market diminished.

*I trust that this may be considered in conjunction with such
other mitigations as the milder winter has rendered possible in
our transport situation.*

PRIME MINISTER TO MINISTER OF WAR TRANSPORT   6 MAR 43

Thank you so much for helping about the flowers.

In 1943 nothing mattered quite as much to Churchill as
maintaining cordial relations with the ever growing number of
US personnel. In particular the brave young men that risked their
lives flying perilous bombing missions over the cities of
Germany.

The note below deals with the practical issue of having
thousands of US military personnel whizzing around the English
countryside in Jeeps and on motorbikes. The content of the
memo makes it clear that it must have taken some time for the
American servicemen to get acclimatized to British roads. Given
that the majority of troops were young, and even now it is the
young who are most accident prone on the roads, it is hardly
surprising that the accident rate would have been high. This is
especially true when you consider that the British drive on the
left hand side of the road and the US drive on the right. I can
imagine the horror of a young US Pilot when he first
encountered a roundabout, a uniquely European invention to
enable the traffic to flow easily at a junction without having to
use traffic lights. When you combine all of this with the
requirement to maintain a blackout whilst driving, you have the
perfect recipe for disaster.

PRIME MINISTER TO FOREIGN SECRETARY   27 FEB 44

*I entirely agree that we should pay out of hand all civil
claims against members of the United States forces over the five
thousand dollar limit, which the Americans are apparently*

constitutionally unable to settle.

2. The remedy for the reckless driving which is causing so much trouble is a conversation between me and Eisenhower. I am sure that if the case is put to him he will exercise a controlling and effective authority. At any rate, we ought to try this first.

3. Surely it is not necessary to make all this long statement in Parliament, which seems to me to be likely to cause a lot of ill-feeling in the United States; and I was not aware that you were subjected to much pressure in the House on this matter. I should greatly prefer to let Eisenhower put his screw on and see what happens, meanwhile confining your statement to the fact that we will pay the claims over five thousand dollars pending further discussion by His Majesty's Government with that of the United States.

The final example I have included, relates to the provision of service personnel with packs of cards. Churchill raised what initially appeared to be a trivial issue into a high priority. It mattered a great deal to a man with firsthand experience of war, that the brave men and women in the forces had something to pass the time with during the long periods of intense boredom, that separated the bouts of active conflict.

PRIME MINISTER TO PRESIDENT OF BOARD OF TRADE   26 JULY 43
I am told that in spite of contributions from civilian supplies there is at present a shortage of playing-cards for use by the forces and workers in industry. The importance of providing amusement for the forces in their leisure hours and in long periods of waiting and monotony in out-of-the-way places, and for the sailors penned up in their ships for months together, cannot be overstated. Nothing is more handy, more portable, or more capable of prolonged usage than a pack of cards.

Let me have a report on this subject, and show me how you can remedy this deficiency. It ought to mean only a microscopic drain on our resources to make a few hundred thousand packs.

PRIME MINISTER TO PRESIDENT OF BOARD OF TRADE   1st AUG 43
Thank you for your note about shortages of playing-cards. What happened to the 1,950,000 produced over and above the

1,300,000 issued in the last twelve months?

2. As to the future twelve months, the demands appear to be well under 2,000,000 packs, against which you propose to make 2,250,000 packs. I should be very willing to support you in getting the twenty more workers and hundred tons of paper necessary to make an additional million, but first I must know what has happened to the 1,950,000 surplus in the last twelve months, and, secondly, what is the reserve you consider necessary to have "in hand for emergency". The important thing is to have the cards freely forthcoming when called for, and although the soldiers should have priority, civilian workers need them too.

The memo's above, and the story of Orde, clearly demonstrate that Churchill enjoyed taking a few moments to show he was human and had consideration for others. As for myself, I can't reel off any list of grand gestures that comes even remotely close to Winston. However, I always go out of my way to demonstrate to the people who work for me, and those I interact with at my company, that I take their wellbeing seriously and that I don't take anything for granted.

I endeavor to respect their personal time and try not to contact them out of business hours, unless it is a dire emergency. At Christmas, I send a personal card thanking everyone for their hard work, at least their families then know how much they are appreciated. If they are involved in any business related issue, they know they can count on my support, so long as they have not broken any major company rules. If they are having a bad day they can talk to me, I will listen and try to help if possible. I go out of my way to praise genuine success, however I am always conscious not to overdo praise as it then loses its value. I've worked with some managers who tell everyone what an awesome job they are doing all the time, no matter what they have done. Everything is always "Great" or "Fantastic". After the first few times no one takes any notice of their praise.

During my time at one business, I had been working with a lady in product development to launch a new service; she had been very helpful and did an excellent job despite some major difficulties. When she left to have a baby, I asked my wife to write down a list of items that a first time mum would find useful and bought her a baby-changing bag filled with baby essentials. A year later when the lady returned to work I discovered that she had told just about everyone in the business about my present, which can't have done my profile within her section of the business any harm.

I don't want to give the impression that I am some sort of pushover, when a person is not doing what they are supposed to or I feel is taking advantage, I am very firm and feel quite comfortable confronting a situation that needs resolving. It is especially true in sales, if someone is not performing you do not let them hide behind the myriad of excuses which can be generated by a salesperson. You offer an honest, if sometimes uncomfortable appraisal of the situation.

As with other chapters, it is not necessary to do extraordinary deeds all the time for people to know that they matter. Whilst the odd one helps, the manner in which the smallest issue is dealt with and the interaction with other people when help is required can quickly give a measure of your attitude to others.

Churchill understood that doing something extra special for someone as and when the right opportunity arose, would generate immense loyalty. The good deed would gain a life of its own and be a force for good. It can also bring a great deal of personal satisfaction to do someone a good turn, especially when it is completely unexpected.

As an incredibly sad footnote to the story of Major General Wingate, unfortunately, towards the end of the war his plane crashed into mountains, on the way back to the Far East. I was devastated when I read this, as was Churchill when he was informed. Like so many other war heroes, Orde Wingate was denied the opportunity of living to enjoy his well-deserved fame. Thankfully he was not forgotten and a number of books were written about him, along with a BBC TV series made in the 1980's that documented his career.

Chapter 11

Compartmentalize

One of the traits of great leaders is the ability to compartmentalize events and problems to enable them to be managed effectively. When reading through Churchill's memoirs I was astonished by the number of issues he dealt with and tracked simultaneously. When you consider the events he described in the main body of his books, and combine them with the memo's he sent regarding different topics on the same day in the appendices, a picture develops of someone who was a master practitioner of the art of compartmentalizing.

If there is too much going on in daily business life, how on earth can things be achieved whilst worrying about the things that there just isn't time for.

How is it possible for concentration to be retained during a discussion or meeting, when a world of worries are competing for a limited amount of attention?

There are hundreds of books that cover time management techniques, and topics and this chapter is not intended to compete with them. I just want to point out a skill of Churchill's that formed one of the cornerstones of his success, for readers to try and emulate, if they wish.

Churchill has to be one of the finest examples of someone who had too much on his plate, and yet he managed to attend meeting after meeting, focusing clearly on the content. He prepared hundreds of speeches and wrote thousands of telegrams. Churchill had developed the skill of compartmentalizing an event or task. If he was dictating to a secretary, he gave it his full attention and blocked everything else out of his mind. If he was in a meeting, he was what training consultants often refer to as being "in the moment." He just gave it his full concentration before moving on to the next task.

I don't profess to know the psychology that enables a person to be better at compartmentalizing than someone else, however, to discover how good the reader might be, I have detailed the habits of those who are probably not compartmentalizing. If the answer is yes to any of these questions, whist in a conversation or during a meeting, then compartmentalizing is not taking place, either at all, or not very effectively.

When someone begins speaking, do you immediately start to think of a response before listening completely to the remainder of the conversation?

Do you start thinking of other things whilst giving the appearance of listening to someone talking?

Do you interrupt someone with the suggestion of a solution before the person has even finished speaking?

If you are in a group conversation, as soon as you have something to say, do you stop listening to the rest of the discussion and concentrate on getting your point across?

Do you finish other people's sentences for them when they hesitate?

Do you find it difficult to focus on what someone is saying when you have something on your mind?

Do you often interrupt other people whilst they are talking?

Do you ever keep talking after you have interrupted someone, until the other person stops?

I always assumed I was fairly good at compartmentalizing until I measured my actions against the list above, in truth I have consistently transgressed any number of the points listed. Now however, whenever I am on a conference call and hear myself start to interrupt, or at a meeting and I lose focus, this chapter pops into my subconscious and I try to stop myself. Being aware of what I am doing and the effect it has on others is the first step on the road to stopping.

People who do not compartmentalize generally do one or other of the above. I once worked with a person who could answer yes to the questions above in nearly every meeting, much to the frustration of colleagues.

Compartmentalizing enables a person to be effective at

whatever they are doing. Colleagues, staff and customers really appreciate it, as they will feel that they have a person's individual attention. By not needing things repeated, a quicker more effective response is possible, freeing up time to get on with the next task.

Failure to compartmentalize can lead to stress and anxiety as dealing with a mass of things at the same time becomes almost impossible. Compartmentalizing doesn't mean that a task is finished regardless of whatever else is being worked on. Churchill had to deal with multiple events happening simultaneously across the globe, it wasn't possible to just simply complete one task at a time, and this is equally true in today's hectic world. It is about giving whatever you are doing your full attention even if it is only for a few minutes before giving you full attention to something else.

The first step to compartmentalizing is to begin to consciously think about doing so when things get very busy. I would describe myself as someone who actively has to think about compartmentalizing in order to achieve it. It does not come naturally to me. The more I practice, the better I am able to deal with the events of the day and the easier it becomes.

As with any business suggestion, what works for one person might not have any benefit for someone else. The scope of this book is to give a flavor of how Churchill achieved what he did during the war and apply it to a modern context. This book is not a complete guide to everything in business and if a reader can take one thing away that helps to improve their business performance, then (hopefully) it has been worth the price.

Without Churchill's incredible talent to compartmentalize the hundreds of pressing matters that landed on his desk every day, he would not have been nearly as effective. I read that Bill Clinton has an incredible ability to do the same thing. Compartmentalizing is one of the foundation stones of successful people.

There are books' covering every facet of business and there will be one that covers the topic of compartmentalizing more thoroughly and effectively than this chapter. I hope that I have managed to communicate the general principle.

Chapter 12

Put on a Show

It is no secret that Churchill was an incredibly charismatic man. He is famous for having a fantastically sharp wit. When he was in company, he would always add a splash of humor or witty comment to the proceedings. Books have been written listing all the one liners and put downs he is said to be responsible for.

The real surprise in his memoirs was the way in which he used this abundance of character to be more effective in the mundane business of waging war. I would have expected his memoirs, written after the war, to be a reflection of his character. I was taken aback that the thousands of memo's in the appendices written during the stress and drama of the war, had the unmistakable stamp of his personality.

If he wrote a telegram, where appropriate he would endeavor to make it interesting for the reader. Churchill was a fantastic writer. By the time he became Prime Minister, he had published numerous books, he was a naturally talented author. His book "My Early Life" written in 1930, is a cracking read and thought to be one of the greatest biographies of the last century.

I have detailed some memo's were Churchill tried to get his point across in an entertaining manner. His memoirs are replete with many such examples.

PRIME MINISTER TO FOREIGN OFFICE   23 APR 45

I do not consider names that have been familiar for generations in England should be altered to study the whims of foreigners living in those parts. Where the name has not particular significance the local custom should be followed. However, Constantinople should never be abandoned, though for stupid people Istanbul may be written in brackets after it. As for Angora, long familiar with us through the Angora cats, I will resist to the utmost of my power its degradation to Ankara.

1. You should note, by the way, the bad luck which always pursues people who change the names of their cities. Fortune is rightly malignant to those who break with the traditions and customs of the past. As long as I have a word to say in the matter Ankara is banned, unless in brackets afterwards. If we do not make a stand we shall in a few weeks be asked to call Leghorn Livorno, and the B.B.C. will be pronouncing Paris "Paree". Foreign names were made for English-men, not Englishmen for foreign names. I date this minute from St. George's Day.

The memo above always makes me smile. Churchill is clearly having some fun, knowing that he couldn't really affect the outcome, which as history has shown, he didn't.

The memo below, and in particular the final paragraph encapsulate Churchill's approach to managing detail, in the entertaining and eloquent manner, that was his hallmark.

PRIME MINISTER TO GENERAL ISMAY 2 AUG 43
Make sure that no code names are approved without my seeing them first.

PRIME MINISTER TO GENERAL ISMAY 8 AUG 43
I have crossed out on the attached paper many unsuitable names.
Operations in which large numbers of men may lose their lives ought not to be described by code words which imply a boastful and over confident sentiment, such as "Triumphant", or, conversely, which are calculated to invest the plan with an air of despondency, such as "Woe betide", "Massacre", "Jumble", "Trouble", "Fidget", "Flimsy", "Pathetic", and 'Jaundice". They ought not to be names of a frivolous character, such as "Bunnyhug", "Billingsgate", "Aperitif", and "Ballyhoo". They should not be ordinary words often used in other connections,

such as *"Flood"*, *"Smooth"*, *"Sudden"*, *"Supreme"*, *"Full force"*, and *"Full-speed"*. *Names of living people, Ministers or commanders-should be avoided; e.g., "Bracken."*

2. *After all, the world is wide, and intelligent thought will readily supply an unlimited number of well-sounding names which do not suggest the character of the operation or disparage it in any way and do not enable some widow or mother to say that her son was killed in an operation called "Bunnyhug" or "Ballyhoo".*

3. *Proper names are good in this field. The heroes of antiquity, figures from Greek and Roman mythology, the constellations and stars, famous racehorses, names of British and American war heroes, could be used, provided they fall within the rules above. There are no doubt many other themes that could be suggested.*

4. *Care should be taken in all this process. 'An efficient and a successful administration manifests itself equally in small as in great matters'.*

I couldn't resist inserting the memo below regarding witchcraft.

PRIME MINISTER TO HOME SECRETARY   3 APR 44
Let me have a report on why the Witchcraft Act, 1735, was used in a modern court of justice.

What was the cost of this trial to the State?-observing that witnesses were brought from Portsmouth and maintained here in this crowded London for a fortnight; and the Recorder kept busy with all this obsolete tomfoolery, to the detriment of necessary work in the courts.

Churchill couldn't believe that time and money was spent prosecuting someone for witchcraft, in fact when I researched the detail it makes fascinating reading, as described below.

The Witchcraft Act 1735 marked a complete reversal in British attitudes to sorcery etc. No longer were people to be hanged for consorting with evil spirits. Rather, a person who pretended to have the power to call up spirits, or foretell the future, or cast spells, or discover the whereabouts of stolen goods was to be punished as a vagrant and a con artist, subject to fines and imprisonment.

The case mentioned by Churchill was of Helen Duncan, the last person to be jailed under the Witchcraft Act, on the grounds that she had claimed to summon spirits. It is often contended that her imprisonment was in fact at the behest of superstitious military intelligence officers, who feared she would reveal the secret plans for D-Day. She came to the attention of the authorities after supposedly contacting the spirit of a sailor on HMS Barham, whose sinking was hidden from the general public at the time. She spent nine months in prison.

Part of Churchill's appeal was his ability to make interaction with him a rewarding experience for those privileged enough to have the opportunity. His skill of compartmentalizing enabled him to focus on any individual even for the briefest moment during a conversation or meeting, making the person feel special, appreciated and valued.

This was particularly useful skill when he dealt with other world leaders and the important people he needed to influence to support the war effort. The force of his personality, along with the focus that he could shine upon a person, must have intoxicated anyone trying to stand up to him, or declining to help Britain. It is difficult to imagine sitting in front of Churchill, attempting to say no to a request, once he had empathized with a situation then asked again for its completion. It would have taken some doing.

Having the ability to influence people and achieve results by making them feel special is an invaluable talent.

With modern day technology, the most likely forms of communication are phone, e-mail, videoconferencing and face-to-face meetings. Gone are the days when sending a telegram was the main form of communication. The value of face-to-face meetings, despite the growth in video conferencing, is still just as high as it was in Churchill's day, you just cannot extend the personal touch needed for those important meetings via a video conference. Churchill took great personal risk travelling the globe to meet the people he needed to influence. He knew that the force of his reputation, along with his charm and personality could make a real difference to the outcome of important events and decisions.

Throughout the war Roosevelt would send personal and military representatives across the Atlantic, both to support Churchill and to inform the USA about the military situation in Britain. Winston always went to great personal lengths to ensure that they were introduced to him, by making personal contact, he knew that he would have a chance to influence them for the benefit of Britain.

I am typical of a lot of people in business today, despite the potential benefits of meeting everyone I would like to, I tend to do a lot of business over the phone, both with customers and within the company I work for. Whilst I have about as much charisma and personality as Churchill had in his big toe, I have found that by endeavoring where possible to make any interaction over the phone rewarding for the other person, they are more willing to help. I covered the aspect of treating people decently in an earlier chapter; entertaining them for a few seconds is just going that one-step further towards greater effectiveness.

It can be as simple as asking someone how they are, listening to the answer and making a pleasant comment. It is rare to find anyone in business with time on their hands, so before making a request it is important to recognize that they are probably already very busy and that the last thing they need is more work. After a request has been made a good line that gets to the nub of when they can complete the task, without being too direct, is to ask how big their to-do list is. Even if they do not have one, they will get the meaning behind the question.

If something needs doing urgently, justify why it is so important and the personal and business benefit that will be delivered with their help. This enables them to personally justify why the request is so vital and helps them prioritize it. Refrain from asking for every request to be urgent, as this will damage that all-important personal credibility.

Even if they state that they cannot give preferential treatment, always finish the call by thanking them anyway, and express appreciation for the difficult situation that asking for a priority request has placed them in. It is amazing how often the request completes early, as if by magic!

The above is just one small example of how planning a call of any nature and making the effort to be pleasant, and where appropriate, entertaining can make a real difference. A humorous observation or a joke at your own expense, which often seems to work well, can break the ice before making a request.

The approach on the phone can work equally well on e-mail and face to face, it just takes a little more thought than a phone call.

Obviously, this style of communication is only suitable in certain situations; it works if the other person has a sense of humor and will not take offence if someone appears to be a bit familiar. Every now and then I will make a call were I completely misjudge the other person's character and have to quickly back track to avoid embarrassment. The overall benefit of the approach however, far outweighs the occasional hiccup.

It is important to compartmentalize any conversation, make sure to avoid distractions during the call. There is nothing more annoying than trying to have a conversation with someone who is reading their e-mail or surfing the internet whilst you are trying to get a point across. There is that slight pause between finishing your sentence and the other person responding. A manager I used to work for had a terrible habit of doing this, I would regularly stop the conversation and ask him if he was reading anything interesting on e-mail, I just knew he wasn't fully listening to me. It is important to concentrate and focus as this enables the other person to feel that you are being sincere.

Churchill had been a politician for forty years before the war started. He had finely tuned his skills of communication and persuasion during his decades spent in government and parliament. Trying to emulate a small fraction of his entertaining ability is not for all people, it requires a certain type of personality.

Everyone, no matter who they are, can follow the basic principles of courteous communication, which in itself can make a huge difference to a person's business effectiveness.

Chapter 13

Never Stop Learning

The first volume of Churchill's WW2 memoirs, (The Gathering Storm) detailed the build up to the War, and why in his view, it needn't have happened. When you read the history and sequence of events the way Churchill recounted them, it is clear that on a number of key occasions the allies could have stood up to Germany and changed the course of history. He was particularly scathing of the manner in which Britain and France handled the issue of the Czechoslovakian territory known as the Sudetenland, which bordered Germany. It was effectively handed over to Germany without a fight at the behest of the British and French. According to the records recovered after the war it was clear that Hitler did not have the armed strength to take what was a well defended frontier by force, he managed to bluff his way to victory without having to fire a single shot. Once the allies had capitulated to Hitler's demands over the Sudetenland, it was only a matter of time before he would demand more. Poland was next and the rest, as they say, is history.

For most of the 30's Churchill was not in government and had to contend with making speeches from the back benches in Parliament, where he was largely ignored. Despite his unfortunate situation, he did not sit back and let the world pass him by. He was 55 in 1930 and could justifiably have kept quiet and waited until he retired. He could have consoled himself with writing the monumental historical work detailing the life of his ancestor the Duke of Marlborough. The four Marlborough books are my favorite amongst Churchill's work, and for most writers they would count as the pinnacle of a writing career. Had the war not intervened that would most likely have remained the case.

Throughout his war memoirs (for which he received the Nobel prize for literature), it is clear that even when he celebrated his sixtieth birthday in 1935 , he did not view his advancement in years as an inhibitor to acquiring knowledge. He was determined to keep up to date with the very latest in military technology, he regularly wrote to the ministers responsible for the Army, Navy, Air force and Home Defense. He enquired about their state of readiness, any new developments, and made suggestions for improvements, based on his own extensive military knowledge.

He increased his understanding by inviting eminent engineers and professors to his home, Chartwell, grilling them about advances in military hardware in Britain and in Germany. Even though he was not a minister, he managed to place himself on a number of important government committees, dealing with the research and development of new weapons, that would ultimately save Britain from the Germans.

Churchill's was happy to admit that he was not a great technical wizard; however to use his own words he instinctively knew "what would help, what would hurt, what would cure and what would kill". He relied heavily on a chap called Professor Lindeman to simplify things for him, he refers to Lindeman in his memoirs as "the Prof", an eminent scientist who stayed with him throughout the war. The Prof was invaluable to Churchill, he had the extremely useful talent of being able to translate the most complex technical detail into plain English. For his invaluable services to the cause Lindeman was made a Lord after the war.

Churchill was on record as stating that Britain was too slow to realize the threat from the Nazi's and was consequently well behind Germany in terms of military production before the war started. At the same time he was also convinced that without some key inventions developed before the war and the application of British engineering ingenuity, the fight could have gone according to Hitler's plan, with Britain cowered by a viscous blitzkrieg in the summer months of 1940 then quickly negotiating peace terms. It had worked everywhere else why not Britain?

Within days of taking over at the Admiralty he immediately

set about putting all his knowledge to good use, one example was a request for a design of new ship to combat the new submarine and air threat.

FIRST LORD TO CONTROLLER   9 SEP 1939
I would ask that a committee of (say) three sea-officers accustomed to flotilla work, plus two technicians should sit at once to solve the following problems:

An anti-submarine and anti-air vessel which can be built within twelve months in many of the small yards of the country. 100 should be built if the design is approved. The greatest simplicity of armament and equipment must be arrived at, and a constant eye kept upon mass production requirements. The role of these vessels is to liberate the destroyers and fast escort vessels for a wider range of action, and to take over the charge of the Narrow Seas, the Channel, the inshore Western Approaches, the Mediterranean and the Red Sea, against submarine attack.

I hazard specifications only to have them vetted and corrected by the committee, viz.:
500 to 600 tons.
16 to 18 knots.
2 cannons around 4-inches according as artillery may come to hand from my quarter, preferably of course firing high angle;
depth-charges;
no torpedoes, and only moderate range of action.

These will be deemed the "Cheap and Nasties" (cheap to us, nasty to the U-boats). These ships, being built for a particular but urgent job, will no doubt be of little value to the Navy when that job is done-but let us get the job done.

A couple of examples of the critical inventions that Churchill kept a close watch on during their pre-war development were RDF (Radio Detection Finding) as it was known in 1935 and ASDICS (Anti Submarine Detection Investigation Committee). Without these fantastic military aids, Britain in the dark days of 1940 standing alone against the might of the German threat, would have been at the most severe disadvantage. RDF is now in use everywhere and today it is widely known as RADAR.

Churchill readily acknowledged that whilst the British

scientist Professor Appleton was developing RADAR, the Germans were also developing the same technology. In 1939, the Germans sent the Graff Zeppelin airship along the south coast of Britain with RADAR detection equipment, trying to discover if Britain had effective RADAR defenses. The Germans wanted to find the locations of Britain's RADAR transmitters. In 1939 Britain had the most sophisticated air defense system in the world. The Germans had their spies and probably knew the British had developed and implemented RADAR. Unfortunately, for the Germans, on the day of the flight, the Zeppelin air ship's detection equipment did not function properly. Even if it had worked, the British knew what they were up to and had switched off the transmitters. It was to be another year before this fantastic achievement of British science and engineering would prove pivotal in determining the future direction of the free world.

As mentioned both of the protagonists at this stage had RADAR; the real difference was how the British had integrated the technology as part of a total defense package. As mentioned in an earlier chapter, at the height of the Battle of Britain this new technology was one of the key factors in stopping the Germans gaining air superiority. The British had built a chain of RADAR stations all along the south and south east coast, the early versions could detect enemy aircraft at a range of sixty miles.

One of the keys to the practical application of RADAR was IFF (Identification Friend or Foe), without which it was impossible to determine at 60 miles if a plane was British or German.

It was the integration of RADAR that provided the crucial difference between the RAF and the Luftwaffe, RAF engineers had linked all the RADAR stations back to Royal Air Force Fighter Command in Uxbridge, just west of London, using thousands of miles of "telephonic communication wire", effectively creating the first national defense network in the world. In addition, fifty thousand people from the observer corps had dedicated phones linking them back to central command. They watched the sky and reported on all plane activities. All of this information was transmitted back to hundreds of people working in fighter command, who then collated and assessed it.

The end result was a huge board, the size of a cinema screen, with different colored light bulbs signifying when planes were in the air, under attack or in reserve. This incredibly detailed and sophisticated communication gave central fighter command up to the minute knowledge of what was happening in the air at any given moment. It was the most advanced air defense capability of its kind in the World in 1940.

The practical manner in which RADAR was implemented made the critical difference. Fighter Command could detect the Germans planes as they flew across the sea and could therefore predict where they would hit land. Spitfires could then be scrambled to make sure they received some warm British hospitality.

A significant proportion of the aerial action took place over the large county of Kent in the south east of England, fifty years later to celebrate the anniversary of the Battle of Britain a Kent based brewer produced a beer called Spitfire with the slogans "Spitfire Beer, no Fokker comes close", "Spitfire Beer, leaves no Nazi after taste" and my favorite "Spitfire Beer, downed all over Kent - just like the Luftwaffe"

Focusing the control from one central point meant that the British could make the best use of available fighters. Without the invention and application of RADAR, the thousand or so fighter pilots who saved the world from German domination, might well have failed in their task.

RADAR development was quickly expanded to include the control of searchlights and anti aircraft guns. On ships, it helped detect the enemy from far away and enabled shelling to take place accurately over a long distance. Planes used it for locating German submarines as they resurfaced to recharge their batteries. RADAR must rank as one of the greatest technological advancements of the last century, based on the simple fact that Britain could well have lost the war without it.

Throughout the war many advances and inventions played their part at crucial times, and another British invention, ASDICS, developed before the war was in active service from the very start of hostilities. It was specifically developed to detect and destroy submarines and is known today as SONAR. At the end of WW1 submarines had significantly advanced in capability, it was vital for the Royal Navy to develop some means of limiting their effectiveness. Having narrowly survived the Battle of Britain, the next task for Churchill was to keep the people nourished by making sure monthly tonnage imports, crossing the oceans of the world, made it safely to British shores. Churchill described this tremendous pitting of German submarine technology against the newly developed British detect and destroy apparatus as the Battle of the Atlantic.

Britain made a point of sharing all of the advancements in technology with America after all it was in Britain's interests for its Allies to receive equal protection. The Americans took the research and with their considerable pool of talented scientists and money, helped refine it, and delivered back to Britain an improved weapon.

Throughout the war Hitler was forever promising his Commanders that the latest and greatest German invention would lead to Britain's downfall. The first example of this was the magnetic mine; deployed early in 1940 it had a devastating effect on shipping around the Channel coast. Previously, mines would only detonate when a boat hit them, the magnetic mine would detonate when the metal hull of a ship passed nearby. Initially, the British had no answer to this devastating new weapon, it took a number of months and some incredible good luck to develop the solution.

An RAF observer noticed a plane dropping what looked like mines off the coast of Southend, a town on the south east coast of England. Mines were regularly dropped by parachute along the English coast with the intention of disrupting local shipping. By chance, the mines landed in soft sand. A bomb disposal team went out to recover them. Churchill was immediately informed about the operation and was given regular updates throughout. He knew how important it was to capture one of these mines in one piece if the Navy were to have any chance of counteracting the deadly menace.

The team took two perilous days to defuse the mines. It was worth all the effort and risk, as at the end of the process they recovered not one but two magnetic mines, intact. The defense research teams then went to work on devising a solution to the threat posed by this new and deadly weapon. The problem was resolved by the development of a process of called degaussing. Degaussing for those who do not know (and I certainly didn't before reading Churchill's books), is as follows, the hull of a ship would have electric wire wrapped around it and an electric current passed through the wire, this offset the magnetic effect of the ship, effectively de-magnetizing it. Once the solution was proven to be effective, a huge project was quickly put in place to degauss every essential ship in the Navy and Merchant Navy, this was completed in three months, rendering the magnetic mines ineffective. Interestingly before the small ships and boats sailed across the English Channel performing the heroic rescue at Dunkirk, they were given a quick degauss. The metal hull was passed over a powerful magnet which applied the same effect as the cable, but only lasted for a few days before wearing off.

In the same way that British scientists battled their opposite numbers in Germany with direction finding beam technology as mentioned earlier, the Navy had to constantly develop counter measures for all the German mine technology. One of my favorites, which conjures up a great image, was the method used to counter the German acoustic mine. These mines were tuned to detect the sound of a large Naval propeller so that they only blew up when a decent sized vessel passed nearby. This avoided wasting an expensive mine on a little boat. To counter the acoustic mine the mine sweepers would tow a submerged box with a working jack hammer inside, 200 yards behind them. Naval scientists had discovered that a jackhammer had similar acoustic properties to a large propeller, the mines would then explode and a new box would be floated behind the minesweeper. The loss of a jack hammer was a small price to pay compared to a large naval vessel and much less than the cost of an advanced German mine.

Without the skill and bravery of the bomb disposal team that defused the magnetic mines, the Navy would have continued to lose ships and would have been powerless to do anything about it. On the subject of bomb disposal, one particular team nicknamed the Holy Trinity, received a special mention in Churchill's memoirs. They illustrate how all the British social classes of the time joined in during the war. The Holy Trinity consisted of The Earl of Suffolk, his seventy-year-old chauffeur and his young personal secretary. They built up a reputation for survival, as a result of successfully defusing thirty-four bombs and saving hundreds of lives in the process. It is a heroic image, the young Earl stuck in a bomb crater with his trusty old chauffeur and young female assistant at hand, courageously helping with the bomb defusing process. Sadly, like so many of the people who trained in that particular profession, they never lived to see the end of the war. They knew when they signed up for the job that it was tantamount to signing their own death warrant. Theirs was a very special kind or bravery that can only be truly understood by fellow bomb disposal experts. Sadly the thirty-fifth bomb disposal operation was their last. I do not know what the average survival rate was for a bomb disposal team during the war but this must have been an heroic effort.

The war was replete with extremely hazardous occupations. Bomber and fighter pilots could be shot down from ack-ack guns on the ground or by the Luftwaffe, many thousands of pilots perished. To be a front line soldier was to be constantly exposed to mortal peril. A sailor in the Navy had to face the constant threat of torpedo attack by a German sub or shelling from a German warship. However the three main fighting services had one thing in common, they were mostly armed and had the possibility of fighting back to a greater or lesser extent.

It is quite ludicrous many years later for a man who has never been in the forces to attempt to compare the bravery of the men and women who fought in the services during WW2. However, a special mention must go to those unsung heroes, the sailors of the Merchant Navy. It must have been the most unnerving experience, sailing across the Atlantic aware that your ship could be sunk at any time, never knowing when it might happen, and remaining completely incapable of defending the ship from the U-Boat menace.

Churchill devoted a significant number of pages to the perils which the brave people of the Merchant Navy faced throughout the war. In the early years shipping losses were measured in hundreds of thousands of tons, on a monthly basis. At the peak of the Battle of the Atlantic, it was common to have fifteen to twenty ships sunk out of a convoy of thirty. To put into perspective the risks that these brave men faced Churchill highlighted one convoy that was sent to Archangel in Russia, only four ships arrived out of a convoy of twenty-nine. All the sailors died in the freezing cold waters of the Barents Sea. In 1940, the worst year, two and a half million tons of supplies sank, comprising hundreds of ships and countless sailors.

The Battle of the Atlantic started in 1940; it was effectively Britain battling to survive the threat from German U boats, whilst trying desperately to get enough weapons, food and materials across the Atlantic. Fulfilling the vital need to nourish the British people and take the fight to Hitler. As well as facing a threat from beneath the waves, merchant ships faced an equally deadly hazard from long-range German bombers.

To counteract the threat, one early method of defense against the bombers involved catapulting a single fighter plane from a merchant ship. Imagine the nerve of the plane's pilot, hundreds of miles out in the middle of the Atlantic and having to quickly scramble into the fighter because a bomber had been sighted. Knowing that before long he would have to bail out into the frozen waters of an uninviting Atlantic Ocean. The plane would be catapulted off the ship, the pilot would attack and shoot down the bomber and would then have to eject from the plane as near to the merchant ship as possible. Hopefully, the crew would then fish him out of the water. It must have taken a seriously brave man to undertake such a mission. Once the Navy had successfully shot down enough bombers the Germans stopped using this method of attack. No point sending bombers out to bomb ships, if there was a high percentage chance that they would be shot down before they could do any damage. The RAF pilot certainly had a great incentive to shoot down the bomber before it could drop its load, otherwise there would be no ship to pick him up.

Churchill was unable to mention in his memoirs the key factor which led to the British victory in the Battle of the Atlantic, it was still top secret when he was writing them. The finest mathematical minds in Britain were assembled in an old manor house called Bletchley Park, in the south of England. Their whole purpose was to act as code breakers for all manner of enemy code encryptions. Their greatest achievement was the cracking of the German Enigma machine which had been retrieved from a sunken U-Boat. By managing after many months to crack the code they turned the table in the battle which raged under the ocean waves. The Enigma machine was vital because it communicated the positions of the German submarines back to the admiralty. Armed with this crucial information the British and American Navy knew where to start the hunt for the U-Boats within the vast watery wilderness of the Atlantic. Increasing the chances of success dramatically. This was the turning point that passed the advantage to the allies, the allies never passed it back.

In the business world sudden changes in technology can have a major impact on a company's prospects, this was brought home to me very forcefully when at the tender age of 25 I joined a well known photocopier company and embarked on a sales career selling copiers. Technological change was rapid, copiers evolved from optical to digital, from black and white to color, from standalone to networked.

Not long after I joined, the company introduced a radical new product to its portfolio of copiers and faxes, it was the forerunner of Windows. This system had a huge black and white screen with picture icons for documents. Printing a customer proposal simply required the dragging of a document icon across the screen onto a printer icon using a mouse. A box would pop up requesting the required number of prints, then a high quality printout would appear from a networked laser printer, in the middle of the office. Pretty standard now, but state of the art for the late 80's, considerably better than the tiny little machines Apple were producing and far more advanced than Windows. Incidentally, a large number of the team responsible for its development ended up working for both Apple and Microsoft!

My companies document systems cost an absolute fortune. At the time you could buy a new car for the same price as workstation and a printer. I had to attend a two week residential training course to learn how to use them. When we produced proposals for clients the documents we created looked dramatically better than our competitors. We were printing on a laser printer that could produce large interesting fonts, whilst our competitors were producing documents that looked as if they had been created on a typewriter. It doesn't seem much but at the time it was a major advancement.

In 1989 a colleague demonstrated Windows, which, including an IBM PC cost about a sixth of the price of my companies system. I remember thinking at the time that it didn't look particularly impressive and that once the cost of our workstations came down a little we would easily be able to compete with this upstart. In fact the first few versions of Windows were not nearly as advanced as the original workstation I sold. However, Windows were rapidly evolving and within a year it had reached parity. Once Windows became available in color and the cost of PC's started to tumble, sales of the large expensive systems rapidly dried up.

Looking back now it is clear that the mistake my company made, was insisting on selling the software plus the workstation and printer as a combined package. The software was incredibly advanced for its time, however my company viewed it merely as means of helping to sell additional equipment. They were at heart an equipment manufacturer that was used to making a nice profit from selling expensive machines to big companies. They weren't interested in selling software for a few hundred dollars a package, where was the money in that! Bill Gates took the opposite approach, concentrating on the software and leaving the hardware to anyone that could make and sell it. Clearly not a bad idea, given that his company has managed to make a respectable little business out of selling software. Had the copier company shown the foresight to develop the software to work on PC based platforms and had not been so fixated on selling the hardware, they might well have given Windows a run for its money in the early days.

To be fair to the copier company, making such a radical change within a very large, long established organization is incredibly difficult. However, it is the large companies that have had the vision and capability to adapt to changing markets and to maximize the potential of new developments and technology breakthroughs that have continued to grow. By keeping themselves fresh they have managed to thrive and survive. My old company are still in business but they are a small fraction of the size they once were.

The copier company consisted mainly of older guys (about my age now) who were used to selling in a certain way and who had been very successful in the past. The world was changing and the old guys were determined to stick to the same routines as long as they could. They were only too happy to quote how much money they had earned a few years ago, bemoaning how the market had changed and how it was everybody else's fault but their own. These people had not adapted to the changing marketplace but had struggled to survive in the new technological world. A fate that will hopefully not befall yours truly.

During three different careers, across eight different businesses, the one constant I have discovered is that about every two years large-scale changes have taken effect. The result of advances in computer technology, making things faster, smaller, cheaper and more or less complex depending on the application.

There is no such thing as a job for life, a technology for life, or a business for life. Staying fresh and in tune with new techniques and technology, adapting to new developments was how Churchill managed before the war. Unfortunately sometimes a business does not, or cannot adapt in time to new external market forces and goes bust.

Throughout a long career, every year I have always found it useful to carry out a personal audit of my current employer and the general state of the business environment. When it has been clear that the market place was in the process of changing, using personal experience, I would assess how successfully my present employer would adapt to the new market conditions. If I didn't believe they were in a position to compete successfully, and there was a good chance that they would need to let people go then I would start looking for another job. I always found it better to leave when I wanted to, than hang on and hope that everything would be alright.

No matter how clever or how good someone is at his or her present job, inevitably the world keeps travelling along a road of progress. Once a person stops the quest to keep up with the latest advances in techniques and technology they start going backwards as the world starts to pass them by.

Before Churchill took charge of the Admiralty and re-joined

the government at the outset of war, he had been out of favor with his own party and significant sections of parliament. He kept up to date with the latest military technologies, and was aware of the devastating consequences the new weapons of war would bring. He tried to warn his colleagues, but received ferocious criticism and was labeled a warmonger. Despite this he persisted in his quest for knowledge. For Churchill even at the age of sixty-five staying fresh was a matter of life and death.

Chapter 14

It Takes all Sorts

Churchill would find one particular aspect of today's society very puzzling. Celebrity culture, the difference between those who achieve success and become famous as a result, and those who are famous without any apparent substance.

In Churchill's day, widespread recognition was earned due to achievement. Fame would follow on from success in fields such as acting, sport, politics, science, business etc.

A chapter dealing with the harsh reality that the majority of successful people have done well because they are more intelligent, or have worked hard for their success is at odds with the expectations of a large section of the population. There are plenty of books promising to help a person achieve wealth and happiness by taking shortcuts, and a large enough audience sufficiently gullible to buy them.

I know quite a few very wealthy people, who have made millions by having an idea and working incredibly hard to make it a success. Some of them would not necessarily be called naturally intelligent by any IQ test measurement. The common trait in all the successful people I know is an exceptionally high degree of will power. This helped them overcome the problems associated with turning an idea into a success.

Churchill would recognize this trait; his final report from school gave no hint of the greatness he was to achieve, marking him out as someone who was likely to aspire to mediocrity. The aim of this book is to point out some of Churchill's unknown skills and by doing so enable the reader to acquire a new perspective with which to approach business matters. Churchill might have received some of the lowest academic grades of his peer group in School however he did have one remarkable skill, which is not easily learnt, a fantastic memory. He won the elocution prize at Harrow, by reciting perfectly 1200 lines of an historic text by a famous historian called Macaulay. He could quote verbatim whole scenes from Shakespeare and was quite happy to correct his teachers if they quoted a line inaccurately. His personal courage and bravery was never in question and at a young age he had the chance to demonstrate it. A great Swordsman came to his school to encourage the boys to join the army. He offered to cut an apple in half horizontally whilst it balanced on the head of a boy and asked for volunteers. The captain of the football team was offered the honor but declined, not surprisingly the other boys were somewhat slow in coming forward, then up sprang Winston who ran from the benches and knelt before the Swordsman to the cheers and relief of his fellow students.

What Churchill demonstrated (which leaps out from the pages of his memoirs), was an unfailing will to succeed, married with an abundance of self-belief. His study of history had taught him that the side with the greater will to win, gained all the great victories in evenly matched battles. This inner strength stopped him succumbing to the pressure from his war cabinet, when on the 26th May 1940 Lord Halifax, the most senior government figure at the time, attempted to persuade Churchill and the other senior ministers to negotiate terms with Hitler, before the inevitable fall of France.

Nobody expected the miracle of Dunkirk; the optimistic predictions envisaged that thirty thousand troops would escape from French soil. Halifax correctly argued that Britain would be able to negotiate better terms with Hitler before the French capitulated. The cabinet took these proposals very seriously, over three days, nine meetings took place. Churchill at this point was new to the job of Prime Minister and was in a relatively weak position, politically. If he had not persuaded the cabinet to fight on, then resignation would have been his only option, leaving peace negotiations to Halifax. It was touch and go right up to the last meeting, with the war cabinet split evenly on what was to be the most important decision they ever made. Halifax actively tried to convince the waverers that Britain stood little chance against the might of the Nazi's, and would be better off doing a deal with Hitler.

Modern history has been hard on the French for surrendering to the Nazi's. I shared this view until I read Churchill's memoirs. The French stood no chance against the incredibly sophisticated and organized German war machine. Many hundreds of thousands of brave French troops died trying to defend their homeland from a hated invader. Many thousands more suffered, whilst heroically resisting the occupation. In the end, the French took the decision I believe the British would have eventually had to make. With all the potential consequences for the world, and which by so thin a margin was avoided in the summer of 1940. The French fought the Germans on their own soil, Halifax was all for a negotiated settlement without a single German jackboot setting foot in Britain.

If Churchill had not won the argument, there would have been no Battle of Britain, no D-Day, and the outlook for America would have been bleak (as described in an earlier chapter). Despite trying to convince Halifax personally on a number of occasions, he would not budge from his position.

Churchill then pulled a brilliant masterstroke; he called a meeting of the full cabinet and explained the position. He finished his presentation by stating that if the story of Great Britain was to come to an end after a thousand years, when countless millions had died, throughout centuries of war, protecting British freedom, such a heritage demanded that Britain go down fighting. The Nazi's would have to fight for every square foot of British soil if they wanted to dominate Europe. The cabinet all cheered him and rushed up to pat him on the back. When he went again to the war cabinet, and told them of the extraordinary reaction of their colleagues, the war cabinet unanimously united behind him, leaving Halifax isolated. He knew he had lost the argument and the topic never surfaced again.

Churchill never mentioned this crucial episode in his memoirs as some of the people involved were still alive when they were published. It was some years later when cabinet papers were released that the magnitude of his achievement became widely known.

There can be few greater examples of one person's will power making such a difference to the history of the world.

Churchill would not recognize modern society's singular desire to measure a person's achievement by the amount of money they have. These days, to be considered successful you have to be rich or famous or preferably both. Using this restricted definition, only those who have plenty of money can be considered a success.

For an Army to win a battle requires soldiers, along with a chain of command back to the Generals making the decisions. Without the hard work, dedication and fighting spirit of the soldier the battle would be lost. A Country needs people whose ambition is to be a soldier, an army could not take the fight to the enemy, if everyone wanted to be an officer.

If a regular business task is boring or mundane, then employing someone who is good at it and happy to complete it ensures a job well done. Not everyone is ambitious and wants to be in charge of a business or to manage people. Successful organizations are able to motivate all staff, to consistently and willingly perform to a high standard, regardless of the job or function.

This was never more important than during the war, to enable the allies to overcome the threat of Nazi tyranny everyone had to play their part. In the memo's below Churchill displays a keen appreciation that all the people taking part in the war effort no matter what role they performed should be valued. In these memo's he is arguing for the fair treatment of women within the anti-aircraft batteries and as the memo's progress it is clear that he is determined to get his way. Women manning anti-aircraft guns shared the same risks as the men and Churchill was adamant that they should be treated as equals. In the 1940's women did not have the rights or the equalities that prevail in the 21st Century, however to Churchill this was irrelevant, anyone regardless of sex, race or color that supported the war effort had his backing.

PRIME MINISTER TO SIR JAMES GRIGG   13.X.40

A hot discussion is raging in the A.T.S. about whether members who marry should, if they wish, be allowed to quit. Nearly everyone is in favor of this. It seems futile to forbid them, and if they desert there is no means of punishing them. Only the most honorable are therefore impeded. Pray let me have, on one sheet of paper, a note on this showing the pros and cons.

PRIME MINISTER TO SECRETARY OF STATE FOR WAR   18 OCT 41
During my visit to the Richmond Anti-Aircraft Mixed Battery I learned, with much surprise, that the present policy of the [Women's] Auxiliary Territorial Service is that A. T.S. personnel in mixed batteries should not consider themselves part of the battery, and that no "battery esprit de corps" was to be allowed. This is very wounding to the A.T.S. personnel, who have been deprived of badges, lanyards, etc., of which they were proud. Considering that they share the risks and the work of the battery in fact, there can be no justification for denying them incorporation in form.

2. In present circumstances it is possible also that the whole efficiency of a battery could be upset by an order from the War Office, A.T.S. Headquarters, moving one of a predictor team to another unit. The A.A. Command has no say in such matters. Obviously this cannot continue when we are relying upon these mixed batteries as an integral part of our defense.

3. I found a universal desire among all ranks that the women who serve their country by manning guns should be called "Gunners" and "Members of the Royal Regiment of Artillery". There would be no objection to the letters "A.T.S." being retained.

PRIME MINISTER TO SECRETARY OF STATE.FOR WAR   29 OCT 41
All this seems to make many difficulties out of fairly simple things.

Women should be enlisted in the A.T.S. and should always wear that badge. This ensures that their special needs in treatment, accommodation, etc., are kept up to a minimum standard wherever they may be by the women influences organizing the A.T.S. When however they are posted to a combatant unit and share in practice with the men the unavoidable dangers and hardships of that unit they should become in every respect members of it. They should wear, in addition to the A.T.S. badge, all regimental insignia appropriate to their rank. Although their well being is still supervised by the

A.T.S. authorities, they should be considered as detached from the A.T.S. and incorporated in the combatant unit. This does not imply any alteration in their legal status, nor need it involve any Parliamentary discussion (although Parliamentary authority could easily be obtained were it necessary).

2. Considering the immense importance of having a large number of women in A.A. batteries and that the efficiency of the batteries depends upon carefully organized gun teams, it is imperative that these women should not be moved without reference to the Battery Command. The idea that there is an army of A.T.S. under its own Commander-in-Chief, part of which lives alongside particular batteries and gives them a helping hand from time to time, is contrary to our main interest, namely, the maintenance of a larger number of A.A. batteries with a smaller number of men.

3. You are good enough to say that I have been misinformed on various points. I should like to go further into this. I shall be glad to have a meeting at 5 p.m. on Tuesday, November 4, at which General Pile and other officers of the A.D.G.B., as well as representatives of the A.T.S., are present, and I trust you and the Adjutant General will also come.

PRIME MINISTER TO SECRETARY OF STATE FOR WAR   9 DEC. 41
(Personal.)

I have considered carefully your minute to me about the A.T.S., and I am willing that the principles you propose should have a trial. It is up to you to make these batteries attractive to the best elements in the A.T.S. and those who are now being compelled to join the A.T.S. I fear there is a complex against women being connected with lethal work. We must get rid of this. Also there is an idea prevalent among the ladies managing the A.T.S. that nothing must conflict with loyalty to the A.T.S. and that battery esprit de corps is counter to their interest or theme. No tolerance can be shown to this. The prime sphere of the women commanders is welfare, and this should occupy their main endeavors.

The conditions are very bad and rough, and I expect will get worse now that large numbers are being brought into the War Office grip by compulsion or the shadow of compulsion. A great responsibility rests upon you as Secretary of State to see that all these young women are not treated roughly. Mrs. Knox and her assistants should be admirable in all this, but do not let them get in the way of the happy active life of the batteries or deprive women of their incentives to join the batteries and to care as much about the batteries as they do about the A.T.S.

I shall be very glad to have a further report from you on how the principles enunciated in your minute are in fact being applied. Every kind of minor compliment and ornament should be accorded to those who render good service in the batteries.

I found Churchill's positive attitude to the women of the ATS fascinating. It showed that he truly valued every type of individual contribution to the war effort, no matter who it came from, or at what level.

Success is a relative measurement. Someone will always be richer or poorer, a better writer, (definitely in my case), a more accomplished singer or musician, greater at sport or brighter academically, the list goes on. Comparing success against a group of peers can be useful; however, the true measurement can only come from within, when someone happily finds their level in life.

No matter how rich or successful a person is, when a plumber is needed to clear the drains or unblock a toilet, it quickly hits home that in the same way as an air force needs everyone from pilots to windshield cleaners, the world only functions when people are prepared to do a job. It functions better when the people doing the job are happy to do it and can do the job successfully.

There is nothing wrong with a person being the best they can be to the limit of their ability, ambition and will power. Without the millions of people who are willing to do jobs at all levels, the world would just not function.

Churchill came from an elitist background; he was a descendent of John Churchill, the Duke of Marlborough, one of Britain's greatest military commanders (son of the first Sir Winston Churchill), who two hundred and forty years before had led an army of European allies to victory over the French army of Louis XIV. Saving Britain and Europe from a tyrant who wanted to impose his regime upon the free world, (Sound familiar?). Churchill was also half-American and could trace his ancestors on his mother's side back to an officer who fought against the British in the war of Independence.

It could have all been so different for Churchill and Britain, at the age of 21 he was one birth away from becoming the Duke of Marlborough.

In 1895, when Consuelo Vander-bilt arrived at Blenheim as the ninth Duke's new bride. Winston's grand-mother, the old Dowager Duchess, who had no time for the young Winston said to her: "Your first duty is to have a child, and it must be a son, because it would be intolerable to have that little upstart, Winston, become Duke!"

Fortunately, Consuelo did give birth to a son, and thereby she did Winston Churchill and Britain a huge favor. Had her marriage remained childless, he would never have become Prime Minister. Upon the death of the ninth Duke in 1934 Churchill would have inherited the titles of his great ancestor. At that time it was impossible for a peer not to take up his seat in the House of Lords. So in the hour of their greatest need the British people would have looked in vain for the man to lead and save them. Isolated at Blenheim, he would have been compelled to watch history take place, instead of shaping it from Downing Street.

With such a rich heritage Churchill must have felt great satisfaction when in 1950, the Queen offered him a similar Dukedom to that of his great ancestor and hero (Which he declined). It would be an understatement to say that Winston added to the illustrious family name.

Despite his background, he knew that in order to win the war it would require everyone across society to work hard for victory. He valued the munitions workers and the Dockers, the farmers and the laborers equally, without everyone pulling together success would have been impossible.

Chapter 15

Comprehension Can be a Test

Throughout the war, there are countless people, from Hitler downwards, who Churchill could have simply contented himself with despising because of who they were, what they did, or the things they stood for. It would have taken a brave person to calmly explain why Hitler became such a tyrant and treated people so appallingly, but that is exactly what Churchill did in his book. Time and again, he would provide an overview of the reasons why he believed other wicked people throughout the war behaved in a certain fashion. He did this in a matter of fact way that did not seek to make any excuses for these people, just to place before the reader the facts as he saw them. He took the time to comprehend his enemy.

The word comprehend is deliberately used instead of understand. To understand might imply a certain sympathy or agreement with a person. To comprehend something allows assimilation of information, whilst remaining completely dispassionate about it.

Comprehending a person might have no influence whatsoever on how they are dealt with. In the case of Hitler, Churchill explained that towards the end of WWI, Hitler was blinded in action temporarily. He was recuperating in hospital when Germany admitted defeat and signed the armistice. Hitler could not understand why this happened, eventually convincing himself that German Jews had somehow betrayed the German nation by forcing them to capitulate. He blamed them for his failure to get a job as an artist, and for the poverty and hardship

Germany suffered after the war. When he rose to power by ruthlessly manipulating and killing his opponents, he used the Jews as an excuse for everything. The German people at the time bought into this fiction, blinded by Hitler's charisma and lies.

Once Churchill had coldly comprehend Hitler's motivations, he devoted himself from the early 1930's to try and force Britain to re-arm. In anticipation of what he correctly predicted was an inevitable war. He then used everything in his power to defeat Hitler. Churchill, even though he had a comprehension of Hitler, judged him by his actions, which were incomprehensibly wicked and despicable. He treated him accordingly.

To coldly comprehend, is to judge a person or a situation by what actions have taken place or are planned, or by how someone treats others, disregarding their motivation or background story. This approach prevents prior knowledge or personal information from clouding an opinion or decision.

One example captured in the memo below relates to the Irish government blocking the Royal Navy from using Irish ports at the outset of the war. This caused tremendous hardship to Britain and grievously upset Churchill, he laid the blame for it squarely with the Irish Prime minister de Valera.

PRIME MINISTER TO SEC OF STATE FOR THE DOMINIONS 22.NOV.40

I think it would be better to let de Valera stew in his own juice for a while. Nothing could be more harmless or more just than the remarks in the Economist. The claim now put forward on behalf of de Valera is that we are not only to be strangled by them, but to suffer our fate without making any complaint.

Sir John Mafley should be made aware of the rising anger in England and Scotland, and especially among the merchant seamen, and he should not be encouraged to think that his only task is to mollify de Valera and make everything, including our ruin, pass off pleasantly. Apart from this, the less we say to de Valera at this juncture the better, and certainly nothing must be said to reassure him.

In 1930 Churchill almost had dinner with Hitler. He was in Germany, researching the locations of his ancestor the Duke of Marlborough's great battles. In particular Blenheim, the location of his most famous victory and the name given to the huge palace built for the Duke by a grateful nation, at huge cost three hundred years ago.

A personal favorite of Hitler, Herr Hanfstaengl who was an excellent English speaker befriended Churchill whilst he was staying at the best hotel in Munich. This was of course no accident. Hitler was keen to meet the famous Churchill and he was probably trying to size up a potential opponent.

After a few days, the assistant said that Hitler was having dinner the following evening and would like Churchill to join him. At this point Hitler was a well-known figure in Germany who Churchill was aware of. At the time he just thought of him as a patriotic supporter of Germany, keen to see his country climb out of economic depression. Churchill had no great reason to refuse to see Hitler. The assistant joined Churchill for dinner the night before the meeting and they chatted about all manner of topics. Churchill asked the assistant why Hitler hated Jews so much, as it seemed odd that a man could have such hatred for a whole race. It was one thing to hate a specific person for something that they had done, however he could not understand how Hitler could despise a complete section of society. The assistant did not offer any answer to Churchill but moved the conversation on to other topics.

The following day the assistant phoned the hotel and advised that Herr Hitler would not be able to make dinner, as something had cropped up. Churchill assumed that the assistant had told him about their conversation and that Hitler no longer wanted to meet him. It is likely that Hitler found it an uncomfortable prospect having to explain his twisted ideology to a person of Churchill's stature. Hitler invited Churchill to meet with him many times after Munich, but by then he had started to display some of his well-known tyrannical qualities. As a result, Churchill always refused the meetings.

Churchill also gave a description of Mussolini, someone he had met quite a few times in the twenties and thirties. He believed that Mussolini wanted to restore the Roman Empire to its former glory, and that he chose to fight alongside the Nazi's because Hitler had promised to give him the British and French African territories without having to spill too much Italian blood.

Mussolini viewed it as the opportunity of a thousand years and was determined to grab it. He vainly wanted the fame associated with Italy's great historic emperors. "I'll Duce" achieved fame for all the wrong reasons; his own people hanged him from a street lamppost.

The Japanese had the same idea, they saw an opportunity to grab the eastern part of the British and Dutch empire along with large parts of China. Japan correctly calculated that Britain had committed all its resources to the fight with Germany, making it difficult to mount an effective defense of the British Eastern Empire. Churchill detailed the hard choices he had to make between fighting the Germans in North Africa, sending troops to the Far East, or defending the colonies. Churchill concluded that victory against Germany required the majority of British resources to be focused on Europe. Allied Eastern command would have to make the best use of the men and equipment available. Whilst no one publicly admitted it at the time, he sacrificed the Far East to allow the deployment of maximum resources against the Germans.

It was the policy of the British government that if Australia or New Zealand came under direct attack from Japan, they would sacrifice the desert campaign. North African troops would run to the defense of "our kith and kin" as Churchill put it.

Early on in the war when Britain was reeling from the Battle of Britain the Australian Prime Minister Sir Robert Menzies made the mistake of sending Churchill a disparaging memo regarding the allied operation to attack Dakar in North Africa. An operation which went badly wrong. I have detailed the sequence of memo's between Churchill and Menzies below, they make fascinating reading and show that Churchill having got the measure of Menzies was going to give back more than he received.

MR. MENZIES TO THE PRIME MINISTER   29.SEP.40
We are very disturbed in regard to Dakar incident, which has had unfortunate effect in Australia. First, as to matter of substance:

It is difficult to understand why attempt was made unless overwhelming chances of success. To make what appears at this distance to be a half-hearted attack is to incur a damaging loss of prestige.

Second, as to matter of procedure:

It is absolutely wrong that Australian Government should know practically nothing of details of engagement and nothing at all of decision to abandon it until after newspaper publication. I have refrained from any public criticism, but privately can tell you that absence of real official information from Great Britain has frequently proved humiliating. Finally, I must say frankly that Australian Government profoundly hopes difficulties have not been underestimated in the Middle East, where clear-cut victory is essential.

PRIME MINISTER TO MR. MENZIES   2.OCT.40

I am very sorry to receive your message of September 29, because I feel that the great exertions we have made deserve a broad and generous measure of indulgence should any particular minor operation miscarry. The situation at Dakar was revolutionized by arrival of French ships from Toulon with Vichy personnel and the manning of the batteries by the hostile French Navy. Although every effort was made, the British Navy was not able to stop these ships on their way. After strongly testing the defenses, and sustaining the losses I have already reported to you, the naval and military commanders did not consider they had the strength to effect and support a landing, and I think they were quite right not to get us committed to a shore operation, which could not, like the naval attack, be broken off at any moment, and might have become a serious entanglement.

With regard to your criticisms, if it is to be laid down that no attempt is to be made which has not got overwhelming chances of success, you will find that a complete defensive would be imposed upon us. In dealing with unknown factors like the degree of French resistance it is impossible to avoid uncertainty and hazard. For instance, Duala, and with it the Cameroons, were taken by twenty-five Frenchmen after their Senegalese troops had refused to march. Ought we to have moved in this case without having overwhelming force at hand? Secondly, I cannot accept the reproach of making "a half hearted attack". I hoped that you had not sustained the impression from these last five months of struggle which has excited the admiration of the whole world that we were "a half hearted Government" or that I am half hearted in the endeavors it is my duty to make. I thought indeed that from the way my name was used in the election quite a good opinion was entertained in Australia of these efforts.

Every care will always be taken to keep you informed before news is published, but we could not prevent the German and Vichy wireless from proclaiming the course of events as they occurred at Dakar before we had received any information from our Commanders.

With regard to what you say about the Middle East, I do not think the difficulties have been under estimated, but of course our forces are much smaller than those which the Italians have in Libya and Abyssinia, and the Germans may always help them. The defection of France has thrown the whole Middle East into jeopardy and severed our communications through the Mediterranean. We have had to face the threat of invasion here and the full strength of Germany's air bombing attack on our cities, factories, and harbors. Nevertheless we have steadfastly reinforced the Middle East, and in spite of all our perils at home and scanty resources have sent over thirty thousand men, nearly half our best tanks, many anti-aircraft guns needed to protect our vital aircraft factories, two of the finest units in the fleet, the Illustrious and Valiant, and a considerable number of Hurricane fighters and Wellington bombers. We have done this in the face of an accumulation across the Channel and the North Sea of barges and shipping sufficient to carry half a million men to these shores at a single voyage and in a single night. Therefore, if the Middle East difficulties and dangers have not been fully met, it is not because the Mother Country has shirked her share of perils and sacrifice. At present the situation in Egypt and the Soudan looks better than we feared some time ago. Still, my dear Prime Minister and friend, as you have allowed me to deem you, I cannot guarantee "clear-cut victory" in the Middle East, or that Cairo, Khartoum, the Suez Canal, and Palestine may not fall into Italian or German hands. We do not think they will, and we are trying our utmost to resist the attacks which are massing against us. But I can make no promises at all of victory, nor can I make any promises that regrettable and lamentable incidents will not occur, or that there will not be disappointments and blunders. On the contrary, 1 think the only certainty is that we have very bad times indeed to go through before we emerge from the mortal perils by which we are surrounded.

I felt it due to your great position and the extremely severe tone of your message to reply with equal frankness.

MR. MENZIES TO MR. CHURCHILL   4.OCT.40
I have received your message of October 2 and am very disturbed by some of its contents.
We were, and are, concerned about the failure at Dakar. My telegram concerning it was somewhat crudely expressed, as I can see on perusing it again. But I still do not understand how it can be construed as containing even the faintest suggestion that you or the British Government are half hearted in policy, spirit, or achievement.

As the recent election here has left my own position extremely precarious and I may therefore soon go out of office, I would like to take the opportunity of saying to you that I have been very proud on behalf of Australia to be associated, even though at a distance, with the efforts of Winston Churchill and the British people. Such machinery as I possess in my own country has at all times been exercised so as to encourage the Australian people to realize that Great Britain is fighting our battles and that her heroism and superhuman cheerfulness and philosophy must be for us not only a shield but an inspiration.

As for yourself praise from me would be an impertinence, but what I cabled you on September 3, the anniversary of the war, represented my whole heart and mind. I am indeed grieved to think that you should have felt my recent telegram to be either carping or discouraging.

I say no more about Dakar ,because it, no doubt, has lessons which it is not necessary for me to underline. Real point I make is that we, at this distance, will learn the lessons of events the more rapidly if information about those events can come to us as promptly and as fully as possible.

As to the Middle East, I have not sought or intended to seek guarantees. All that we asked and I am sure it is granted before the asking, is that the Middle East should be as fully reinforced *and equipped as is humanly possible. Your telegram has given me great satisfaction on this point. .*

You point out that if the Middle East difficulties and dangers have not been fully met it is not because the Mother Country has shirked her share of the perils or sacrifice: this is, of course, splendidly true. But I hope that you do not entertain any idea that Australia is shirking her share. We have many thousands of men in the Middle East, as many as shipping has been able to take. We have in camp in Australia further Expeditionary Force approximating eighty-five thousand men, many of whom will shortly be moving to the Middle East.

In spite of much public doubt caused by a real fear of what Japan may do, my Government has raised naval, air, and military forces and pledged our resources to munitions production on a scale previously unknown and regarded only a year ago as impossible.

We have done this notwithstanding the parochial interests and issues which in the recent elections succeeded in defeating us in the all important State of New South Wales. We have set no limit to our contribution, because we know that there is no limit to the total British risk.

I mention these matters because I desire to make it clear that our anxiety about our main overseas theatre of actual participation in the war is not only intelligible but acute.

Please, my dear Prime Minister, do not interpret anxieties arising from these facts as either fearful, selfish, or unduly wrongheaded. And, above all, please understand that whatever interrogative or even critical telegrams I may send to you in secret, Australia knows courage when it sees it and will follow you to a finish, as to the best of my abilities I certainly shall.

PRIME MINISTER TO MR. MENZIES   6.OCT.40

I am deeply grateful for your generous message. Forgive me if I responded too controversially to what I thought was somewhat severe criticism. I am having an account prepared of the Dakar incident, in all its stages, which I will send for the confidential information of yourself and your colleagues. I do not propose to defend myself at any length in Parliament, as such a spectacle would only gratify the enemy. I am deeply grateful for all that Australia has done under your leadership for the Common Cause. It has been a great comfort having some of the Australians here during these anxious months. I greatly admired their bearing and spirit when I inspected them. They had just received twenty-four good field guns. They are soon going to join the rest of the Australian Army in the Middle East, where they will probably be in the forefront of the fighting next year. We shall do everything in our power to equip them as they deserve. For the moment it seems that the situation in the Middle East is steady. Should the armies engage Mersa Matruh the forces available during the next month or six weeks would not appear to be ill-matched in numbers. This should give a good chance to General Wilson, who is reputed a fine tactician and the excellent troops he has. The Londoners are standing up magnificently to the bombing, but you can imagine the numerous problems which a ruthless attack like this upon a community of eight million people creates for the administration. We are getting the better of our difficulties, and I feel confident that the act of mass terror which Hitler has attempted will fail, like his magnetic mines and other deadly schemes. All good wishes personally for yourself.

I am certain that Mr. Menzies would have been far more careful in his choice of words in any subsequent memo's.

The Japanese did such a good job of conquering the British colonies that New Zealand and Australia in particular felt very threatened, despite the logistical impossibility (as Churchill saw it) of a large-scale Japanese invasion. Churchill concluded that if Britain could hold out from an invasion with only 21 miles of sea between the Nazi's and the White Cliffs of Dover, then the likely -hood of Japan successfully invading the vast territory of Australia with supply lines stretching thousands of ocean miles, was just simply too fantastic to imagine. However, Britain could not offer a 100% cast iron guarantee to Australia, and as the North Africa campaign became increasingly difficult in the year following the memo's, the labor government demanded that large numbers of troops had to be withdrawn from the campaign and sent home. Churchill repeatedly argued that transporting the troops to Australia would put them in mortal danger from enemy attack whilst on board ship. General Alexander complained bitterly about the withdrawal of such high quality troops from the field of battle. Eventually the Royal Navy ran great risks to ship the soldiers back.

In fairness to the Australians, they supported Britain at the outset of war; their soldiers distinguished themselves in many conflicts, including Greece, Crete and North Africa. They did not pull out of the war completely and continued to play a reduced role.

Churchill was greatly troubled by the possibility that Japan would attack India. This was not helped by India having such a dislike of Britain. Six years before independence significant Indian factions would have preferred the Japanese to attack. With everything else Churchill had to contend with, India caused him great difficulties. India wanted Britain to grant independence immediately, in return for access to their ports. Britain only wanted access to the ports to defend India from Japanese attack. India's politicians eventually concluded that continuing as part of the British Empire was preferable to life under a Japanese flag. Churchill correctly argued that it would have been impossible to deal with the complex nature of independence whilst fighting a world war. Once it was over India would be granted independence. It took a considerable amount of time and effort to reach agreement with India's politicians, which was an unwanted distraction for Churchill. He balanced his criticism of Indian opportunism, by stating that many thousands of brave Indian soldiers fought and died supporting the war effort in the Far East and Europe.

The Japanese made their big mistake when they decided to attack America. Pearl Harbor not only spelled the doom of Japan but also sealed the fate of Hitler. Japan hugely miscalculated Pearl Harbor's effect on American public opinion. The USA instantly went from opposition, to direct involvement in the war, and an overwhelming desire for retribution upon the nation who committed such a terrible act of aggression. It seems inconceivable that Japan could have been so stupid as to directly attack America and then not expect the mighty American military machine to eventually recover and seek revenge. They clearly underestimated America in the same way that Germany underestimated Britain.

Had Japan limited its greed and concentrated on China along with the British and Dutch colonies in the far east, they would probably have been a lot more successful. Without the direct attack, the American public was unlikely to have ever allowed troops to be committed on such a huge scale in Europe and Asia, to fight and die in someone else's war. Roosevelt in his election campaign of 1940 had stated categorically "your boys will not be sent overseas to war". Without Pearl Harbor, enormous amounts of military aid would not have flowed as easily to Russia. It did not do Hitler any favors, he would have had a better chance against a Russian army that was not receiving all the latest military equipment from America and Britain.

Hitler had gone out of his way to avoid conflict with America, allowing them to increase support to Britain and in the case of the Atlantic convoys, allowing the US Navy to guard British merchant ships against German U-boat attacks. When the US Navy encountered a U-Boat, they would directly radio its position to a British sub and if a U-Boat fired upon the US Navy they would immediately retaliate. Germany would have declared war on any other country that committed such acts of aggression. However, Hitler was rightly afraid of entering a war with America whilst he had so many other commitments. As it turned out, with very good reason.

Who can know what would have happened if Japan had taken a different course. One thing is clear from Churchill's memoirs, all these events are interrelated in a way that it is difficult for the general public to comprehend. What happens on one side of the world can have a direct effect on another military campaign thousands of miles away. Churchill firmly believed that once America came in to the war, it was a matter of when and not if the Germans would be defeated.

Roosevelt developed into a great supporter of Britain in fact he was probably one of the best friends Britain has ever had. Harry Hopkins a great personal friend of Roosevelt and a man who Churchill greatly admired, passed a private message from Roosevelt to Churchill twelve months before Pearl Harbor. He asked Harry to tell Churchill, "for as long as I live I will not see Britain go down to the Nazi's" and that "Britain's war is

America's war". It was just a matter of time before he could convince the American public to send their boys overseas. Roosevelt stayed true to his word, right up to his dying breath, writing letters to Churchill about war matters, literally hours before he knew he was going to pass away. Churchill did not know he was so gravely ill and felt terrible for troubling him when he was in such bad shape. Political leaders were made of strong stuff in those days. One of Churchill's biggest regrets was that he could not pull himself away from the War to attend Roosevelt's funeral. He stated that if he'd had his time again, he would have gone.

Churchill does not actually say it in his memoirs, but you can read between the lines that Roosevelt was determined to get America into the war and was convinced that only something dramatic would change public opinion. Roosevelt had only just managed to persuade congress by one vote to bring back the draft; he had no chance of persuading them to vote for war even though he was personally convinced of the need for America to become directly involved. US Intelligence had been able to decipher Japanese radio transmissions long before Pearl Harbor, Churchill thought it inconceivable that someone high up in the US military did not know what was going to happen. He suggests that Roosevelt may have prevented any advanced warnings of the impending attack, encouraging an outraged America to go to war. Roosevelt and his senior advisers knew what could happen if they stood on the sidelines of the European conflict for too much longer. If they did really allow the attack to happen, then they did so in the full knowledge that they were doing the right thing and who can argue that history has proven them correct.

At the time of Pearl Harbor, British nuclear research was far in advance of the USA. If the worst had happened and America had stayed out of the war, after defeating Russia, the Nazi's might have successfully invaded Britain. They could have gained access to Britain's nuclear research. Some years later it might have been a German bomber, flying from an old British aircraft carrier, dropping an Atom Bomb on a US city. Who knows…?

Whilst Roosevelt recognized that Germany should be defeated before Japan, significant factions in the US military were not convinced. Churchill had to work hard to win the argument, writing many letters and sending large military delegations across the Atlantic to argue the position. As was the case right up until the latter part of the war, Winston got what he wanted and the planning began for Operation Overlord, the D Day landings.

Churchill found it difficult to comprehend why Japans military treated Allied soldiers so badly. According to Churchill, Japanese tradition was to despise anyone who surrendered to the enemy, believing they would have to face their ancestors and be shamed for eternity. They would sooner commit suicide than surrender, preferring what they believed to be an honorable death over a dishonorable life. A westerner would have real difficulty comprehending this attitude to life. If a captured soldier was staring down the barrel of a gun, better to surrender with dignity and try to escape later. At the very least, they would have a chance of seeing their homeland and loved ones again. Western opinion did not see any shame in being a prisoner of war. As they would not consider doing such a thing themselves, the Japanese had no respect for prisoners who surrendered and dreadfully mistreated them.

It is one thing to comprehend why the Japanese did what they did. This does not mean that there is even the slightest excuse for the way they behaved.

Churchill took time to comprehend his enemies and his friends, at no point did he consider that by gaining an understanding of both, he would put himself in a position where his judgment would be clouded.

In businesses, as in life in general the same principle applies. It can only increase a person's effectiveness in their work if they have a thorough knowledge of their own business and its goals along with as much information about the goals and objectives of the companies that operate in the same business environment, either as suppliers or competitors.

This same principle also applies to people, in the same way that Churchill wanted to gain an understanding about the key personnel of the enemy, he spent equal if not greater effort getting to know the key personnel of the friendly countries. The more a person knows (within reason) about the people they work with and those that they will come up against in business the more effective they are likely to be.

The principle is to comprehend without empathizing or judging a situation or person. If this can be done with the people, company and issues on both sides of a business situation, from a support, billing, sales or any other perspective then better decisions are likely to be made. In addition this approach will also have the benefit of reducing any misunderstandings.

In the immensely complex situations that Churchill had to deal with throughout the war, his skill of being able to coldly comprehend a situation and then determine the right course of action was in constant use.

Chapter 16

Dealing with the difficult people

One of the toughest business tasks is dealing with difficult, ungrateful customers. For some, no matter how much hard work takes place on their behalf, they adopt the attitude that it is never good enough. Constantly expecting more, even when behind the scenes everyone is trying their utmost to help. For some reason companies spend fortunes on training people to negotiate, present and sell, but very little on the subject of dealing with nightmare customers. Over the years through trial and error, people develop some method of coping with these situations. Not all customers are difficult to deal with, it is normally limited to one or two individuals that do their utmost to make life difficult and unpleasant.

The way Churchill dealt with the Soviet Union during the war was like reading a handbook on how to treat this complicated and difficult subject. Since finishing Churchill's memoirs my approach to such situations has changed considerably.

In 1939, at the outset of war, Russia under the rule of Stalin was not directly fighting Britain. However, they were actively helping the Germans by providing food, iron ore and other war materials to help defeat the British. Communist backed agitators in Britain tried to make things difficult for the government by spreading anti war propaganda. Stalin regularly denounced Britain in broadcasts and newspaper articles. As Germany conquered more and more of Europe, Stalin pressured neighboring countries such as Ukraine and Lithuania to become Soviet satellite states. When Germany invaded Poland, the

Soviet Union annexed a section of Poland as part of a deal struck with the Germans.

Up until June 1941, the Soviet Union formed part of the axis of powers ranged against Britain. Whilst they had no direct military involvement, they wanted Germany to defeat Britain. They were looking forward to receiving their share of the British Empire, a reward for supporting the German war effort with raw materials.

Hitler was simply following his usual process of trying to defeat one enemy at a time, keeping the next one in line deluded, whilst finishing off his current victim, in this case Britain.

The codename for the campaign against Britain was operation Sea Lion, under such directives, all the planning required to defeat a country was coordinated. For the Russians the codename for the attack was Barbarossa. Hitler gave his order to prepare the plans for the Russian invasion in November 1940, eight months before the Germans invaded.

Churchill in his books tried to tell it like it was, sometimes being self-critical, and on occasion, criticizing others. Considering that Russia had become the biggest threat to world peace by the time he wrote his memoirs, he does not spare Stalin or the rest of the people responsible for Soviet war direction from his honest opinions.

In his view the Germans played the Soviets like a violin, right up to the day before they invaded. Churchill believed Stalin showed himself to be completely inept in his relations with Hitler. He accepted the guarantees of a charismatic man, who had said the same thing to the last ten countries he had conquered. On the day before the invasion of Russia the Germans used high speed freight trains to extract the last few tons of supplies from the unwitting Soviets before they declared war. They had amassed the biggest single army the world had ever seen on the Russian front, however, Stalin refused point blank to accept all the warnings given to him by well-informed people. Churchill sent Stalin a personal message warning him that the Germans were going to invade which he completely ignored.

Churchill then made a speech in parliament a few days before the invasion, predicting it would happen. This was widely reported on the night before operation Barbarossa began. Stalin denounced Churchill, and Britain, for attempting to stir up trouble between Russia and its German allies. Churchill, as a result of Britain's spy network and the ability to decipher German secret communications, actually set aside time to write a speech with his response to the invasion, before it was actually launched.

There is a well-known conversation that Churchill had with one of his generals the weekend before the Germans attacked Russia. During a discussion about the content of the radio broadcast, the general asked Churchill how he would treat the Soviets after they were invaded, taking into account what they had said and done to Britain since the war began. Churchill replied candidly that any enemy of Germany was an ally of Britain, no matter what had gone before. If Hitler had invaded hell, Churchill stated that he would find a way to make a favorable comment about the devil.

By invading Russia before conquering or quelling the British Isles, Hitler changed his winning formula of defeating one country at a time, this change in strategy effectively cost Germany the war. Instead of making a second attempt to invade Britain in 1941, preceded by another effort to gain air superiority, Hitler decided to leave Britain to one side, strangle its supplies by the use of U-Boats, then come back and finish the job after he had dealt with the Russians. It probably seemed like a good plan at the time!

Operation Barbarossa should have been launched by mid-May 1941, however it was mid-June before the attack began. The delay was due to Britain unexpectedly sending fifty thousand men to help Greece defend their homeland from a combined German and Italian attack. The Germans could not afford the loss of prestige associated with a failure to conquer Greece. Originally Hitler expected the Italians to do the job, but once the British sent re-enforcements he knew that the Italians would not be able to handle the situation. As a result, he had to send enough German troops guarantee victory. This temporarily caused crucial forces to be diverted from the Russian front. Whilst the brave Greeks were ultimately defeated, Churchill was confident that the months' delay caused by the conflict was a vital factor in preventing Russia from collapsing under the German onslaught before the end of 1941. Churchill contended that the additional months' delay caused by the British troops aiding the Greeks, stopped the Germans reaching Moscow (and they were within thirty miles). It was physically impossible to fight in the midst of a harsh Russian winter. Had they started a month earlier, as originally planned, they would definitely have reached Moscow, which would have tipped the war in their favor. When the campaign renewed in the spring of 1942, the Russians, helped by the Allies, had regrouped and re-armed, enabling them to go on and ultimately defeat the Germans.

Churchill couldn't believe his luck when Russia was invaded, he hoped it would bring some relief to Britain from constant German bombing and the Battle of the Atlantic, but it did nothing of the sort. For the first twelve months, it caused Britain great difficulties. The passing of the American lend-lease bill a couple of months before the attack meant Britain was finally beginning to receive vast supplies of arms from America. As they were being shipped across the Atlantic, large portions of these arms had to be diverted to Russia. Equipment earmarked for the defense of the British Empire in the Far East went instead to Russia, contributing to the ease with which the Japanese captured Hong Kong, Burma and Singapore. It was during this period that Churchill discovered how difficult it was to deal with Stalin and the Russians.

Post war analysis of German records clearly indicated that the Russians had it coming, betrayal was planned and inevitable, it was only a matter of timing. In 1941, the Russians appeared to be disappointed in the British for not losing, holding them responsible for changing the course of the war to their disadvantage. Whilst this was technically correct, what Stalin failed to realize was that if Britain had been defeated, Russia would have had no chance against the Germans. It would have just delayed the inevitable.

Rudolf Hess had flown to Scotland on his own a few months before the Russian invasion, he had been a friend of Hitler's before the war, however, his influence had waned since the start of the conflict. He hoped to regain Hitler's confidence by persuading the King of England that Adolf was a friend and admirer of Britain, who would like to make peace. Post war records showed that Hitler did not even know about the visit, denouncing Hess as a traitor, once the mission became public. Ever suspicious, the Russians harbored the belief that Britain had made a pact with the Germans, enabling them to invade Russia, without "The Englanders" giving them too many problems during the operation. Stalin quizzed Churchill about the Hess incident, when they met in 1944, and would not accept Churchill's emphatic denial.

Churchill worked hard to create a strong dialogue with Roosevelt, he wrote to him almost every day. He tried to get something similar going with Stalin, but he was not interested. Communications from Stalin were always matter of fact and cold.

Churchill showed extraordinary patience and tact when dealing with Stalin especially considering the circumstances. Stalin, who would have delighted in seeing Britain under Nazi rule, now demanded that Britain give up all new American arms in their favor. Churchill related a story to illustrate his point. On a mission to Moscow two months after the attack, a Russian guide was showing around a British security guard. "That is King George railway station formerly Goering Station. This is Beaverbrook Street formerly Ribbentrop Street and that is Churchill Square formerly Hitler Square", he then asked the British soldier if he would like a cigarette, to which he replied "yes thank you comrade, formerly b*$!%&d" No matter what Britain did or the risks they took getting weapons to Russia, it was never good enough. The Russians rarely, if ever, said thank you or showed any appreciation, even when hundreds of British sailors died trying to help them.

As soon as the attack on Russia took place, Stalin insisted that Britain open up a second front by attacking Northern France. This was impossible in 1941, anyone with a rudimentary knowledge of warfare knew that it would take years before Britain could have the slightest chance of successfully invading France. The Russians did not accept any of the detailed arguments put forward by Churchill and his commanders. Regardless of how many times the facts were reiterated, they continued insisting that France should be invaded immediately.

Forcing troops and planes to be drawn away from the eastern front, even if this meant exposing Britain to mortal peril. All this from the country that was quite content to stand back and support Germany's attempt to invade Britain. The British communists suddenly started painting the slogan "Second Front Now" across the land, trying to encourage the British to invade France and draw German troops away from Russia.

Churchill having tried to replicate the same friendly approach he had with Roosevelt, concluded that the only way to deal with the Russians was by sticking to the facts. No matter what arguments they put forward for their demands, he would stay resolute and firm in his dealings with them. In Stalin, he was dealing with someone who had a completely different belief system to Roosevelt, a man who believed in democracy based on western Christian values. I have no idea what belief system Stalin had. Based on Churchill's dealings with him, it appeared the only people Stalin cared about were himself and a few specific Russians. He had no consideration for the problems facing the British or anyone else. He would have been content to see Britain give up all available weapons to Russia and place the country at great risk, without the slightest consideration.

Once Churchill understood this, dealings with Stalin, whilst always difficult, became easier to rationalize. Churchill would ensure he did the best he could to help Russia, making decisions about them based on his own belief system. By approaching his dealings with them in this way, he avoided upset every time they discarded tremendous British sacrifice without thanks or appreciation. It simply became the expected response, not something to cause annoyance. It was how Russia did business, nothing anyone could do was going to change them.

Despite his laidback approach, one incident really annoyed Churchill. Stalin sent him a letter of complaint regarding a delay in shipping equipment to Russia. The Germans were desperate to stop Britain supplying weapons to the Soviets and heavily targeted convoys on the long and dangerous journey across the freezing waters to Archangel. Given the strains on the Royal Navy, it was often difficult to defend large convoys for the whole journey. As a result, the Merchant Navy suffered terrible losses regularly losing over half of a convoy. The shipments had to be suspended, in order to explore a safer means of delivery. Churchill wrote to Stalin to tell him that it was becoming impossible to continue sending convoys, predicting that he would not get a fair response Churchill went into great detail to explain the reasons for the decision. It made no difference as can be seen in the sequence of memo's below.

PRIME MINISTER TO PREMIER STALIN   17 JULY 42

We began running small convoys to North Russia in August 1941, and until December the Germans did not take any steps to interfere with them. From February 1942 the size of the convoys was increased, and the Germans then moved a considerable force of U-boats and a large number of aircraft to North Norway and made determined attacks on the convoys. By giving the convoys the strongest possible escort of destroyers and anti-submarine craft the convoys got through with varying but not prohibitive losses. It is evident that the Germans were dissatisfied with the results which were being achieved by means of aircraft and U-boats alone, because they began to use their surface forces against the convoys. Luckily for us however at the outset they made use of their heavy surface forces to the westward of Bear Island and their submarines to the eastward. The Home Fleet was thus in a position to prevent an attack by enemy surface forces. Before the May convoy was sent off the Admiralty warned us that the losses would be very severe if, as was expected, the Germans employed their surface forces to the eastward of Bear Island. We decided however to sail the convoy. An attack by surface ships did not materialize, and the convoy got through with a loss of one-sixth, chiefly from air attack. In the case of P.Q.17 however the Germans at last used their forces in the manner we had always feared. They concentrated their U-boats to the westward of Bear Island and reserved their surface forces for attack to the eastward of Bear Island. The final story of P.Q.17 convoy is not yet clear. At the moment only four ships have arrived at Archangel, but six others are in Nova Zembla harbors. The latter may however be attacked from the air at any time. At the best therefore only one third will have survived.

I must explain the dangers and difficulties of these convoy operations when the enemy's battle squadron takes its station in the extreme north. We do not think it right to risk our Home Fleet east of Bear Island or where it can be brought under the attack of the powerful German shore-based aircraft. If one or two of our very few most powerful battleships were to be lost or even seriously damaged while Tirpitz and her consorts, soon to be joined by Scharnhorst, remained in action, the whole command of the Atlantic would be [temporarily] lost. Besides affecting the food supplies by which we live, our war effort would be crippled; and above all the great convoys of American troops across the ocean, rising presently to as many as 80,000. in 1 month, would be prevented and the building up of a really strong Second Front in 1943 rendered impossible. .

My naval advisers tell me that if they had the handling of the German surface, submarine, and air forces, in present circumstances, they would guarantee the complete destruction of any convoy to North Russia. They have not been able so far to hold out any hopes that convoys attempting to make the passage in perpetual daylight would fare better than P.Q.17. It is therefore with the greatest regret that we have reached the conclusion that to attempt to run the next convoy, P.Q.18, would bring no benefit to you and would only involve dead loss to the common cause. At the same time, I give you my assurance that if we can devise arrangements which give a reasonable chance of at least a fair proportion of the contents of the convoys reaching you we will start them again at once. The crux of the problem is to make the Barents Sea as dangerous for German warships as they make it for ours. This is what we should aim at doing with our joint resources. I should like to send a senior officer of the R.A.F. to North Russia to confer with your officers and make a plan.

Meanwhile we are prepared to dispatch immediately to the Persian Gulf some of the ships which were to have sailed in the P.Q. convoy.

Believe me, there is nothing that is useful and sensible that we and the Americans will not do to help you in your grand struggle. The President and I are ceaselessly searching for means to overcome the extraordinary difficulties which geography, salt water, and the enemy's air power interpose. I have shown this telegram to the President.

Having taken great care to lay out his case, Churchill was furious with the rough and surly answer from Stalin. This was the kind of response he would have to endure many times throughout the war.

PREMIER STALIN TO PREMIER CHURCHILL   23 JULY 42

I received your message of July 17. Two conclusions could be drawn from it. First, the British Government refuses to continue the sending of war materials to the Soviet Union via the Northern route. Second, in spite of the agreed communiqué concerning the urgent tasks of creating a Second Front in 1942 the British Government postpones this matter until 1943.

2. Our naval experts consider the reasons put forward by the British naval experts to justify the cessation of convoys to the northern parts of the U.S.S.R. wholly unconvincing. They are of the opinion that with goodwill and readiness to fulfill the contracted obligations these convoys could be regularly undertaken and heavy losses could be inflicted on the enemy. Our experts find it also difficult to understand and to explain the order given by the Admiralty that the escorting vessels of the P.Q.17 should return, whereas the cargo boats should disperse and try to reach the Soviet ports one by one without any protection at all. Of course I do not think that regular convoys to the Soviet northern ports could be effected without risk or losses. But in war-time no important undertaking could be effected without risk or losses. In any case, I never expected that the British Government would stop dispatch of war materials to us just at the very moment when the Soviet Union in view of the serious situation on the Soviet-German front requires these materials more than ever. It is obvious that the transport via Persian Gulf could in no way compensate for the cessation of convoys to the northern ports.

I hope you will not feel offended that I [have] expressed frankly and honestly my own opinion as well as the opinion of my colleagues on the questions raised in your message.

Churchill explained that Stalin's contentions were not well-founded. So far from breaking "contracted obligations" to deliver the war supplies to Soviet ports, it had been specifically stipulated at the time the agreement was made, that the Russians were to be responsible for conveying the armaments from Britain to Russia. Recognizing the difficulties for the Soviets, Britain out of goodwill and the desire to support the Russian fight against the Nazi's, endeavored to help.

Faced with such a one sided view and a complete lack of empathy from Stalin, Churchill decided that it wasn't worthwhile to continue to argue the practicalities of the situation with the Soviets, who had been willing until they were themselves attacked to see Britain totally destroyed and to share the booty with Hitler. Stalin even in the common struggle could hardly spare a word of sympathy for the heavy British and American losses of both men and ships incurred in trying to send them aid.

Churchill let Stalin's bitter message pass without any specific rejoinder. He did not wish to dignify it with a response.

He talked the situation over with Roosevelt who advised him that he should ignore Stalin's offensive attitude and see if it was possible to try again, it was clear that the allies best interest lay in helping Russia to kill Nazi's. Two months later a massive fleet of destroyers and a new small aircraft carrier escorted a large convoy of merchant ships into Archangel, having undergone fierce fighting with U-Boats, German destroyers and countless attacks from the Luftwaffe.

Churchill organized the overwhelming protection of the convoy in response to Roosevelt's request, it was a matter of politics to be seen to make a supreme effort to help the Russian's in their time of crisis. It was however completely impractical to continue repeating the deliveries by this method, as it left enormous gaps in Britain's Naval defense. The convoys stopped, it was a year later when Stalin asked for the convoys to resume.

Having received the request from Stalin, Churchill wrote back to him confirming that Britain would once again do the best it could to help. As can be seen in the series of memo's below Stalin was to cause even greater offence with his response to Britain's offer.

PRIME MINISTER TO PREMIER STALIN   1 OCT 43
I have received your request for the reopening of the convoys

to North Russia. I and all my colleagues are most anxious to help you and the valiant armies you lead to the utmost of our ability. I do not therefore reply to the various controversial points made in M. Molotov's communication. Since June 22,1941, we have always done our best in spite of our own heavy burdens to help you defend your country against the cruel invasion of the Hitlerite gang, and we have never ceased to acknowledge and proclaim the great advantages that have come to us from the splendid victories you have won and from the deadly blows you have dealt the German armies.

2. For the last four days I have been working with the Admiralty to make a plan for sending a new series of convoys to North Russia. This entails very great difficulties. First the Battle of the Atlantic has begun again. The U-boats have set about us with a new kind of acoustic torpedo, which has proved effective against the escorting vessels when hunting U-boats. Secondly, we are at very full stretch in the Mediterranean, building up an army in Italy of about 600,000 men by the end of November, and also trying to take full advantage of the Italian collapse in the Aegean islands and the Balkan peninsula. Thirdly, we have to provide for our share of the war against Japan, in which the United States are greatly interested, and whose people would be offended if we were lukewarm.

3. Notwithstanding the above it is a very great 'pleasure to me to tell you that we are planning to sail a series of four convoys to North Russia in November, December, January, and February, each of which will consist of approximately thirty-five ships, British and American. Convoys may be sailed in two halves to meet operational requirements. The first convoy will leave the United Kingdom about November 12th arriving North Russia ten days later; subsequent convoys at about twenty-eight-day intervals. We intend to withdraw as many as possible of the merchant vessels now in North Russia towards the end of October, and the remainder with returning convoy escorts.

Churchill wanted to avoid any new charges of a breach of faith from the Soviet Union, should Britain's efforts to help them be in vain, he inserted a safeguarding paragraph:

4. However, I must put it on record that this is no contract or bargain, but rather a declaration of our solemn and earnest resolve. On this basis I have ordered the necessary measures to be taken for the sending of these four convoys of thirty five ships.

He then proceeded with a list of grievances regarding the treatment of British sailors in North Russia.

5. The Foreign Office and the Admiralty however request me to put before you for your personal attention, hoping indeed that your own eye may look at it, the following representations about the difficulties we have experienced in North Russia.

6. If we are to resume the convoys we shall have to reinforce our establishments in North Russia, which have been reduced in numbers since last March. The present numbers of naval personnel are below what is necessary, even for our present requirements, owing to men having to be sent home without relief. Your civil authorities have refused us all visas for men to go to North Russia, even to relieve those who are seriously overdue for relief M. Molotov has pressed His Majesty's Government to agree that the number of British Service personnel in North Russia should not exceed that of the Soviet Service personnel and trade delegation in this country. We have been unable to accept this proposal, since their work is quite dissimilar and the number of men needed for war operations cannot be determined in such an unpractical way. Secondly, as we have already informed the Soviet Government, we must ask to be the judges of the personnel required to carry out operations for which we are responsible. Mr. Eden has already given his assurance that the greatest care will be taken to limit the numbers strictly to the minimum.

7. I must therefore ask you to agree to the immediate grant of visas for the additional personnel now required, and for your assurance that you will not in future withhold visas when we find it necessary to ask for them in connection with the assistance that we are giving you in North Russia. I emphasize that of about one hundred and seventy naval personnel at present in the North over one hundred and fifty should have been relieved some months ago, but Soviet visas have been withheld. The state of health of these men, who are unaccustomed to the climatic and other conditions, makes it very necessary to relieve them without further delay.

8. We should also wish to send the small medical unit for Archangel to which your authorities agreed, but for which the necessary visas have not been granted. Please remember that we may have heavy casualties.

9. I must also ask your help in remedying the conditions under which our Service personnel and seamen at present find themselves in North Russia. These men are of course engaged in operations against the enemy in our joint interest, and chiefly to bring Allied supplies to your country. They are, I am sure you will admit, in a wholly different position from ordinary individuals proceeding to Russian territory. Yet they are subjected by your authorities to the following restrictions, which seem to me inappropriate for men sent by an ally to carry out operations of the greatest interest to the Soviet Union:

(a) No one may land from one of H.M. ships or from a British merchant ship except by a Soviet boat in the presence of a Soviet official and after examination of documents on each occasion.

(b) No one from a British warship is allowed to proceed along-side a British merchantman without the Soviet authorities being informed beforehand. This even applies to the British admiral in charge.

(c) British officers and men are required to obtain special passes before they can go from ship to shore or between two British shore stations. These passes are often much delayed, with consequent dislocation of the work in hand.

(d) No stores, luggage, or mail for this operational force maybe landed except in the presence of a Soviet official, and numerous formalities are required for the shipment of all stores and mail.

(e) Private Service mail is subjected to censorship, although for an operational force of this kind censorship should, in our view, be left in the hands of British Service authorities.

10. The imposition of these restrictions makes an impression upon officers and men alike which is bad for Anglo-Soviet relations, and would be deeply injurious if Parliament got to hear of it. The cumulative effect of these formalities has been most hampering to the efficient performance of the men's duties, and on more than one occasion to urgent and important operations. No such restrictions are placed upon Soviet personnel here.

11. We have already proposed to M. Molotov that as regards offences against Soviet law committed by personnel of the Services and of the ships of the convoys, they should be handed over to the British Service authorities to be dealt with. There have been a few such cases no doubt, partially at any rate due to the rigorous conditions of service in the North.

12. I trust indeed, M. Stalin, that you will find it possible to have these difficulties smoothed out in a friendly spirit, so that we may help each other, and the common cause, to the utmost of our strength.

Churchill considered these were modest requests considering the efforts the British were about to make. As no answer to his memo was received for nearly a fortnight, becoming anxious that time was running out to co-ordinate the shipment, he wrote to Britain's man in Moscow.

PRIME MINISTER TO SIR A. CLARK KERR (MOSCOW)   12 OCT 43

I have received no answer to my long telegram of October 1 about resuming the Arctic convoys. If the cycle of convoys is to begin on November 12 we must have an early reply to our requests about personnel. Several dozens of wireless operators and signals personnel, on whose work the safety of the convoys may well depend, are to leave the United Kingdom, together with about one hundred and fifty reliefs for men due to return home, by destroyers sailing from the United Kingdom on October 21. Pray therefore press for an answer. Meanwhile we are preparing the convoys in the hope that the Soviets still desire them.

Churchill received his answer from Stalin the next day. It could hardly have been more offensive.

PREMIER STALIN TO PRIME MINISTER   *13 OCT 43*

I received your message of October 1 informing me of the intention to send four convoys to the Soviet Union by the Northern route in November, December, January, and February. However, this communication loses its value by your statement that this intention to send Northern convoys to the U.S.S.R. is neither an obligation nor an agreement, but only a statement, which, as it may be understood, is one the British side can at any moment renounce regardless of any influence it may have on the Soviet armies at the front. I must say that I cannot agree with such a posing of the question. Supplies from the British Government to the U.S.S.R., armaments and other military goods, cannot be considered otherwise than as an obligation, which, by special agreement between our countries, the British Government undertook in respect of the U.S.S.R., which bears on its shoulders, already for the third year, the enormous burden of struggle with the common enemy of the Allies, Hitlerite Germany.

It is also impossible to disregard the fact that the Northern route is the shortest way which permits delivery of armaments supplied by the Allies within the shortest period to the Soviet-German front, and the realization of the plan of supplies to the U.S.S.R. in appropriate volume is impossible without an adequate use of this way. As I already wrote to you earlier, and as experience has shown, delivery of armaments and military supplies to the U.S.S.R. through Persian ports cannot compensate in any way for those supplies which were not delivered by the Northern route.

By the way, for some reason or other there was a very considerable decrease in the delivery of military goods sent by the Northern route this year in comparison with those received last year; and this makes it impossible to fulfill the established [Soviet] plan of military supplies [to the armies] and is in contradiction to the corresponding Anglo-Soviet protocol for military supplies. Therefore, at the present time, when the forces of the Soviet Union are strained to the utmost to secure the needs of the front in the interests of success of the struggle against the main forces of our common enemy, it would be inadmissible to have the supplies of the Soviet armies depend on the arbitrary judgment of the British side. It is impossible to consider this posing of the question to be other than a refusal of the British Government to fulfill the obligations it undertook, and as a kind of threat addressed to the U.S.S.R.

2. Concerning your mention of controversial points allegedly con-tained in the statement of M. Molotov, I have to say that I do not find any foundation for such a remark. I consider the principle of reciprocity and equality proposed by the Soviet side for settlement of the visa question in respect of personnel of the military missions to be a correct and indeed a just one. The reference to the difference in the functions of the British and Soviet military missions, and that the numbers of the staff of the British military mission must be determined by the British Government only, I consider to be unconvincing. It has already been made clear in detail in the previous aide-memoires of the People's Commissariat for Foreign Affairs on this question.

3. I do not see the necessity for increasing the number of British Servicemen in the north of the U.S.S.R., since the great majority of British Servicemen who are already there are not adequately employed, and for many months have been doomed to idleness, as has already been pointed out several times by the Soviet side. For example, it can be mentioned that, owing to its non-necessity, the question of the liquidation of the British port base in Archangel was put forward several times, and only now the British side have agreed to liquidate it.. There are also regrettable facts of the inadmissible behavior of individual British Servicemen who attempted, in several cases, to recruit, by bribery, certain Soviet citizens for Intelligence purposes. Such instances, offensive to Soviet citizens, naturally gave rise to incidents which led to undesirable complications.

4. Concerning your mention of formalities and certain restrictions existing in Northern ports, it is necessary to have in view that such formalities and restrictions are unavoidable in zones near and at the front, if one does not forget the war situation which exists in the U.S.S.R. I may add that this applies equally to the British and other foreigners as well as to Soviet citizens. Nevertheless the Soviet authorities granted many privileges in this respect to the British Servicemen and seamen, about which the British Embassy was informed as long ago as last March. Thus your mention of many formalities and restrictions is based on inaccurate information.

Concerning the question of censorship and prosecution of British Servicemen, I have no objection if the censorship of private mail for British personnel in Northern ports would be made by the British authorities themselves, on condition of reciprocity, and also if cases of small violations committed by British Servicemen which did not involve court procedure would be given to the consideration of the appropriate military authorities.

The reply was cabled to Churchill via his man in Moscow, Churchill was furious, but he decided not to get into an ongoing spat with Stalin which was unlikely to ever reach a satisfactory outcome. Instead he contacted Anthony Eden the foreign secretary who by chance was on his way to Moscow for a conference, and gave him a draft copy of a letter (below) to show Molotov, Eden's Russian equivalent. In the draft he lays out his response in no uncertain terms, he instructed Eden to explain to Molotov that if the Russians wanted the military supplies they had better start being reasonable, otherwise they could forget it.

PRIME MINISTER TO PREMIER STALIN   15 OCT 43

It is impossible for His Majesty's Government to guarantee that the four convoys mentioned can be run irrespective of the military situation on the seas. Every effort and heavy loss and sacrifice would however be made to do so if the Soviet Government attaches importance to the receipt of their cargoes. I cannot undertake to do more than my best, and His Majesty's Government must remain the judge of whether any particular operation of war to be carried out by their forces is in fact practicable or not.

2. The running of these four convoys would be a very great burden to the Royal Navy, and involves the diversion of much-needed flotillas from the anti-U-boat war and from the escorting of troop and other important convoys. It also exposes the main units of the Fleet to serious risks. His Majesty's Government. would be very glad to be relieved of the task of running the convoys if the Soviet Government do not attach importance to them.

3. *In particular the refusal of the request of the British Government in respect of the reliefs and small increases in the few hundreds of British Servicemen in the north of the U.S.S.R., and in particular the signals personnel, on which the safety of these convoys to some extent depends, raises an insuperable obstacle. His Majesty's Government would be very glad to withdraw the handfuls of Service personnel from North Russia, and will do so as soon as they are assured that it is not the desire of the Soviet Government to receive the convoys under the modest and reasonable conditions which the British Government consider necessary.*

At the same time that Eden was talking to Molotov, Churchill wanted to make his annoyance clear to Stalin. A new Russian ambassador had just arrived in London and a meeting was scheduled with Churchill. Towards the end of the discussions the Ambassador pulled out the official copy of Stalin's unpleasant letter and handed it over, Churchill received the letter and then explained to the Ambassador that as he knew the contents to be extremely offensive to Britain he did not wish to accept it. By doing so he would have to pen a reply which would include a number of home truths, which whilst accurate, would not help the situation. He then gave the letter back unopened. This approach left a strong impression on the Russians, with Molotov commenting on it to Eden several times. It clearly demonstrated to Stalin that Churchill would not fall for the standard bullying tactics, which he usually employed to great effect.

Churchill was dealing with a man and a regime that had a completely different belief system to that of the allies and he had to treat the regime and the people accordingly. I have used the phrase "belief system" in the absence of any better description available to me. It attempts to describe the values a person adopts within a given group, section of society or culture. Not in a particularly religious way although that might play some part, but as a way of explaining why some individuals behave differently, treat people differently or have different values and expectations than others. This can apply to diverse sections of the same society and to different regions of a country. Some French friends of mine would confirm that the only people the French dislike more than the English are the Parisians. They are perceived by the rest of France as being rude and ungrateful in the way they treat everyone.

This also applies to the way people behave in business. Over the years, I have worked with colleagues, managers and customers that adopt Stalin's approach to business. Additional effort put in on their behalf is taken for granted, they do not acknowledge it and simply expect more and more. The greater the help offered, the more they seek to take advantage. These type of people look at the world entirely from their own point of view, everyone else appears to exist only to be of service to them. Like Stalin, whilst their own belief system revolves entirely around themselves, they also recognize that someone with a more reasonably balanced belief system is ripe for exploitation. They are entirely comfortable manipulating people who are helpful to their own advantage.

The trick in business, when dealing with these characters, is to avoid letting them get into ones head and under ones skin. Treat the Stalin's of this world fairly and firmly, stick to the facts in any dealings with them. Whilst the Stalin's will "try it on" constantly, by demonstrating to them that they cannot manipulate the situation to their advantage, boundaries are set for the business discussion. In the same way that Churchill behaved after receiving the dreadful response from Stalin when it became untenable to carry on delivering convoys, don't let bullying influence a decision, just continue to do the right thing even if that means benefiting the bully. The right thing to do is the right thing to do, regardless of any hackles raised.

One trick Stalin types often employ is to deliberately try and cause a person to lose their temper, believing they have the upper hand when this happens. Nothing better indicates to a Stalin that someone cannot be intimidated than when they stay calm and rational throughout an argument or heated discussion. A Stalin might well begin to shout, pretend to be angry or personally upset. These are just some of the tricks of the trade that often helps a Stalin get what they want. It is easier to remain calm and deal rationally with a Stalin when the facts are adhered to, and despite their efforts to stray into speculation, feigned emotion or upset, the discussion remains anchored to reality.

During my time at one company, my boss pulled me to one side and asked if it would be possible to add a very difficult account to my portfolio of customers. The owner of the company had been complaining to my boss about the ineffectiveness of his account manager. Just to complicate matters my business had just employed an ex member of his staff, against his wishes. At the time, they were a relatively small account. I vividly remember the first meeting we had in his boardroom. His wife who worked with him, was also present.

After the usual pleasantries, he forcefully stated that he was very annoyed with my company, and that unless I could give him certain assurances regarding the access that his ex-employee had to his companies account information, then he would be moving all his business to a competitor. He delivered this statement in a very confrontational way. I stayed calm and explained how the internal systems worked and that it was very unlikely that his ex-employee could gain access to the information. Not content with this he then demanded that I give him a cast iron guarantee that his ex employee was not able to gain access, I stated that I could not. Knowing the systems as I did, I repeated that it was very unlikely that it could happen. He then insisted that the systems should be re-designed in order that he could have his guarantee. I explained that this was not possible. He then reached the peak of his anger and stated that it was not good enough; and he was going to move his business.

Whilst appearing calm on the outside but inwardly quite shaky I decided that his account was beyond salvation and no amount of re-stating or explanation was going to change the situation. I explained that I was very disappointed that I had not been able to meet his expectations and that he would have to do what he felt was best for his business. I silently began to put my things away on the basis that the meeting had concluded.

He then realized that he had pushed things further than he wanted them to go. Whilst the business I worked for was not perfect, it was without doubt the best service provider compared to the competition at the time. He was aware that new products were just about to be launched, which he could profitably resell.

He also realized that whilst he did not like what he was hearing, at least he had an honest answer from someone with integrity and resolve. He then offered me a coffee and asked me to talk him through some of the new products due to launch, considerably softening his tone in the process. After another hour the meeting finished on a positive note. He went on to become one of my old companies biggest customers. It turned out that his bark was much worse than his bite and over the next few years we developed a very amicable working relationship, based on mutual respect.

With regularity, business situations arise which can be rather uncomfortable. Often a team member will need me to deliver some bad news to a client, or an irate customer (that does or does not have a valid complaint) wants to bring attention to a particular issue. Some customers will be reasonable and recognize that you are doing your best in difficult circumstances, however they want to register their dissatisfaction. Others are just plain tortuous to deal with and go out of their way to be as obnoxious as possible, no matter what is said.

Whilst never looking forward to this type of meeting or conference call, over the years my ability to deal with these situations has improved. Without realizing it, this improvement has been the result of moving closer to the way Churchill handled the same type of problem. Staying calm, sticking to the facts and not responding emotionally to any aggressive behavior. Since reading his memoirs, I am now even more confident that the approach I take is the best method for me to deal with tough situations.

One of the most difficult challenges is to treat a Stalin in exactly the same way as the great people that form part of daily business interaction. It is only natural to do your utmost for the decent customers and the absolute minimum for the nightmare ones. The problem, is that this makes the nightmare customers worse. The trick, and it is a difficult one to master, is to try to do as much for the nightmare ones as those who are decent. By dealing with everyone equally, it makes business much more straightforward. Even though satisfaction can be derived from doing the absolute minimum for the nightmare customer, in effect when this happens, they win. In making a decent person behave in this way, they have exported part of their own belief system, which can only be detrimental.

It is important to be anchored to one's own belief system when dealing with people who's system is clearly different. It is much easier to deal with people effectively, when working within a set of comfortable personal business boundaries. In essence, this is how Churchill managed to deal with Stalin and the rest of the unsavory characters during the war.

Chapter 17

It Just Happens

This chapter does not include a secret skill of Churchill's. It deals with the harsh reality of an unexpected loss of employment. The way the British people treated Churchill after he dedicated his life to defeating the Germans beautifully illustrates the point.

The British war government between 1940 and 1945 was a coalition of all the parties. Party politics stayed subdued in parliament during the war, largely due to the universal desire to win. The pettiness of politics paled into insignificance compared to a life under a Nazi jackboot. Once victory started to look inevitable, party politics became more prevalent. After Victory in Europe, it went in to overdrive. Churchill tried to persuade Clement Attlee, the opposition leader, not to press for an election until victory over Japan. It seemed wrong for Britain to hold an election whilst the army was still fighting in the Far East. Victory over Japan seemed a long way off, but Attlee did not want to wait any longer than necessary, figuring an early election was to his benefit. Atlee, the opposition Labor Party leader, was entitled to ask for an election. He had concluded an agreement with Churchill in 1940 that permitted him to call for a vote once the Nazi's had been defeated.

Atlee ran a brilliant campaign distinguishing between Churchill the war leader and Churchill the conservative politician. Atlee argued that the Labor party would take greater care of the returning soldiers than the conservatives. Given his pre-war political credentials and track record, Churchill is often assumed to have the equivalent political outlook of a right wing Republican. One of the truly surprising sides to Churchill which only reveals itself when you read through the thousands of memo's in the appendices' of his books, is how much his outlook was similar to that of a democrat. One clear example was the argument he had with the treasury regarding war widows pensions, detailed below. There are innumerable examples detailed in the memoirs of left leaning policies and decisions which Churchill took or supported throughout the war. The British electorate might well have voted for him in greater numbers, had they been aware that he was no longer the right wing politician who became Prime Minister in 1940.

PRIME MINISTER TO CHANCELLOR OF THE EXCHEQUER   4 MAY 41
Is it true that the widow of a Service man killed by enemy action on leave gets only half the pension she would if her husband were killed on duty?

PRIME MINISTER TO CHANCELLOR OF THE EXCHEQUER 10 MAY 41
Do you think this distinction is justifiable? Is there much money in it? I was told of a case of a sailor who was drunk on duty and drowned in consequence, his widow getting full pension; while another sailor on well-earned leave, killed by enemy action, was far worse treated in respect of his wife. I doubt very much whether treating leave earned by service as equivalent to service for these purposes would cost you much, and it would remove what seems to be a well founded grievance.

PRIME MINISTER TO CHANCELLOR OF THE EXCHEQUER 16 MAY 41
I draw a dear distinction between deaths arising from the fire of the enemy and ordinary accidents. This is the line of demarcation which we have successfully maintained in the Bill dealing with compensation for war injuries. The air attack on this country is novel and sporadic, and can also quite safely be kept in a compartment by itself. Therefore I reject the arguments about the concessions spreading to ordinary accidents, and from the armed forces to persons in employ on a part time system, such as air-raid wardens and the like. I consider that in a regular service persons bound by discipline on permanent engagement have a right to be considered when on leave as enjoying the same privileges in regard to pensions for their widows, etc., as when they are with their units. Here again is a

frontier which can be effectively maintained.

In a regular disciplined force leave is regarded as earned, and is part of the normal system of the force, and it breeds contempt of the governing machinery when one man's widow is left with half the pension of the other merely because he was hit by the enemy's fire while on leave.

Let me know what would be the expense if the regulations were amended as I have here suggested.

The great Churchill historian Roy Jenkins believed he did not run a particularly effective campaign, making quite a few errors of judgment in the way he referred to the Labor Party. Churchill had a great weight on his mind; while Britain was full of the euphoria of victory he was deeply troubled about Russia's plans for Europe. Churchill had to keep a brave face on what he believed were the early warning signs of a potential cold war.

In his memoirs Churchill argued that his own campaign was at a major disadvantage as most of the people who ran the regional party machine still hadn't returned from the war. A far larger part of Labor's organization was still in-tact as the Labor parties active political supporters were plentiful among the essential skilled workers who stayed at home to work in the munitions factories.

None-the-less, Churchill could not believe that after everything he had done for Britain, the British public would not allow him to remain in office after the war, to help with the reconstruction. It certainly didn't do Britain any favors in terms of the relationship with the USA, as the Labor party were wrongly perceived by the Truman administration as being too closely aligned with communism. When the Labor government went cap in hand to the USA for money to help fund their election promises, it took an intervention from Churchill to persuade the US administration that the Labor government were decent people to do business with.

The election took place just shortly before Churchill went off to attend the victory peace conference with the Russians and Americans in Potsdam, Germany. The declaration of the result was delayed for three weeks because all the soldiers' votes from around the world needed to be counted. Everyone at the conference was confident that Churchill would win, however Churchill took Attlee along in the role of observer, just in case. Before the conference was finished, Churchill and Attlee returned to Britain for the result. In one of the great election upsets of all time, Churchill lost. He never went back to Potsdam.

In a now famous quote Clementine told Churchill, it was a blessing in disguise. He replied "at the time it was very well disguised". In reality, it probably did Churchill a favor. Whilst reading the memoirs it became clear just how much death and heartache Churchill had to endure during his five years as Prime Minister.

He related a particularly heart wrenching story about how he sailed to America in the brand new battleship the Prince of Wales, shortly after Pearl Harbor. How much he enjoyed the company of the Captain, how he vividly recalled the emotional service he attended on the ship's deck, jam packed with the combined US and British Navy on what was a bright, crisp, Sunday morning. He described how Roosevelt and the crew sang hymns to stir the heart as they joined in the march to victory. Then, how three months later the captain and crew of the Prince of Wales whom he had befriended during his voyage across the Atlantic, were all dead. Sunk by a Japanese torpedo air attack trying to defend Singapore. This was just one example, the books are packed with stories of heroic figures who died for their country and the cause of freedom, many of them close friends of Churchill's. How he could cope with the remorseless pain and sorrow, whilst carrying on so effectively, is a mystery, and one that nobody should ever have to learn by experience again. What Churchill's books grimly illustrate is the random nature by which all these people died. Death could visit any one of them at any time.

Churchill was devastated at losing the election and took a long time to get over it. He spent the next six years publishing his memoirs, which made him a great fortune. At the same time he toured the world receiving accolade upon accolade as the grateful nations of the world fell over themselves to thank him for saving them from Nazi tyranny. During this time he remained leader of the Conservative party and in 1951 at the age of seventy six the British public gave him his old job back, as he became leader of the country once more, staying in power for four years, running what is widely considered to be a very successful government. Towards the end of his time as Prime Minister, his lifestyle started to catch up with him and his health started to fail, he had a couple of strokes and he was largely a symbolic figurehead.

As Churchill discovered, a person's value to a population or indeed a business is limited to what they believe that person can do for them in the future, not on the achievements of the past. It never ceases to amaze me when people complain about having committed their heart and soul to a job for years, only to receive a redundancy notice without ceremony, assuming their company had a memory and would be grateful for what they did. Companies do not show loyalty, because they cannot. There is no such thing as corporate memory, or corporate feelings. Businesses do not have a heart, they exist on paper to generate money for investors and shareholders. It is only individuals that can show loyalty to one another and it is individuals that constitute a company.

Soldiers go to war for a cause but fight and make sacrifices for the people with whom they fight. They have the greatest loyalty to the men and women they train and fight with and it is these soldiers they do not want to let down in battle.

True loyalty as opposed to corporate loyalty, tends to limit itself to the immediate group of people someone works with. The amount of loyalty reflects the way people actually treat each other. Fine words and all the right noises will make no difference when it comes to the crunch. When you really need someone's help, they will only be prepared to go the extra mile if you have shown sincere commitment to them, and gone the extra mile yourself.

Good businesses often try to create an environment which encourages loyalty and that is a good thing. In order to create loyalty they provide employees with good services and benefits seeking to create a pleasant and rewarding working environment. Employees who feel valued and enjoy their job will be more productive.

Working for a good company can be extremely enjoyable, putting in long hours and working hard to help make something a success. This is easy to confirm from personal experience.

No matter how hard someone works, or how good they are, for no reason they can find themselves out of a job. It just happens sometimes. They might be the most knowledgeable person with regard to a particular technology and feel completely secure in their position. The next day a rival with a similar technology acquires the company, they retain their own staff and shortly afterwards tickets to the dance are delivered in the post, "the redun-dance". It just happens.

When something like this occurs, it can have unfortunate personal side effects. A person might be flat broke living from pay-check to pay-check. It is sad, it is personal to those involved but the company will soon forget and move on.

During many years of employment no dance tickets have ever been delivered to me (yet), although there have been a few close scrapes. At one company early in my career, the entire sales and support staff were invited to a meeting at a hotel near head office on a Monday morning. Half the group were asked to go into one room and the other half into the adjoining room. My half kept their jobs the other half had to go back to the office collect their belongings and hand in their car keys. (To this day, I am always suspicious of large meetings in hotels).

More recently, a company I worked for was taken over by a competitor, something of an arch rival. Given the way this company had behaved in the past I was convinced that my days were numbered and that any time I would be handed the black spot. (If you have ever seen any old pirate movies, the crew give the captain a piece of paper with a black spot drawn on it when they want to get rid of him). My company was downsized by a third, I had never been through a formal mass redundancy procedure before and didn't know what to expect. The process dragged on across three long months. The new company did their very best to keep everyone informed, and actually proved themselves to be an excellent organization, doing their utmost to mitigate what was a very difficult process. During this time snippets of information would come to light, one day it pointed to me keeping a job the next day it seemed certain I was doomed.

It was impossible to ignore the rumors and speculation, during what was a very debilitating and stressful time, both for me and my family.

Crunch day came when the new organizational structure for my division was announced, I remember like it was yesterday. It was winter and I stopped my car on the journey home. It was pitch black and I was in the middle of the countryside when my boss phoned me to give me the news. It wasn't good, the company had decided to completely eradicate everyone of my managerial level. I had known my boss for many years and we sat and chatted through the new organizational structure. What instantly became apparent, both to me and my boss was how the new structure was completely untenable. There was no way my boss could have coped with so many people reporting to him. Whilst I accepted my situation with good grace I pointed out that the division would quickly grind to a halt under the proposed structure. He had only just been given the information and the reality of the situation was rapidly unfolding. He told me he would speak to his manager and come back to me shortly. I continued my journey through the darkness wondering what lay in store, if I would have to break the bad news to my wife when I got home. Ten minutes later and a few miles down the road my boss phoned, I had a stay of execution. He had persuaded his manager to re-think and had proposed a way around the situation. For the next few hours my valiant boss argued the case for keeping me and a colleague within the business, as he went to sleep he still hadn't managed to convince his manager who said he would mull the idea over during the night.

The next morning I sat in my study anxiously awaiting a call which when it came was fantastic news, not only had I kept my job but I was to be given a slightly different role which I quickly calculated had better prospects than my old one. The only change was to my title, I was no longer to be called a manager, my remarkable boss had succeeded in getting around the issue by giving me a different job title that paid the same, had the same responsibilities but with a different name. As I said to my boss they can print "Chief Cook and Bottle Washer" on my business card, so long as I have a job I enjoy and I have a reasonable chance of earning a decent wage. I quickly found out how much of a close shave it had been, out of 30 people at my level employed as managers, only 4 survived.

I have had a few lucky escapes, there are a million stories of people who have not been so lucky. Eileen from New York is one example. My wife and I started chatting to Eileen whilst on holiday in Bermuda. She was a senior engineer, having worked her way up the corporate ladder of a well known American TV company. After eighteen years, Eileen had achieved real success having put heart and soul into her job. You only had to be in Eileen's presence for 10 minutes to know that she was a warm hearted person who simply fizzed with energy. There was a company take-over, to give an indication of the type of people who bought the company, her boss read about her redundancy in a newspaper. Two days later Eileen was given the black spot. Thankfully, Eileen was able to relate this story with a smile as she was quickly snapped up by a rival broadcast network. Whilst she was treated pretty badly, at least Eileen had a happy ending.

As an example of wicked treatment at the hand of an employer the business world can have few parallels with the brutal treatment of a person who for five long years gave his all night and day for his country. Continuously pushing himself to the very limit of human endurance whilst suffering terrible emotional trauma and hardship. Then to be kicked out on his ear within weeks of delivering the country from the grip of an evil tyranny. It is no comfort to anyone who has lost their job to know someone had it worse, but it is worth mentioning. These things just happen!

Chapter 18

Meritocracy

The principal of a meritocracy, where a person achieves success based on their effort, talent, ability, knowledge and how well suited they are for a particular role seems a fairly straight forward proposition in the 21st Century. It is an idea that most people would agree with, and one which most company owners or managers would like to delude themselves with the thought that it applied to their business. It might do, but it is far more likely that it doesn't. Even with the best of intentions and the most sincere effort, politics, personalities, race, religion, gender, weight, disability along with any number of other factors will stop the idea being applied in practice.

The message of this chapter is inspired by the surprising observation that Churchill actively pushed a meritocratic agenda into the armed forces. Winston recognized early on in the war that the only person who should be in a job was the person who was best suited for it, based on their capability to carry out the task. He expressly wanted to avoid selection based on favoritism, commonly known in Britain at the time as "the old boys' network". It's equivalent today would be "it's not what you know but who you know". The wrong person doing the wrong job making bad decisions could cost lives. Whilst Churchill placed enormous emphasis on applying the principle of meritocracy it would be foolish to say that he was completely successful. However, by having the abiding principle of meritocracy at the core of his decision making, he minimized the number of occasions that ill suited people filled the wrong positions. By the leader setting the example he gave those below the direction and courage to continue the process.

It is an important distinction to point out that he didn't just choose "nice" people that could do a good job he had no issue putting someone in place that was prepared to ruffle feathers. One example of this was General Hobart, who it appears from the content of the memo below to be thoroughly disliked by his superiors. He must have rocked the boat a little too much as despite his obvious ability they didn't want to have him in the regular army. Churchill was having none of it.

Prime Minister to C.I.C.S.   19.OCT.40

I was very much pleased last week when you told me you proposed to give an armored division to Major-General Hobart. I think very highly of this officer, and I am not at all impressed by the prejudices against him in certain quarters. Such prejudices attach frequently to persons of strong personality and original view. In this case General Hobart's original views have been only too tragically borne out. The neglect by the General Staff even to devise proper patterns of tanks before the war has robbed us of all the fruits of this invention. These fruits have been reaped by the enemy, with terrible consequences. We should therefore remember that this was an officer who had the root of the matter in him, and also vision.

In my minute last week to you I said I hoped you would propose to me the appointment that day, i.e., Tuesday, but at the latest this week. Will you very kindly make sure that the appointment is made at the earliest moment.

Since making this minute I have carefully read your note to me and the summary of the case for and against General Hobart. We are now at war, fighting for our lives, and we cannot afford to confine Army appointments to persons who have excited no hostile comment in their career. The catalogue of General Hobart's qualities and defects might almost exactly have been attributed to most of the great commanders of British history. Marlborough was very much the conventional soldier, carrying with him the goodwill of the Service. Cromwell, Wolfe, Clive, Gordon, and in a different sphere Lawrence, all had very close resemblance to the characteristics set down as defects. They had other qualities as well, and so I am led to believe has General Hobart. This is a time to try men of force and vision and not to be exclusively confined to those who are judged thoroughly safe by conventional standards.

I hope therefore, you will not recoil from your proposal to me of a week ago, for I think your instinct in this matter was sound and true.

In the footnotes Churchill gave a quick overview of the General, who it transpired had been an excellent soldier throughout the war.

General Hobart at this time a corporal in the Home Guard was accordingly appointed to command an armored division and in that capacity rendered distinguished service to the very end of the war. I had a pleasant talk with him on the day we first crossed the Rhine in 1945. His work was then highly esteemed by General Montgomery.

Hobart was a classic case of the sort of person who might rub people up the wrong way but could actually do a good job. When I read the memo about him it immediately brought to mind a manger I worked with in my last company. He was a very frustrating colleague, one day he would be fine the next he was incredibly irritating, whilst occasionally he would do or say something so arrogant or offensive that you felt you wanted to strangle him. He had an arrogant air of superiority which did not appear to have any substance to justify it. His one redeeming feature, which is why I immediately thought of him when reading about Hobart was his ability to achieve results. Over the few years I worked with him he consistently delivered against his targets. I was not alone in the view I held of my colleague, and I would quite often find myself defending his abilities to other people within the business when they complained about his lack of sensitivity.

He must have been a challenging employee, sometimes when I mentioned my colleagues name in conversation with his manager I could sense that they had recently come to close quarters on some issue or other. Despite the difficulties, through many re-shuffles when it would have been easy to let him go, his manager clearly stuck to the Churchillian principle that the person who could deliver the best results was the most suitable for the job. My colleague and I had what would best be described as a healthy tolerance of each other. He rankled both myself and others fairly often, but he didn't overstep the mark of being so unbearable, that despite his own success, his presence had a detrimental effect on the business. Whilst it would be ideal to work in a perfect world where everyone got along famously and achieved success. Given the choice between working with someone I liked a great deal but who didn't deliver the goods, or working with a Hobart who irritated whilst putting in a strong performance, I would choose a Hobart every time.

War had only just been declared and Churchill had his mind set on sweeping away outdated Naval traditions and practices from the cozy decades before the war. He was determined to radically change the whole recruitment and promotion program within a Royal Navy that had been used to doing things a certain way. Churchill had the foresight to appreciate the best people needed to be in charge, regardless of their background. The day when a small group of privileged, clipped voiced, private school educated elites would exclusively command the Navy had come to an end. It was just a case of making sure that everyone understood that people were to be promoted based on their experience and ability. The best were to progress no matter what their background or the job they currently performed, either below deck or above deck. This change did not happen overnight but Churchill made sure it took place, he realized that the future success of the Royal Navy and therefore the safety of Britain depended upon it.

To get the ball rolling Churchill asked for a list of all the Naval professions and the ability with which each individual profession could progress up the promotion ladder.

FIRST LORD TO SECRETARY   4.OCT.39

Let me have a list at once of the branches to which promotion from the lower deck still does not apply. What proportion do these branches bear to the other branches?

As can be seen below Churchill was not impressed by the response.

FIRST LORD TO SECOND SEA LORD, PARLIAMENTARY SECRETARY
AND SECRETARY.   7.OCT.39

Will you kindly explain to me the reasons which debar individuals in certain branches from rising by merit to commissioned rank? If a cook may rise, or a steward, why not an electrical artificer or an ordnance rating or a shipwright? If telegraphist may rise, why not a painter? Apparently there is no difficulty about painters rising in Germany!

I like Churchill's humor in the last line of the above memo, he is referring to the fact that Hitler was originally a painter. Churchill swept aside the red tape that stopped certain categories from progressing, it took a while but he achieved his objective. It is still the case today that in the British Royal Navy anyone can rise to any rank based solely on their ability.

The last memo I shall use to demonstrate Churchill's meritocratic approach completely stunned me. I assumed that like everyone else from his era, Churchill would have probably been classed by today's standards as racially prejudice. Given that the Royal Navy discriminated against white people that didn't come from the correct background, a person of color realistically would have stood no chance of rising through the ranks. In 1939 the way colored minorities were treated especially in the US would be considered shocking by today's enlightened standards. In 1939 the thought of a black man named Barrack Hussein Obama becoming President of the USA in 2009 was just not conscionable. In 1939, racial prejudice in America and in the American armed forces was so institutionalized, and attitudes so ingrained, that the treatment of minorities wasn't even considered racist. It was just the way things were. Things wouldn't really start to improve for another 30 years. The phrase African American would not pass across peoples lips for decades.

Britain didn't have the same extreme of prejudice that prevailed in America, but it is certainly true that what would be considered racism by modern standards was rife. The Britain of 1939 was still predominantly Anglo Saxon white. It would be another 15 years before large scale immigration from the colonies would take place and begin to shape a 21st Century multicultural society. Churchill when it came to the war didn't care about a person's skin color so long as they could point a gun at a Nazi or help in the war effort.

The note below shows just how far ahead of his time Churchill was, he clearly wanted to prove this to the world when in 1947 he included the memo in the appendices of Volume 1 of his memoirs "The Gathering Storm". Even though Churchill was ahead of his time, he knew how difficult it would be for the vast majority of the Navy to accept non white people in senior Naval positions, he tempered his instruction with practical advice.

FIRST LORD TO SECOND SEA LORD AND OTHERS CONCERNED AND SECRETARY.   14.OCT.39.

There must be no discrimination on grounds of race or color [in the employment of Indians or Colonial natives in the Royal Navy]. In practice much inconvenience would arise if this theoretical equality had many examples. Each case must be judged on its merits, from the point of view of smooth administration. I cannot see any objection to Indians serving on H.M. Ships where they are qualified and needed, or, if their virtues so deserve, rising to be Admirals of the Fleet. But not too many of them, please.

The memo about racial equality really came as a complete bolt from the blue, and was right at the very back of the appendices. I can't imagine that Roosevelt sent a similar memo, or any President or Prime Minister sent this type of memo for many years to come. The fact that Churchill was quite comfortable seeing an Indian or a Black man from the Caribbean becoming an Admiral in 1939 is simply astounding. Especially when you consider the prevailing attitude of the time. Based on this memo I have to believe that Winston would have been delighted to see Barrack become President of the United States of America, based solely on the principal of meritocracy. If

Winston were around to pass on any advice, he would probably advise that it takes a lot more than being a great public speaker, to make a world class leader. As I have endeavored to identify throughout my book, a great leader needs a diverse range of skills. The same is true of people in business.

Chapter 19

Delegation

Of the secret skill's that I endeavor to identify, the absolute cornerstone or bedrock of Churchill's success was built on his ability to delegate. In my humble opinion he was quite simply a master practitioner. To prove this point, I would recommend that anyone who wants to learn how to delegate effectively should read the appendices section of any one of Churchill's six volumes of memoirs. Each book contains hundreds of examples, detailing the requests for information he required and the guidance by which Churchill was to receive back exactly what he was looking for. For those without the time or inclination, some memo's are detailed below. I have drawn out what I consider to be some of the salient points.

First example – Being Specific

PRIME MINISTER TO CHANCELLOR OF THE EXCHEQUER 13.JULY.42
Pray let me have the following information. What is the difference in the yearly pay of a British soldier anywhere and an American soldier quartered in this country? You should take allowances into consideration and give me a simple block figure.

What would be the cost to the Exchequer of advancing the British pay (taking allowances, etc., into consideration) half-way up to the American level, on condition that the Americans reduced theirs to meet us and paid the surplus to their troops as a nest-egg in the United States?

I am deeply concerned about the troubles that will arise here and the tremendous demand that maybe made upon you to equalize upwards. I therefore wish to explore the possibilities of equalizing downwards. There is no need for you to argue the matter at this stage, because anyone can see the disadvantages. But let me know the figures. They may indeed be staggering.

In the example above Churchill was very specific about what he wanted and what he didn't want. As a very busy leader he needed detailed information without an opinion. He used this style of request consistently.

Second Example – Length of response

PRIME MINISTER TO MINISTER OF FOOD   6 DEC 41
Amid your many successes in your difficult field, the egg distribution scheme seems to be an exception. I hear complaints from many quarters, and the scarcity of eggs is palpable.

I send you a note which the Minister of Agriculture has furnished on his side of the problem. Will you please give me a very short statement of your plans and policy.

Churchill endeavored to read every piece of correspondence sent to his office, he didn't want edited versions stuck under his nose by civil servants with a vested interest in pushing a particular angle. This was especially true with intelligence reports which he insisted were received unedited from the field. Because of the colossal amount of detail he wanted to digest, Churchill would regularly dictate the length of response he required. In the case above he asked for a very short response. In situations where he wanted a person's opinion or expert view on a topic, he would request the length of response required in terms of the number of pages he wished the reply to be limited too.

Third Example – Observation with a call to action

PRIME MINISTER TO SECRETARY OF STATE.FOR WAR   12 OCT 41
I see some odd court-martial cases mentioned in the papers. First, a sergeant who told a Home Guard lieutenant "So what?" and "Put a sock in it" in the presence of troops, but who was merely reprimanded. He should surely have been reduced to the ranks. Second, some soldiers who were heard calling the sergeants "b*%$£rds with three stripes", but who apparently

were honorably acquitted on the grounds that this was a word of common use in the Army. The major giving evidence said he had often turned a deaf ear to it when used about himself.

In sharp contrast, two Canadians who deserted in Canada, and made their way over here after great adventure in order to fight, received sixty days.

All this seems to require very clear guidance from you and the Army authorities.

(Action this Day)

FIRST LORD TO FIRST SEA LORD, SECOND SEA LORD AND SECRETARY. 18.SEP.39

I have just approved the message to the Northern Patrol. about the Newfoundland fishermen: the boat work of the Newfoundlanders was an important thing to render this effective in the stormy winter months. These men are the hardiest and most skilful boatmen in rough seas who exist. They long for employment. Please propose me measures at once to raise 1,000 R.N.V.R. in Newfoundland; drafting the necessary letter to the Dominions Office and outlining terms and conditions. They have nothing to learn about the sea, but almost immediately some method of training and discipline could be brought into play. In ten days at the outside this should be working in Newfoundland.

In the two memo's above he gives clear guidance for when things need to happen, (Action this Day) in the first and 10 days to get the scheme up and running in the second.

Fourth Example – Who to get help from

PRIME MINISTER TO GENERAL ISMAY, FOR CHIEFS OF STAFF COMMITTEE 1 JUNE 41

Adverting to my wish that the West African Brigade should be returned from East Africa to Freetown forthwith, and that the captured Italian arms should be used to equip the Shadow Brigade now forming at Freetown or thereabouts, I have had a talk with General Gifford. He says that the West African battalions require an average of eighty British officers and non-commissioned officer personnel, and that these will be lacking for the Shadow Brigade, and that even if supplied they would be better employed on handling any modern equipment we can find. It has been suggested to me that the great plethora of Polish officers in Polish divisions, amounting to several thousands, might be married up to this West African Shadow Brigade. I am sure that General Sikorski could easily be persuaded to find two or three hundred, and they would be very good.

Pray let this be examined and a plan made. General Giffard should be consulted, and should like to have a report before he leaves the country, the object being the transfer of the West African Brigade from east to west, and the development of the Shadow Brigade on Italian equipment and Polish white infusion.

Churchill made a request and then gave guidance as to where the people tasked with responding should get help from.

The examples above give an indication of how Churchill used to delegate. One of the minimum requirements needed to be successful in business is the ability to delegate effectively. By doing so, the person making the request doesn't end up wasting time by repeating themselves when they don't get the response they want. Just as importantly they don't waste the time of colleagues by sending them on wild goose chases trying to respond to a vague request. It is equally important for the person receiving a request to have the courage to push back and ask for more guidance, when a manager or another member of staff make a request that is open to misinterpretation. It can be useful to gain agreement at the time the request is made, to ensure the timescale for completion is reasonable. It is then important to ensure that responses to a request are delivered when they are supposed to be, otherwise people will continually ignore deadlines.

I recall learning this lesson very quickly when I first became a manager with responsibility for a small sales force early on in my career. If I asked for a report or some information from my team of six and I wasn't specific, I would receive six different responses in six different format's and end up wasting my time re-shaping each individual response into a format I could use. After doing this a few times I quickly got the hang of basic delegating. Over the years my ability has improved, although it was some time before I plucked up the courage to ask questions regarding a vague request. I was concerned that I might give the impression of not knowing what I was doing. Eventually I came to the conclusion that if someone didn't know how to delegate properly, then I wasn't going to waste my time worrying, I would just simply seek some clarification before responding. This approach has stood me in good stead throughout the balance of my career. Until I started reading through Churchill's memo's I thought I was a pretty good delegator, however it doesn't do any harm to pick up additional tips from a master practitioner.

One other area I would like to touch upon in this chapter is a method Churchill used to improve the quality and fighting capability of the British tanks during WW2. After Britain's initial successes in 1941 against the Italian tanks in North Africa, it quickly became apparent once the Germans arrived, that the British tanks were no match for the latest German panzers. In what was an early version of a brainstorming session, Churchill came up with the idea of putting together a Tank Parliament. His idea was to gather everyone who had any involvement with tanks into a forum, where they could each contribute towards the design of the ideal tank. This was a very radical approach for the time, the people invited were steel producers, designers, shippers, manufacturers, maintenance engineers, tank battalion commanders, tank commanders, drivers, gunners and radio operators.

The Tank Parliament was set up to mirror the workings of the English parliament, hence the name. Everyone in the room was treated as an equal and was able to make proposals, criticize and ask questions. The person in charge of controlling the group acted like the speaker of the House of Commons, he was independent and made sure that questions were relevant and a level of politeness was observed. People who started prattling on were asked to get to the point. Crucially, once any modification or change to a design had been debated there was a democratic vote to determine who was in favor or against it, the majority decision determining the outcome.

Up to that point, the tank designers and manufacturers would produce designs in conjunction with a few senior army commanders, which they believed to be suitable for battle. Churchill concluded that there was no point designing a fast light tank, when the people on the front line might have preferred a slightly slower tank with heavier armor, able to withstand the impact of an enemy shell, without killing them. Maintenance aspects in the field were also critical, quickly fixing the wear and tear that tanks were prone to had an important influence on the overall design. The list of competing elements was considerable. The outcome of the first tank parliament was the Churchill tank (what an original name!) which delivered a vast improvement on previous versions, and was the technological equivalent of the American Sherman, the best tank the allies had at the time.

British Parliament's sat regularly, and the same was the case for the Tank Parliament. Throughout the war they would regularly meet, with new members added and removed as required. This approach ensured that Britain kept up with what was in effect an arms race in tank technology.

Most of the techniques Churchill used are covered today by current business practices such as mind mapping, brainstorming and focus groups. (Plenty of literature is available on these techniques). The key to the success of the Tank Parliament was making sure that the people invited had actual practical experience or involvement with a particular aspect of the tank process. He insisted that it wasn't a talking shop for people with opinions that were not based on actual experience. It is quite often the case in business that committee's and focus groups are formed with colleagues who have an opinion, as opposed to having direct knowledge gained at the coalface. Often these people will express a view based on information that is many years old. The benefit of the Tank Parliament approach to design was just like members of parliament who are regularly voted in and out of office, the people who constituted the tank parliament would only be drawn from those with active, current knowledge.

By today's standards the Tank Parliament seems a fairly simple and obvious idea, at the time however, it was a radical approach to improving Britain's chances of success, Churchill used this approach time and again throughout the war.

Chapter 20

The Case of the Cadets
(A Short Story)

This chapter does not follow the format of all the preceding chapters and is not intended to highlight any specific skill of Churchill's.

After reading through his memoirs twice in preparation for this book I thought I would try and tackle the appendices at the back of volume 1 "The Gathering Storm". Each book has at least 100 pages of memo's written in very tiny print. All selected by Churchill and detailing the massively complex and widely varied issues he had to contend with on a daily basis. Being candid it was hard work, even for a Churchill devotee like myself. There were quite a few interesting insights which I thought could add an extra dimension to the chapters of my text, however, it was not until the very end that the story of the special entry cadetships unfolded in memos across the last few pages. I found it gripping and was hooked on knowing what happened. The outcome of the story was revealed in the last memo on the last page. I was really taken with it.

In my opinion the way Churchill approached the problem encapsulates the reason why he became the iconic figure he is today. For a bit of out and out self indulgence I decided to blend fact with fiction and put the memo's within the context of a short story. The person at the centre of the tale absolutely existed, although he was not called Andrew, Churchill memo's are real, the rest is my own lame attempt at story writing. It would be fair to say that J K Rowling has nothing to fear.

When war broke out Andrew resolved to join the Royal

Navy. Winston Churchill had been First Lord of the Admiralty for a few days when Andrew submitted his request to become an officer, he was determined to do his bit for King and Country. Little did he know, that as he sat at the kitchen table in his East London terraced house, filling in the application forms on that unusually warm and sunny September morning, that he would come face to face with Winston, and cause an archaic system of Naval recruitment to be tossed overboard like unwanted fish from a trawler.

Andrew had always dreamed of joining the navy, he came from a proud Naval family with a long tradition of service, his dad joined the Navy in 1917 and 22 years later he had progressed through the ranks to become a 1st class engineer. His grandfather had been in the Navy, and had been involved in the conversion of the Royal Navy from coal to oil. A decision Winston Churchill had taken many years before when he was First Lord of the Admiralty during WWI, a decision which had far reaching consequences. Once the greatest Naval power in the world (as Britain was at the time) converted to oil then the security and supply of oil became of prime importance. It was then critical that the countries supplying the oil continued to do so, if a foreign government became unstable, then a country like Britain wouldn't flinch from intervening to make sure the oil still flowed. (History continues to repeat itself in one guise or another.)

Andrew decided at the age of 10 that he wanted to be an officer. He was proud of what his dad had achieved in his 22 years, but he saw the toll that all the physical work had taken upon him, he had every one of the 22 years of service, etched into the leathery skin of his face, a patina that only years spent down below at the business end of a warship could produce. Andrew wanted to be an officer, his ambition was to be able stand on deck making the decisions and giving the orders.

Having set his sights high Andrew knew that for an East London boy to go straight into the Navy as an officer, he would need to show exceptional ability. His dad had always encouraged him in his ambition, but he was only too aware that most new officer recruits had clipped accents that only a private school education could bring. Naval officers had the schooling costs of their children paid for by the Navy, thus ensuring that there would be ready supply of officers specially groomed for the job, and eager to enlist. This system had been working just nicely for years, making sure the officer ranks were of a certain background and breeding. It wasn't going to be easy for Andrew to break into this cozy self serving circle.

The system might have worked in peacetime but it was singularly ill suited for the requirements of WW2. With the massive expansion of the Navy and the loss of life that was to come, Britain simply needed as many qualified men as possible to step forward and train as officers.

Andrew was the sort of son that a parent would beam with pride about every time his name was mentioned. He was 6ft 2inches tall, athletically built, his wavy blond hair and piercing blue eyes making him stand out in a crowd. All of the local girls were envious of Iris, his childhood sweetheart, they had first met when they were 11 and had been inseparable ever since. At 11 Andrew was tall and gangly and covered in spots, they had become close friends and then over the next seven years they had somehow fallen in love. Neither of them could recall the date when their friendship had blossomed into something much deeper, they just knew they would spend the rest of their lives together. They were the perfect couple, both kind and considerate, never hesitating to help others in need. Both were hard working and determined to move onwards and upwards, to build a better life for the big family they planned to have once they were married. But first Andrew needed to become an officer in the Navy.

Andrew's headmaster was confident that his exceptionally gifted pupil would be able to sail through the Naval board exam. Had Andrews parents been wealthy, he was certain that Andrew could have passed the entrance exam to either Oxford or Cambridge. Such was the caliber of this outstanding young man.

It was November when the response came from the Naval board. He was to be interviewed on the November 4th and would sit his exam on the 18th. In the meantime he had an interim job working at Covent Garden market helping out a friend of his Dad's. At long last the day came, he looked fantastic wearing a dark blue suit walking up the steps of admiralty house. After waiting what seemed like an eternity he was ushered in to a large wood paneled room and asked to stand and salute, when ordered he was to sit down. He was 5 paces away from a long dark wooden table. Six men, dressed in their Naval uniforms all with dark blue suits, gold braid, gold buttons and gold rope in abundance, sat behind the table. These men were clearly very senior, Andrew guessed that the average age must have been about 60, these guys were long past their active service sell by date.

Each candidate was allotted 15 minutes for interview. Andrew recalled some of the questions, why did he want to join the Navy, why join as an officer, had he considered becoming an engineer, what school had he been to, what marks had he achieved. He remembered the final question. What special qualities did he have that made him suitable to become an officer? He checked his watch as he stood, saluted and left the interview, he had been in and out in 9 minutes. He took this as a good sign, clearly he had done so well that they didn't need to use the full 15 minutes to determine how suitable he was.

Andrew walked out of Admiralty house into a miserable November day. It had been freezing cold when he walked in but now the wind had picked up and it had started raining. The angle of the wind caused the rain to drive hard into his face as he walked down the road into Westminster Square. Big Ben chimed for 12.00pm and hundreds of people in military uniform hustled and bustled about. He had to keep looking up to avoid walking into the new sandbag gun emplacements, which had sprung up since the last time he had been to Westminster. The weather was miserable and he would have to stand in the freezing cold for a long time before his bus arrived, (the service had deteriorated dramatically since the start of the war) it didn't matter, as it was all worth it. All he had to do was pass the entrance exam and he would be certain of a place.

Over the next 2 weeks Andrew closely followed events at sea, during what could only be described as the phony war period. The Royal Navy had been engaged in plenty of action with Ships and U-Boats, thousands upon thousands of soldiers had been shipped off to France as part of the BEF (British Expeditionary Force) but there had been no action at home to speak of. Plenty of air raid warnings but no bombing, it was

November 1940 the beginning of the real war was a few months away.

Two weeks later and back again up the steps of the Admiralty building, after being searched Andrew enquired at reception were the exam was taking place. Passing through a labyrinth of wood paneled corridors he eventually reached a large room about 100ft by 40 ft. This had more dark wood paneling on the walls and a really ornate guilt ceiling with 10 huge crystal chandeliers, unusually there were no windows. The desks were laid out in 4 columns and 10 rows, each desk had an exam paper turned upside down, with a pencil, a sharpener and rubber placed on top. It reminded him of his final exams at school, the only difference was that this exam would determine the future direction of his life.

At exactly 1.00pm the exam commenced, each candidate had 4 hours to complete a grueling exam, with detailed questions encompassing Math, English, Science, Geography and History. 3 hours and 16 minutes later Andrew put his pencil down, completely confident that he had done his absolute best and feeling convinced that he would get a high score.

Back down the steps of the Admiralty and out into the darkness as he re-traced the journey home he had taken 2 weeks earlier. As the old red London bus rattled along the embankment he started day dreaming about what it would be like on his first day of basic training down in Plymouth. He was expecting to receive his joining papers within the next 2 weeks.

It had become a ritual, every day Andrew would wait in the living room overlooking the road outside between 9.30 and 10.00am waiting for the postman. This had gone on for 9 straight days, the waiting was taking its strain not only on Andrew but on his mother and father. At last the letter arrived, by chance it was on the one day that Andrew was unable to wait at home in the morning. He had to leave early to collect his gas mask, the queue seemed to go on forever, he stood impatiently, checking his watch every few minutes, desperate to return home, hoping that today would be the day.

Andrews poor Mother and Father waited what seemed like an eternity for their lad to return home, they were desperate to know if he had been accepted. In those days there was no way of contacting the kids, they didn't even have a phone, today they would have dropped him a text, how things have moved on.

They all sat together at the kitchen table, the moment had finally arrived, Andrew opened the letter, after reading it Andrews face dropped, all the color drained from his cheeks, the letter slipped out of his hands and fell slowly onto the kitchen table. His father immediately picked it up, reading it his face went the opposite of Andrew's, a deepening angry maroon. Whilst his son sat motionless and unable to speak, Andrews father launched into a tirade of abuse directed at the stuck up idiots that had rejected his son, his genius son! The same boy that came top of the class at everything, who everyone liked. He had been in the Navy 22 years and he knew officer material when he saw it, and his Andrew was 100% premium grade officer material.

It only really sank-in the following day, everything Andrew had worked for had been cruelly taken away, he didn't know what to do for the best. His father did, he wrote to the Admiralty recruitment office and demanded to know on what grounds his son had been rejected. Six days later he received an irritatingly short and polite response stating that "We regret that your son was not considered suitable to be an officer, however, it is not the policy of the Admiralty recruitment board to disclose the rationale used for assessing candidates. This does not preclude your son from applying for other positions in The Royal Navy"

Andrews dad wondered why his son had even bothered. It was all down to class prejudice and making sure the cozy officers mess wasn't infected by working class people, with their common habits and dreadful accents. Far better to have a mediocre candidate from the right school than an outstanding candidate with the wrong pedigree. These people were living in cloud cuckoo land, how did they expect to win a war with such antiquated attitudes. It was a disgrace, but he had been around long enough to know that you couldn't beat the system. Christmas was 2 days away, and rather than a joyous celebration, with what he anticipated would probably be his son's last Christmas at home for some time, it was likely to be a miserable affair, with everyone putting on a brave face. Pretending to enjoy themselves whilst nursing the resentment that Andrew had been cast aside for no good reason.

By Boxing Day dad was still not over the disappointment, he seethed with anger, it was so difficult to shake off his feeling of disgust, did he really want his son being put in mortal peril to preserve such an obnoxious class system. He turned the radio on, it was 11.00am and Churchill was giving a speech. Listening to Churchill detail how the Navy were beating the Germans lifted his spirits, he had always liked Churchill, at least he had stood up for Britain before the war. He alone had complained about the lack of investment in the armed forces, at least he had been prepared to hold the people with their head in the sand to account. He didn't much like his politics but he got the sense that somehow Churchill wasn't one of "them". And then like a light going on in his head he had an idea, he would write to Churchill and tell him that Andrew hadn't been accepted, even though he was confident that he was more than good enough. He would put Churchill to the test and see if he was one of "them" or not.

Dear Mr. Churchill,

I would like to bring to your attention a matter regarding my son Andrew.

He applied to become an office in your Navy and was rejected, despite the fact that he is eminently qualified. He was the brightest boy in his school and has the character and bearing to become a first class officer. I have been an engineer in the Royal Navy for 22 years and I would consider myself a reasonable judge of what makes a good officer. Sir, despite the fact that Andrew is my son, I am confident that he exceeds the criteria by some margin.

If I might be so bold as to suggest a reason for his rejection, I believe it is because of his background. With Andrew going to a normal state school and me being an engineer I have to conclude that he was passed over because he was too "common" to be an officer.

Forgive me for troubling you with such a small matter, when you have all the tasks of the Navy to deal with, but I feel a great injustice has been perpetrated which stains the reputation of His Majesty's Royal Navy. I would be most grateful if you could ask one of your staff to enquire upon this matter.

I have enclosed documents detailing my son's qualifications and his Naval application along with the response to my subsequent appeal

Little did Andrews father realize that he was about to stir up a hornets' nest within the Admiralty. Churchill was adamant that he wanted the best people for any given job no matter what background they came from. The recruitment board were about to discover that Churchill was not a man to be trifled with. Unlike previous First Sea Lords he had his own opinion and he was used to getting what he wanted.

Churchill wrote to the second Sea Lord who had responsibility for recruitment, copying the contents of the letter from Andrews father.

SPECIAL ENTRY CADETSHIPS   FEB 40

It seems very difficult to understand why this candidate should have been so decisively rejected in view of his high educational qualifications, his service connections, and his record as set out by his father in his letter of January 4. One has to be particularly careful that class prejudice does not enter into these decisions, and, unless some better reasons are given to me I shall have to ask my Naval Secretary to interview the boy on my behalf, before assuming responsibility for writing to his father as proposed.

Churchill was clearly not happy with the response. The Second Sea Lord was obviously upset with the meddling from above and pretty much told Churchill that it was none of his business. That he shouldn't interfere in the workings of the long established recruitment board. The Second Sea Lord clearly had a lot to learn about Winston Churchill, his response was like a red rag to a bull, or should I say bulldog. Churchill wrote back and put him in his place.

FIRST LORD TO SECRETARY   FEB. 40
CANDIDATE FOR THE NAVY ENTRANCE EXAMINATION NOVEMBER,

FAILED

I do not at all mind "going behind the opinion of a board duly constituted", or even changing the board or its chairman if I think injustice has been done. How long is it since this board was re-modeled? I could not help being unfavorably struck with the aspect of the Dartmouth cadets whom I saw marching by the other day. On the other hand I was enormously impressed with the candidates for commission from the ranks who I saw drilling and being trained on the parade ground at Portsmouth. They were of course much older, but a far finer looking type.

Not only shall my Naval Secretary see the boy, but I shall hope to have time to see him myself. Who are the naval representatives on the board of selection? Naval officers should be well represented.

Action accordingly.

Let me have a list of the whole board with the full records of each member and the date of his appointment.

On the 6th February 1940 Andrew was again recalled to the Admiralty. The letter had requested that he attend a further interview in connection with his application to be an officer. After battling through the snow, once again he climbed the steps of the Admiralty building.

After clearing security he reported to the reception desk and handed his letter across to a very stern faced clerk. The clerk went over to the corner of the room and made a phone call. Andrew noticed the clerk giving him an odd glance, then as he put the phone down he did it again. It was almost as if the clerk wasn't sure that the instructions he was receiving over the phone were correct. Andrew was instructed to sit in the waiting area, the clerk's curt attitude seemed to have changed and for some strange reason he was now being very friendly. A couple of minutes later a man dressed in a Captains uniform came through a very imposing looking door and asked for him.

After winding through a labyrinth of corridors Andrew was shown into a room where straight in front of him was a policeman standing bolt upright and cradling a Thompson machine gun across his folded arms. He was guarding a pristine, highly polished black door. Things were becoming more surreal by the minute, the guard opened the door and as he entered a familiar sounding voice greeted him. "Good morning I'm the First Lord of the Admiralty Winston Churchill, welcome to my office" Churchill reached out his hand to shake Andrew's hand, and with a twinkle in his eye asked him to take a seat.

It took Andrew what seemed like an eternity to get over the shock, there he was 19 years of age shaking hands with the famous Winston Churchill, he had to pinch himself to make sure he wasn't dreaming. Churchill explained the impact of his father's letter and over the course of what seemed like hours, but was in fact just 10 minutes Churchill asked him a number of questions about his father, his background, schooling, why he wanted to be an officer etc. Churchill referred occasionally to a brown file which Andrew concluded must have been about him.

At the end of the conversation Churchill stood up to indicate to Andrew that the meeting was over. He told him that he was extremely impressed with his academic record and by his attitude and general bearing. He went on to say that the Navy needed more men of Andrews clear capabilities, to help in what was undoubtedly going to be a long and difficult struggle. He came around his desk and shook Andrews hand again, he told him that he would shortly be hearing from the Navy. Churchill had discovered that Andrew wasn't the only boy who had been passed over on the grounds of prejudice, and after finishing with Andrew he went on to interview 2 other boys.

Andrew walked down the steps of the Admiralty building with a huge beaming smile across his face, he had just met Winston bloody Churchill! He couldn't wait to get home and recount the whole story to his mum and dad, which he did, again and again, as they kept on asking more and more questions making sure no tiny detail was missed in the retelling.

The next day Churchill wrote once again to the Second Sea Lord.

FIRST LORD TO SECOND SEA LORD.   FEB.40

I have seen the three candidates. Considering that these three boys were 5th, 8th and 17th in the educational competitive examination out of more than ninety successful, 320 qualified, and 400 who competed, I see no reason why they should have been described as unfit for the Naval service. It is quite true that A .... has a slightly cockney accent, and that the other two are the sons of a Chief Petty Officer and an Engineer in the Merchant Service. But the whole intention of competitive examination is to open the career to ability, irrespective of class or fortune. Generally speaking, in the case of candidates who do exceptionally well in the examination, the presumption should be that they will be accepted. Similarly, those who do very badly in the educational examination may nevertheless in a few cases be fit to serve. But the idea of rejecting boys at the very top of the list, unless some very grave defect presents itself, is wholly contrary to the principles approved by Parliament.

I am sure if the Committee, when they had these boys before them, had known that they were among the cleverest in the whole list, they would not have taken so severe a view and ruled them out altogether on the personal interview. It seems to me that in future the Committee ought to conduct the interview after the examination, and with the results of it before them. Furthermore, it is wrong that a boy should be allowed to sit for examination, with all the stress and anxiety attached to it, when it has already been settled that, even if he is first on the list, he has already been ruled out.

I also feel that there is no need for any mention of a disqualifying standard for interview and record. The Interview Board should also be instructed that they may award different marks to the same candidate for different branches of the Service. It is obvious that a boy may be much more suitable for the Paymaster than the Executive Branch, and the Committee should be able to differentiate accordingly.

There will of course be no need for the Interview Committee to see all the candidates. There must be a qualifying educational standard. This is 400 marks at present, out of a total of 1,350. I notice that all the successful boys in the last examination had well over 600 marks. Surely it would ease the work of the Interview Committee if the qualifying educational standard were raised?

Pray make me proposals for rearranging the present system so as to achieve the above conditions.

Cadetships are to be given in the three cases I have

mentioned.

On the 9th February a letter arrived from the Admiralty stating that Andrew had been selected to become an officer in His Majesty's Royal Navy. He was to report to Dartmouth college two weeks hence. His dad's letter to Churchill had changed forever the situation for Andrew and the two other cadets who had been discriminated against due to their background. It also ensured that the Royal Navy would be in a stronger position to defeat the Nazi threat going forward as applicants would henceforth be chosen on merit

So it turned out that Churchill was not one of "them" after all, despite coming from an incredibly privileged background, he viewed the people who had rejected Andrew and the other two candidates with disdain, he sorted them out once and for all. He knew that a system based on class prejudice could not possibly serve the interests of the Royal Navy, so he swept it away in his own inimitable style.

I love a story with a happy ending.

Chapter 21

Churchill's Final Speech

At the back of volume six "Triumph and Tragedy", the last in the series of Churchill's war memoirs, he published his victory speech, this was the last he gave as Britain's war leader. I hadn't come across this speech in the many books I had read about Churchill, I include it here because it is effectively Churchill's own summary of the war, as would be expected it is brilliantly written, I hope you enjoy it.

PRIME MINISTER'S VICTORY BROADCAST, MAY 13, 1945

It was five years ago on Thursday last that His Majesty the King commissioned me to form a National Government of all parties to carry on our affairs. Five years is a long time in human life, especially when there is no remission for good conduct. However, this National Government was sustained by Parliament and by the entire British nation at home and by all our fighting men abroad, and by the unswerving cooperation of the Dominions far across the oceans and of our Empire in every quarter of the globe. After various episodes had occurred it became clear last week that so far things have worked out pretty well, and that the British Commonwealth and Empire stands more united and more effectively powerful than at any time in its long romantic history. Certainly we are - this is what may well, I think, be admitted by any fair minded person in a far better state to cope with the problems and perils of the future than we were five years ago.

For a while our prime enemy, our mighty enemy, Germany, overran almost all Europe. France, who bore such a frightful strain in the last great war, was beaten to the ground and took some time to recover. The Low Countries, fighting to the best of their strength, were subjugated. Norway was overrun. Mussolini's Italy stabbed us in the back when we were, as he thought, at our last gasp. But for ourselves - our lot, I mean, the British Commonwealth and Empire - we were absolutely alone.

In July, August, and September 1940 forty or fifty squadrons of British fighter aircraft in the Battle of Britain broke the teeth of the German air fleet at odds of seven or eight to one. May I repeat again the words I used at that momentous hour: "Never in the field of human conflict was so much owed by so many to so few." The name of Air Chief Marshal Lord Dowding will always be linked with this splendid event. But conjoined with the Royal Air Force lay the Royal Navy, ever ready to tear to pieces the barges, gathered from the canals of Holland and Belgium, in which a German invading army could alone have been transported. I was never one to believe that the invasion of Britain, with the tackle that the enemy had at that time, was a very easy task to accomplish. With the autumn storms the immediate danger of invasion in 1940 passed.

Then began the Blitz, when Hitler said he would "rub out our cities". That's what he said, "rub out our cities." This Blitz was borne without a word of complaint or the slightest sign of flinching, while a very large number of people - honor to them all - proved that London could "take it", and so could our other ravaged centers. But the dawn of 1941 revealed us still in jeopardy. The hostile aircraft could fly across the approaches to our Island, where forty six millions of people had to import half their daily bread and all the materials they needed for peace or war. These hostile aircraft could fly across the approaches from Brest to Norway and back again in a single flight. They could observe all the movements of our shipping in and out of the Clyde and Mersey, and could direct upon our convoys the large and increasing numbers of U-boats with which the enemy bespattered the Atlantic - the survivors or successors of which U-boats are now being collected in British harbors.

The sense of envelopment, which might at any moment turn to strangulation, lay heavy upon us. We had only the North-Western Approach between Ulster and Scotland through which to bring in the means of life and to send out the forces of war.

Owing to the action of the Dublin Government, so much at variance with the temper and instinct of thousands of Southern Irishmen who hastened to the battle front to prove their ancient valor, the approaches which the Southern Irish ports and airfields could so easily have guarded were closed by the hostile aircraft and U-boats. This was indeed a deadly moment in our life, and if it had not been for the loyalty and friendship of Northern Ireland we should have been forced to come to close quarters or perish for ever from the earth. However, with a restraint and poise to which, I say, history will find few parallels, His Majesty's Government never laid a violent hand upon them, though at times it would have been quite easy and quite natural, and we left the Dublin Government to frolic with the Germans and later with the Japanese representatives to their hearts' content.

When I think of these days I think also of other episodes and personalities. I think of Lieutenant-Commander Esmonde, V.C., of Lance-Corporal Kenneally, V.C., and Captain Fegen, V.C., and other Irish heroes whose names I could easily recite, and then I must confess that bitterness by Britain against the Irish race dies in my heart. I can only pray that in years which I shall not see the shame will be forgotten and the glories will endure, and that the peoples of the British Isles, as of the British Commonwealth of Nations, will walk together in mutual comprehension and forgiveness.

My friends, when our minds turn to the North-Western Approaches we will not forget the devotion of our merchant seamen, and our minesweepers out every night, and so rarely mentioned in the headlines. Nor will we forget the vast, inventive, adaptive, all embracing, and, in the end, all controlling power of the Royal Navy, with its ever more potent new ally, the Air. These have kept the life line open. We were able to breathe; we were able to live; we were able to strike. Dire deeds we had to do. We had to destroy or capture the French Fleet, which, had it ever passed undamaged into German hands, would, together with the Italian Fleet, have perhaps enabled the German Navy to face us on the high seas. This we did. We had to make the dispatch to General Wavell all round the Cape, at our darkest hour, of the tanks, practically all we had

*in the Island and this enabled us as far back as November 1940
to defend Egypt against invasion and hurl back with the loss of a
quarter of a million captives and with heavy slaughter the Italian
armies at whose tail Mussolini had already planned to ride into
Cairo or Alexandria.*

*Great anxiety was felt by President Roosevelt, and indeed by
thinking men throughout the United States, about what would
happen to us in the early part of 1941. The President felt to the
depths of his being that the destruction of Britain would not only
be an event fearful in itself, but that it would expose to mortal
danger the vast and as yet largely unarmed potentialities and the
future destiny of the United States. He feared greatly that we
should be invaded in that spring of 1941, and no doubt he had
behind him military advice as good as any that is known in the
world, and he sent his recent Presidential opponent, the late Mr.
Wendell Willkie, to me with a letter in which he had written in
his own hand the famous. lines of Longfellow which I quoted in
the House of Commons the other day.*

*We were, however, in a fairly tough condition by the early
months of 1941, and felt very much better about ourselves than
in those months immediately after the collapse of France. Our
Dunkirk army and field force troops in Britain, almost a million
strong were nearly all equipped or re-equipped. We had ferried
over the Atlantic a million rifles and a thousand cannon from the
United States, with all their ammunition, since the previous June.
In our munitions works, which were becoming very powerful,
men and women had worked at their machines till they dropped
senseless from fatigue. Nearly one million of men, growing to
two millions at the peak, although working all day, had been
formed into the Home Guard. They were armed at least with
rifles, and armed also with the spirit "Conquer or die".*

*Later in 1941, when we were still alone, we sacrificed
willingly, to some extent unwittingly, our conquests of the winter
in Cyrenaica and Libya in order to stand by Greece; and Greece
will never forget how much we gave, albeit unavailingly, of the
little we had. We did this for honor. We repressed the German-
instigated rising in Iraq. We defended Palestine. With the
assistance of General de Gaulle's indomitable Free French we
cleared Syria and the Lebanon of Vichyites and of German*

aviators and intriguers. And then in June 1941 another tremendous world event occurred.

You have no doubt noticed in your reading of British history and I hope you will take pains to read it, for it is only from the past that one can judge the future, and it is only from reading the story of the British nation, of the British Empire, that you can feel a well grounded sense of pride to dwell in these islands, you have sometimes noticed in your reading of British history that we have had to hold out from time to time all alone, or to be the mainspring of coalitions, against a Continental tyrant or dictator, and we have had to hold out for quite a long time: against the Spanish Armada, against the might of Louis XIV, when we led Europe for nearly twenty-five years under William III and Marlborough, and a hundred and fifty years ago, when Nelson, Pitt, and Wellington broke Napoleon, not without assistance from the heroic Russians of 1812. In all these world wars our Island kept the lead of Europe or else held out alone.

And if you hold out alone long enough there always comes a time when the tyrant makes some ghastly mistake which alters the whole balance of the struggle. On June 22, 1941, Hitler, master as he thought himself of all Europe, nay, indeed, soon to be master of the world, so he thought, treacherously, without warning, without the slightest provocation, hurled himself on Russia and came face to face with Marshal Stalin and the numberless millions of the Russian people. And then at the end of the year Japan struck a felon blow at the United States at Pearl Harbor, and at the same time attacked us in Malaya and Singapore. Thereupon Hitler and Mussolini declared war on the Republic of the United States.

Years have passed since then. Indeed, every year seems to me almost a decade. But never since the United States entered the war have I had the slightest doubt that we should be saved, and that we only had to do our duty in order to win. We have played our part in all this process by which the evildoers have been overthrown and I hope I do not speak vain or boastful words, but from Alamein in October 1942, through the Anglo American invasion of North Africa, of Sicily, of Italy, with the capture of Rome, we marched many miles and never knew defeat. And then last year, after two years' patient preparation and marvelous devices of amphibious warfare, and mark you, our scientists are not surpassed in any nation in the world, especially when their thought is applied to naval matters, last year, on June 6, we seized a carefully selected little toe of German-occupied France and poured millions in from this Island and from across the Atlantic, until the Seine, the Somme, and the Rhine all fell behind the advancing Anglo-American spearheads. France was liberated. She produced a fine army of gallant men to aid her own liberation. Germany lay open.

Now from the other side the mighty military achievements of the Russian people, always holding many more German troops on their front than we could do, rolled forward to meet us in the heart and centre of Germany. At the same time, in Italy, Field-Marshal Alexander's army of so many nations, the largest part of which was British or British Empire, struck their final blow and compelled more than a million enemy troops to surrender. This Fifteenth Army Group, as we call it, British and Americans joined together in almost equal numbers, are now deep in Austria, joining their right hand with the Russians and their left with the United States armies of General Eisenhower's command. It happened, as you may remember, but memories are short, that in the space of three days we received the news of the unlamented departures of Mussolini and Hitler, and in three days also surrenders were made to Field-Marshal Alexander and Field-Marshal Montgomery of over two million five hundred thousand soldiers of this terrible warlike German Army.

I shall make it clear at this moment that we never failed to recognize the immense superiority of the power used by the United States in the rescue of France and the defeat of Germany. For our part, British and Canadians we have had about one third as many men over there as the Americans but we have taken our full share of the fighting, as the scale of our losses shows. Our Navy has borne incomparably the heaviest burden in the Atlantic Ocean, in the narrow seas and the Arctic convoys to Russia, while the United States Navy has had to use its immense strength mainly against Japan. We made a fair division of the labor, and we can each report that our work is either done or going to be done. It is right and natural that we should extol the virtues and glorious services of our own most famous commanders, Alexander and Montgomery, neither of whom was ever defeated since they began together at Alamein. Both of them have conducted in Africa, in Italy, in Normandy, and in Germany battles of the first magnitude and of decisive consequence. At the same time we know how great is our debt to the combining and unifying command and high strategic direction of General Eisenhower.

And here is the moment when I pay my personal tribute to the British Chiefs of Staff; with whom I worked in the closest intimacy throughout these heavy, stormy years. There have been very few changes in this small, powerful, and capable body of men, who, sinking all service differences and judging the problems of the war as a whole, have worked together in perfect harmony with each other. In Field-Marshal Brooke, in Admiral Pound, succeeded after his death by Admiral Andrew Cunningham, and in Marshal of the Royal Air Force Portal, a team was formed who deserved the highest honor in the direction of the whole British war strategy and in its relations with that of our Allies.

It may well be said that our strategy was conducted so that the best combinations, the closest concert, were imparted into the operations by the combined Staffs of Britain and the United States, with whom, from Teheran onwards, the war leaders of Russia were joined. And it may also be said that never have the forces of two nations fought side by side and intermingled in the lines of battle with so much unity, comradeship, and brother hood as in the great Anglo American Armies. Some people say, "Well, what would you expect, if both nations speak the same language, have the same laws, have a great part of their history in common, and have very much the same outlook upon life, with all its hope and glory? Isn't it just the sort of thing that would happen?" And others may say, "It would be an ill day for all the world and for the pair of them if they did not go on working together and marching together and sailing together and flying together, whenever something has to be done for the sake of freedom and fair play all over the world. That is the great hope of the future."

There was one final danger from which the collapse of Germany has saved us. In London and the south eastern counties *we have suffered for a year from various forms of flying bombs perhaps you have heard about this, and rockets, and our Air Force and our ack ack batteries have done wonders against them. In particular the Air Force, turned on in good time on what then seemed very slight and doubtful evidence, hampered and vastly delayed all German preparations. But it was only when our armies cleaned up the coast and over ran all the points of discharge, and when the Americans captured vast stores of rockets of all kinds near Leipzig, which only the other day added to the information we had, and when all the preparations being made on the coasts of France and Holland could be examined in detail, in scientific detail, that we knew how grave had been the peril, not only from rockets and flying bombs, but from multiple long range artillery which was being prepared against London. Only just in time did the Allied armies blast the viper in his nest. Otherwise the autumn of 1944, to say nothing of 1945, might well have seen London as shattered as Berlin.*

For the same period the Germans had prepared a new U-boat fleet and novel tactics which, though we should have eventually destroyed them, might well have carried anti U-boat warfare back to the high peak days of 1942. Therefore we must rejoice and give thanks, not only for our preservation when we were all alone, but for our timely deliverance from new suffering, new perils not easily to be measured.

I wish I could tell you tonight that all our toils and troubles were over. Then indeed I could end my five years' service happily, and if you thought that you had had enough of me and that I ought to be put out to grass I tell you I would take it with the best of grace. But, on the contrary, I must warn you, as I did when I began this five years' task and no one knew then that it would last so long that there is still a lot to do, and that you must be prepared for further efforts of mind and body and further sacrifices to great causes if you are not to fall back into the rut of inertia, the confusion of aim, and "the craven fear of being great". You must not weaken in any way in your alert and vigilant frame of mind. Though holiday rejoicing is necessary to the human spirit, yet it must add to the strength and resilience with which every man and woman turns again to the work they have to do, and also to the outlook and watch they have to keep on public affairs.

On the continent of Europe we have yet to make sure that the simple and honorable purposes for which we entered the war are not brushed aside or overlooked in the months following our success, and that the words "freedom", "democracy", and "liberation" are not distorted from their true meaning as we have understood them. There would be little use in punishing the Hitlerites for their crimes if law and justice did not rule, and if totalitarian or police Governments were to take the place of the German invaders. We seek nothing for ourselves. But we must make sure that those causes which we fought for find recognition at the peace table in facts as well as words, and above all we must labor that the World Organization which the United Nations are creating at San Francisco does not become an idle name, does not become a shield for the strong and a mockery for the weak. It is the victors who must search their hearts in their glowing hours, and be worthy by their nobility of the immense forces that they wield.

We must never forget that beyond all lurks Japan, harassed and failing but still a people of a hundred millions, for whose warriors death has few terrors. I cannot tell you tonight how much time or what exertions will be required to compel the Japanese to make amends for their odious treachery and cruelty. We like China, so long undaunted have received horrible injuries from them ourselves, and we are bound by the ties of honor and fraternal loyalty to the United States to fight this great war at the other end of the world at their side without flagging or failing. We must remember that Australia and New Zealand and Canada were and are all directly menaced by this evil Power. They came to our aid in our dark times, and we must not leave unfinished any task which concerns their safety and their future.

I told you hard things at the beginning of these last five years: you did not shrink, and I should be unworthy of your confidence and generosity if I did not still cry: Forward, unflinching, unswerving, indomitable, till the whole task is done and the whole world is safe and clean.

Dear Reader,

If you have made it this far, then I would like to thank you for taking the time to read my book.

I hope you found it enjoyable and that a few of the chapters struck a chord.

If you have any feedback please don't hesitate to contact me.

Kind Regards

Binden

binden@kernelwarden.com

www.ingramcontent.com/pod-product-compliance
Lightning Source LLC
Chambersburg PA
CBHW060545200326
41521CB00007B/498